The Best Talk in Town

The Best Talk in Town

by
Scott Young
and
Margaret Hogan

Clarke, Irwin & Company Limited
Toronto/Vancouver

Canadian Cataloguing in Publication Data:
Main entry under title: The best talk in town
Includes index
ISBN 0-7720-1257-1

1. Canadian orations (English)*   2. Speeches, addresses, etc.
I. Young, Scott, 1918-   II. Hogan, Margaret, 1939-

PS8335.B48   C815'.0108   C79-094888-5
PR9197.4.B48

©1979 by Clarke, Irwin & Company Limited
ISBN 0-7720-1257-1

1 2 3 4 5   83 82 81 80 79

Printed in Canada

CONTENTS

The Best Talk in Town

CHAPTER ONE

A Meeting at Webb's

Once upon a time in Toronto of long, long ago there was a place called Webb's Restaurant at which it was acceptable to eat or drink, for a particular kind of Torontonian. In those days he was the Torontonian of law, business, education, the clergy or medicine, often with a direct or familial British connection, who liked to step out of his office at noon and stroll a block or two, or travel longer distances by horse-drawn carriage or motorcar or the newish electric trolley, to take lunchtime food and drink and discussion among his own kind. He was, in short, fairly akin to the kind of Torontonian Rupert Brooke defined a few years later as "Souls for whom the wind is always nor'- nor'-west." (That is to say, always favourable.) "They sail nearer success than failure, and nearer wisdom than lunacy. . . . They support civilization. You can trust them with anything, if your demand be for nothing . . . absurdly altruistic."

We join a few of these with their collars turned up against the chilly day's-end early darkness of November 18, 1903, hurrying to where the door at Webb's, when opened, threw out light and warmth. One was a militia lieutenant-colonel and lawyer, James Mason. A few days earlier he and a friend had been discussing by telephone what they saw as a crisis in Canadian life: a sudden and widespread turning against the

9

English in a way that seemed to pose a serious threat to Canada's future
as a loyal participant in the British Empire. To men of their class at that
time, nothing was more important than Canada's British connection.
Could this threat somehow be countered? The dinner meeting of a few
influential men at Webb's had been called to seek out a way.

They felt beleaguered. For weeks, Canadian newspapers had been
front-paging angry reports about how Britain's Lord Alverstone, sitting on a judicial tribunal with two Canadians and three Americans,
had sided with the Americans. The 4-2 vote had given to the United
States several islands plus a long stretch of coastline called the Alaska
Panhandle, shutting off, thundered editorialists, 210,000 square miles
of North-West Canada from the sea. The towering anger of Canadians
at what they considered a British sell-out could be read about every
day. The *Globe* alone devoted its lead editorial to the subject for
eighteen consecutive days. The perfidy of the Americans, Canadians
seemed to have expected; they understood self-interest as a motive.
But for the British to show themselves so eminently squeezeable (a
term used earlier by Sir John A. Macdonald) was, said many editorials,
betrayal.

From every side, the anti-British fire thus touched off was being
doused with gasoline. The prime minister, Sir Wilfrid Laurier, rose in
the Commons the day after the decision of the Alaskan Boundary
Tribunal was announced, and demanded Canadian control over her
own foreign affairs. John A's letter to Sir Charles Tupper seventeen
years before, warning Tupper to be as wary as a fox as the senior
Canadian in another tri-nation tribunal on another matter, was quoted
by one newspaper: "American members have found our English
members of so squeezeable a nature that their audacity has grown
beyond all bounds. (Their aim) is to go to England with a treaty in their
pockets (that must be put into effect unchanged), no matter at what cost
to Canada. The effect produced is that British protection is a farce."

The *Globe* reprinted what was being said and written on the matter in
England. The *Saturday Review* there expressed amazement "at the
way papers here [in England] are telling Canada, as if she were a child,
not to mind the Alaska smack in the face." *The Economist*, more
moderately, wrote: "We cannot but hold that the King's government
appear to have acted with a haste for which it is difficult to see
justification." The British prime minister, Arthur Balfour, chimed in

10

disdainfully: "The islands, the loss of which to Canada has aroused such feeling, are really valueless from a strategic and military point of view." That as if only Britain's assessment of such considerations counted; not caring a whit that by the decision a good portion of Canada north of British Columbia had been cut off from the sea.

In all those circumstances, Canadians who took a longer view of what they called "the Imperial bond," felt set upon. This cast of mind was in those who met at Webb's with Col. Mason in the chair. Some were members of the long-established and often opinion-moulding Canadian Club of Toronto—but felt that the Canadian Club was laying too low in face of the anti-British public temper. The new club they were meeting to form would, like the Canadian Club, have weekly luncheons addressed by prominent men speaking with authority on the issues of the day, but there was a specific rider: "having also a distinctive basis of British unity in its work and policy."

The next day, a few of them began drafting the new club's constitution. When word got out, the new organization was dubbed a secessionist movement from the Canadian Club, possibly because one enthusiast said that those who now stayed in the Canadian Club would be demonstrating that they were no longer loyal to Britain and the crown. The *Globe* pooh-poohed this in an editorial, saying that most members of the Canadian Club were still imperialists of one stripe or another with few wanting Canada to break its ties with Britain. This mild controversy helped the word get around, however, and a week after the first meeting, sixty-one men gathered to consider the draft constitution and pick a name. After discarding several suggestions, including "the Dominion Club," the majority voted to name it The Empire Club of Canada. Col. Mason was elected president. Membership was restricted to British subjects (there was no Canadian citizenship at the time) who would pay dues of $1 a year, with a maximum membership of 500. Within a month membership exceeded 300. A year or two later the club had a waiting list of those wishing to join.*

"I can quite understand that to many persons the formation of a club

---

* Eventually membership reached nearly 3,000, with several hundred members each year choosing to belong to both of the city's major lunchtime forums, the Canadian Club as well as the Empire Club.

of this kind will seem a very little thing," said the first luncheon speaker on December 3, 1903, a clergyman and professor, William Clark. If he had had the gift of prophecy, he might then have said that in the next three-quarters of a century hundreds of the world's most distinguished men would follow him to that podium, discussing wittily, informatively, entertainingly (and sometimes boringly) many of the great issues of the century in a manner which would constitute a kaleidoscope of Canadian and world experience.

Clark addressed two issues of that time, both of which were to be more or less disposed of, by time itself. "Certainly there are some, but they are very few indeed, among us who can look forward with equanimity to separation from the Mother Country," he said. "This is supposed to mean either independence, or else absorption by our neighbours in the United States." But he thought there was only one alternative, not two: "An attempt at separation would probably come to an end in a very speedy absorption. I do not seek to belittle the great Republic alongside of us. I esteem and respect the United States without wishing to become one of them. We have the most perfect liberty. What could we gain?"

It was in a sense a keynote speech for decades to come, a reference point noted consciously or unconsciously by all who spoke in subsequent years, including in that host Mackenzie King, Robert Borden, and every other prime minister of Canada; ex-president William Taft, soon-to-be president Richard Nixon, Stephen Leacock, Vilhjalmar Stefansson, cabinet ministers, royalty, generals, scientists, and Captain A. T. Hunter.

Captain A. T. Hunter?

No aficionado of early Empire Club speakers could rightfully list those who impressed him without recalling the joy of discovering Captain A. T. Hunter. He shows up first on February 4th, 1904, with an address entitled "The Fatuous Insolence of Canadians." He liked the idea of the Empire Club, he said. He had spoken once at the Canadian Club and "expressed with the frankness of the common Canadian a number of opinions, some of which I then held, and others of which I thought would be novel and interesting," but: "They never invited me again." He mentioned another club, the Anglo-Saxon Union, but it had Americans as well as Canadians and therefore speakers, wishing to offend neither nationality, tended to discuss issues in terms of "gushful blandishments."

The Empire Club, in contrast, was "magnificently organized for both beginning and ending those family quarrels which make home life dear to us, and with whose progress we suffer no outsider to interfere." Here, among citizens loyal to the Empire, he could "vehemently admire or despise" particular opinions. He proceeded forthwith to poke fun at some of them. He mentioned a new book of the time, on the Builders and Makers of Canada.

"The honest truth is that Canada has by the hand of man been neither built nor made. All the Canadians that have ever been—English, French or nomadic Indians—have never made a conquest of Canada; they have merely hacked at the fringe of her robe.

"It is a matter of pride with our orators that in the North-West wheat can be successfully grown some 800 miles north of the International boundary, and that the Territories can support a population of fifty millions. That this should be a matter of pride is merely another instance of the strange things men take pride in. Had we peopled the North-West the pride would be legitimate. But our scanty settlers stand out to view like the pins with which you tack down a map to prevent it being blown away. With today the bulk of her lands untilled, unoccupied, unexplored and unguarded, Canada remains the unlocked storehouse of nature, the unallotted prize of the ultimate masters of the world."

He warned that Canadians now were in peril, having told all and sundry "and for the first time have had the misfortune to be believed, that we Canadians have a glorious heritage, meaning thereby that we have the forests of timber which we are too penurious to cut; the unwrought mines which a short time ago we used as a pretext for selling each other all kinds of weird and wonderful mining shares; and the vacant granary of the North for which, if we don't make more haste in its occupation, someone else will find a tenant.

"As they say in police circles, we have been 'showing our wad.' The advertising mischief has been done. We cannot disadvertise. Canada is now known to be worth stealing."

Captain Hunter was a youngish Toronto lawyer at the time he spoke, establishing that speakers who came with wit and irony had as much a place as one such as Mackenzie King, who first came with the most dry-as-dust pedanticism that ever caused waiters to signal the end of an Empire Club speech by going around awaking the listeners. But from Prof. Clark's opening musings to the most recent speech given to a modern Empire Club audience more than seventy-five years later, each has been printed and bound in annual volumes reflecting and recording history as it appeared at that moment for more than two thousand lunchtimes since the first one at Webb's.

CHAPTER TWO

The Span of a Generation

The first decade of the new century in Canada was marked by rapid industrialization and expansion, a surge of immigration (277,376 newcomers in the banner year of 1909 alone) and, proof positive of a coming of age of sorts, a national debt of seventy million pounds sterling by 1909. Prosperity and self-evident progress informed the enthusiastic—and sometimes awed—optimism of the times. At the end of the 1904 fiscal year, E. P. Heaton of the insurance department of the Canadian Manufacturers' Association, marvelled:

> The property, real and personal, of the people of the country was insured against loss by fire in companies licensed to do business in Canada to an amount exceeding sixteen hundred and fifty millions of dollars.
> [The sum was $1,657,712,735 precisely, a figure] so large as to be almost meaningless even to businessmen.

We've come a long way, chaps, was the burden of a light lunchtime lesson in history by Frank Yeigh titled "The Span of a Canadian Generation":

15

A generation ago in Canada there was no nine-province Dominion as we have it today: there was no Greater Britain in the 20th-century sense: there was no Empire spirit as we understand it today. Indeed, there was no Canadian spirit such as today exists.

The Canadian of pre-Confederation days had to do without a great many things that he has today. He could not sit in his office and throw his voice into a telephone and have it thrown back at him from a gramophone. He had no bicycle with which to run a human being down; there was no automobile to run down the man on the bicycle who ran down the other fellow. . . .

A generation ago we missed many things that we have today. The people who lived then missed the thrill of these modern days of standing in front of a bulletin board, with open eyes and bated breath, until it is discovered whether Casey made a home run at a baseball match! They missed the thrill then, that we may now enjoy, of getting the very latest sporting extra from the press and finding that some two-year-old mare, of which one had never heard, had won a race away down in Lexington. So we are living in live days when things are being done in a live way. . . .

A generation ago the Rocky Mountains were practically undiscovered; the rich gold-fields of the Yukon were not dreamed of; the French-Canadian blacksmith, LaRose, had not stumbled on a piece of ore up in Cobalt, leading to the mining since then of $85,000,000 worth of silver; the navvies building the C.P.R., digging through a Sudbury hill, had not laid open the great hidden storehouse of nickel.

A generation ago Edmonton was only a shack on a hill; a generation ago there was no Calgary, no Regina, no Saskatoon, no boom towns or boom lands in the West. A generation ago the provinces down by the Atlantic were looking askance at Confederation schemes. Upper and Lower Canada were quarrelling like children, under the Union Act, and certain English statesmen even ventured the opinion that Canada was a millstone around the neck of the Mother Land. That is only the span of a generation ago.

In those pre-Confederation days Canada's future must have seemed dark indeed; it must have required great optimism and faith on the part of her statesmen to foresee the future in all its fullness. The pulse of nationhood had only begun to beat very faintly through its hitherto unrelated parts, and all this was the condition of things nationally only a generation ago.

But this is the day of today, and what a change has come over the scene since the beginning of this span about which I am speaking. Since Confederation we have, as Kipling tells us, "macadamized some stretches of our road towards nationhood": we are taking a hand in the Imperial game: we have been and are working out some experiments in government, the results of which may benefit the whole Empire; we are making history, and we are making a new country very rapidly.

The "new country" was the Canadian West and the northlands, from the Ontario hinterlands to the Arctic—the latter the subject of a compelling series of luncheon-chair excursions during the Club's first decades. In 1909 Captain J. E. Bernier, a French Canadian, self-styled a sailor, described his flag-planting voyages in the wake of expeditions sent from Britain in search of Sir John Franklin, who "gave his life to find the North-West Passage." "I am sure it was simple work," Bernier began, "to follow those great men [who] gave to Canada all the Northern territory. . . ."

My mission on the first trip was to go to Hudson's Bay, and leave some Royal Mounted Police at different quarters, and build two stations. We did that. . . . The second year my mission was to patrol the Northern waters of Canada, and annex the islands during the time that was at my disposal that summer. Going along Greenland, I went into Pond's Inlet to secure Esquimaux and to find the ice conditions before I went farther; also to meet some of those Scotch whalers who were supposed to be in that neighbourhood. I did see them and collected dues for the Government for fishing. It is not a very large amount, but, in this case, we wanted these people to admit our claims—not only the Scotch whalers, we should not charge them anything because it was their fathers who had given us that land—we had this object in view and wanted Canadian control admitted. There were strangers fishing there, and we wanted them to give a little towards our expenses. It is nothing but right that we should have something as a recognition that these were our lands. I did manage to secure $500 from whaling licenses, and $1,000 for

17

custom house duties on goods that were imported from the other side, and from the United States. . . .

I found an American gentleman in the North who had been hunting musk-ox and deer, and one fine night in Baffin Land, inside a bay, I noticed a small light. It was then about 11 o'clock at night, and I made for the light and when I got there I found an unknown schooner, *The Jenny,* from Newfoundland. And I sent the second officer to find out and pay my compliments to the Commander of that vessel, because at that time of the night I did not want to trouble him. The Captain came on board with my mail so that was a good find.

And at the same time Mr. Harry Whitney, of New York, came on board and commenced to tell me of all the game he had killed, and after he was through I said, "Will you have a glass of wine?" We talked for a while, and I said, "Will you have a cigar, sir?" Afterwards I said, "Now that we are through, I would like to have a private talk with you." I said, "Now, according to our statutes and laws you are entitled to get your license and I can give you a license for the sum of fifty dollars." He looked at me. "Well," I said, "I am the representative of the Canadian Government and here are my credentials." I showed that I had taken possession of Baffin Land. There were the papers of the land, and he did pay. And his cheque was paid in time in New York. . . .

In annexing those lands we have annexed probably in the neighbourhood of eight thousand Esquimaux, and when I took possession of Bank Land on the ninth of November, the King's birthday, I told them that they had become Canadians and therefore they were subject to our laws. Well they could not see that, but I tell you they saw it when they came on board my vessel to a dinner to which I had invited them, and they had everything they wanted, and then they commenced to realize that it was a good thing to be a Canadian. . . .

Is it necessary that I should give the names of the islands that I have put the flag on? We have planted our flag on Baffin's Land, Violet Island, Griffith's Island, North Coronet, Bank Land, Victoria Island, King William Island, and many others. On the first of July last year, on Confederation Day, I had a slab made and on that slab I wrote, "This memorial is erected here today to commemorate the taking possession of all the Arctic Archipelago.'' I was doing a wholesale business. . . .

There are yet two little islands here on the map, but I am inclined to believe that they are only one by what I know at present. It was sighted by Peary two years ago and sighted again by Dr. Cook, but all he has of it is some photographs, and I have asked him to allow me to have some prints of them so that I can really learn when I go North if he has been there. [Laughter] At the present moment these two islands are the only ones that we know of where the flag of Canada has never been placed. . . .

If Captain Bernier was for the most part content to describe his experiences, Vilhjalmur Stefansson went farther, into prophecy. Stefansson, of Icelandic stock and by profession an anthropologist, brought up in the cattle country of Dakota but born in Manitoba, had been stranded in the Arctic on his first expedition in 1906 and lived for thirteen months with the Eskimos:

These Eskimo are a resource to the country because they are the only people who can ever make that country of any value so far as we can see, unless minerals are discovered there, which I hope may not be the case, for the sake of the Eskimo. [Laughter] These Eskimo hunt for a living with bows and arrows and spears and harpoons; they had not heard the report of a rifle or seen a sulphur match lighted until I came—at least those around Dolphin and Union Strait had not, and the ones from the Coppermine east to Grace Bay had not. . . .

On account of their weapons and the peculiar conditions of their country, they live for three months of the year on caribou, which they shoot with bows and arrows, and for nine months they live on seals. The caribou are there in millions. The Eskimo hunt them in the summer, kill only as many as they need, and hunt them at a season when the animals are fat and the skins are suitable for clothing. Now, the traders are beginning to come in; their rifles will soon replace the bows and arrows; and then the Eskimo will find that they can easily kill caribou at any time of year, so that instead of living on caribou for three months they will live on caribou for twelve months. This will quadruple the consumption of caribou.

Another feature is that the dog among the Eskimo today is not a

19

draft animal primarily, he is a hunting animal; he is used by the Eskimo for the finding of seal holes under the snow. Consequently our hunter has only one dog; he hasn't any more because it is not convenient for him under the present arrangement to support any more. But the coming of the rifle will make it easy to support any number of dogs, and the Eskimo will develop large dog teams. The same thing happened in the Baillie Island District and the Mackenzie District a few years ago. In that District they had one dog to a family twelve years ago, and now they have fifteen to a family. Here is another thing that will increase the consumption of caribou. . . .

In Alaska there is a great market for caribou skins among the miners and Eskimo. The caribou of Alaska have been destroyed by carelessness; no one took steps to save them, and they are now a thing of the past. If the Government takes no precautions, traders will come into our districts and buy caribou skins, and the Eskimo will begin with their modern rifles and hunt them for the market. I have known men who in August and September killed three or four hundred caribou, and by October they were starving. The same thing will happen with the caribou which happened with the buffalo. . . .

There is, on the American side of the line, the saying that the only good Indian is a dead Indian; that was so because the Indian, as well as the buffalo, encumbered the farmer's land. But in the north the only good Indian is a live Indian, because he secures furs. That is one of the reasons why the Hudson's Bay Company had a policy so diametrically opposed to the policy of the American Government. That is one of the reasons that has kept the Indian in the northern part of this country. If it be true of the Indian in the Hudson Bay and Mackenzie River Districts that the only good Indian is a live Indian, it is more true of the Eskimo, because he inhabits the fringe of your country, which cannot be used by anybody so well as by him. At present, in most of the tribes that I discovered, the Eskimo kill only enough caribou to clothe themselves; some do not kill enough; the tribe at Cape Bechsell kill only about half enough for sleds and bows, and they buy in skins to dress from other tribes. The Eskimo in Victoria Land district will trap wolves, when traders go in and sell them traps. Wolves live on caribou, and there are many wolves there.

Each wolf killed means a great many caribou saved, and you can double the consumption of caribou (above the present rate) and still keep the balance even by killing the wolves. . . . If the Government will step in now, before the habits of the Eskimo change, and pass wise laws which they have the machinery to enforce, the caribou in millions can be protected forever as one of the resources of Canada and the Eskimo will also be protected. If you let the caribou be killed off, the Eskimo will do as they now do in Mackenzie District, they will dress in the Hudson Bay blanket. Those Eskimo cannot go out in winter; that was never true while they dressed in caribou skins.

George Black, who represented the Yukon in Parliament in the Twenties, brought his recollections of gold-rush days to the podium:

We did not have much currency, or, as they called it there, cheechako money—cheechako being the Indian word for "tenderfoot." Everybody carried his gold sack, a little bag or sack made of chamois or moose-skin, and carried a certain amount of gold dust in that to use for change. There was a gold scale in every place of business, and every office. A client went into a law office to consult counsel; he was charged not so many dollars but so many ounces, and the lawyer proceeded to weigh out his fee on his own gold scale.

The handling of money, the handling of gold, was careless. Everybody got into careless ways. They seemed to lose sight, really, of the value of money. The care-free miner would go into a saloon with thousands of dollars of gold dust in his coat pocket, and go up to the open bar and proceed to call up the host of men and treat them to wine at $15 a pint—and it cost some money. The banks were usually more careful in the handling of gold, but I am going to tell you of an actual fact. One of the leading banks of the town did business for a great many years in a little old log building near the bank of the river. They had their assay office on the same lot, a little distance away from the bank, and millions of dollars' worth of gold passed through that bank and through that assay office. About ten years after the rush, when the production was at its peak, a former employee of that bank went back to Yukon and made arrangements with the then manager of the bank to give him what he called a "leg," that is, a working lease on the ground, on the surface gravels of that bank lot. The lot was next door to where I lived, and I gave him the use of the garden hose. He constructed a set of man-power sluice boxes, and

21

proceeded to run through the sluice boxes, with water, the surface gravels lying between the bank building and the assay building; and, would you believe it, he cleaned up three thousand dollars in gold, in dust and nuggets and crucible buttons which had not been put there by nature, but had simply been carelessly spilled in the operations of the bank's business. He cleaned up thousands. That was a surprise to the bank manager, but that former employee knew his business; he had been there in the old days. After that fellow got through, the contractor who had the contract to move the buildings had a "go" at it, and he cleaned up a nice respectable little pocket; and after that my small boy went at it, and recovered something over $100—he and a school chum of his. That shows you the way they scattered money. [Laughter.]

Vilhjalmur Stefansson—almost incidentally—had announced at the conclusion of his speech in February of 1913 his plans for a third expedition into the Arctic. That mission completed, he returned to the Club. As part of his speech he untethered his hobby horse—the cultivation of the musk-ox as a domestic animal. It was Armistice Day when he spoke, and he noted the "glorious expansion of the Empire by force of arms in Africa, the South Seas, and elsewhere." He had sailed in different waters, unaware for a whole year that the war was on:

Seeing that the expedition was in many ways the most extensive polar enterprise that has ever been undertaken, it is manifestly impossible to go over its history in half an hour. . . . The thing of greatest consequence about our expedition I can explain in five minutes: it is that we have introduced a new method into polar exploration. We had a sumptuous outfit, a large scientific staff, all the equipment that forethought could devise, and the advice of all our friends. To give an idea of the special nature of some of the equipment, I will say that some of the scientific instruments used in oceanography were not on the market anywhere in the world, and were to be had only from the Prince of Monaco, the greatest of living oceanographers. It would not be compatible with royal dignity to write him saying, "Dear Sir, Enclosed please find so many dollars; please send so and so." We had to go about the matter in a more diplomatic way, and finally the Prince of Monaco presented us with the oceanographic equipment which no money would have bought for us anywhere. . . .

In the early stages of the expedition, the Karluk, the largest of our three vessels, was taken out of our hands by the force of circumstances; she drifted in the ice from Alaska northwestward, and her equipment and her staff of men (some of our very best) were taken out of the sphere of operations. We then faced the problem of doing, without our equipment and without many of our men, the things that we had intended to do with the help of those men and by the use of that equipment.

Here we were, with our ship taken away from us, about seven hundred miles away from where we wanted to be; in other words . . . we had to make a trip of six or seven hundred miles if we were to do our work: otherwise we had to come home, and the expedition would have been a failure. Of course that was scarcely to be thought of. . . . In my first and my second expeditions . . . we had sometimes for a year at a time lived on the animals of the land—caribou mainly. It occurred to me that perhaps on this third expedition (now that the ship was lost to us) we could do our work by relying on the animals of the sea, as we had previously lived on those of the land, for the Government had assigned to us the task of exploring the ocean that lies north of Alaska, and west of the previously known British Islands in the Canadian archipelago. I therefore put before the remaining men of our expedition a proposition. . . .

My proposition was this: "In my belief, seals in the Polar sea live mainly on shrimps and similar animals; the shrimp is not confined to the vicinity of land, but will be found anywhere in the upper layers of the ocean. . . . I believe we shall find seals wherever there is ocean, because they will follow the food. We know that the frequent winds are sure to break up and readjust the polar ice every few days; the polar ice is always in motion, always breaking in different sized cakes, with open lanes of water between: I feel sure that in those lanes we shall find seals feeding on the shrimps that are sure to be there, and we can live on those seals or even on the shrimps directly." To all this the men replied that it sounded very interesting, but it was academic, and that they did not think they ought to be called on to risk their lives on a proposition of that kind. . . .

The work would have stopped then if there had not been two Norwegians on the coast of Alaska, who thought a certain money equivalent would compensate them for the risk that they would have to undergo: and for $25.00 a day I engaged those men to take the chance of a journey with me. Members of our own party supported us to the distance of fifty miles from shore. At that point I sent back instructions saying that if we did not return to Alaska whence we had started, our non-return was to be considered presumptive evidence that we had gone to Banks Island; that was a journey of about 700 miles in the direction we intended to go. But so strong was the impression with every whaler who was then wintering on the north coast of Alaska, and with every Eskimo and white man who was there, that we could not live on food provided by our rifles, that when we did not come back to Alaska, the story grew up that we were dead. . . . As a matter of fact we made our journey of 700 miles in 96 days, 40 days with food we brought from home and 56 days securing the food as we went. We landed where we said we would land, without losing a day, with every one of our six dogs fat, and without having missed a meal ourselves. [Applause]

If one suspects the business and professional men of the Empire Club did not fully share Stefansson's vision of Canada's northern frontier, they were certainly involved in a direct way in the affairs of the "boom lands" of the Canadian West, the domain of the new "Canadian spirit" which Frank Yeigh and other speakers noted. Settlers streamed West in the decades before and after the founding of the Club, land-seekers drawn from the United States (where nearly all of the free homestead lands had been occupied by 1890), from Europe, and from other parts of Confederation.

The high hopes, confidence and buoyancy of Westerners impressed Rev. G. C. Pidgeon of Toronto. A friend, he said, "visiting one of the rising communities of the West, met a recent immigrant from the South who had brought into this new land all its optimism. He said, 'This is the grandest country on earth, and this is the finest town; we've got them all skinned to death already.' My friend the next morning counted the houses and shacks, and they numbered just twenty-three. . . ."

Western settlers were not pioneers in the accepted sense of the term but denizens of the industrial age, selling a product and living on profit.

And, not incidentally, contributing mightily to Eastern bank accounts. The surge of settlers and occupation of land coincided with railway expansion, the subject of a cheerleading speech in 1907 by D.B. Hanna of the Canadian Northern Railway ("the second largest railway in Canada . . . only a chastened humility prevents me enlarging upon the fact"):

I am not here to laud the particular enterprise to which I devote my working hours, or to defend it from criticism to which, in common with other systems, it is subjected. But as it is essentially a Canadian undertaking, projected and governed by typical Ontario men—may I localize it, and say Toronto men?—it is perhaps not unfitting that some note should be taken of what has actually been accomplished to meet such a situation as is embedded in the immigration and census figures. . . .

I shall refer exclusively to the lines west of Lake Superior. Ten years ago—in 1897—we operated 100 miles of railway through a then unsettled country. Traffic was light and the train service limited. Our equipment consisted of three locomotives and some eighty cars all told, a working staff of less than twenty men altogether, and a pay-roll for the year under $17,000. The gross revenue for the first year was under $60,000, but it was more than sufficient to pay our debts. During that year we handled 25,700 tons of freight and carried 10,343 passengers. There is nothing particularly impressive in these figures.

Today, or ten years afterwards we are operating—or shall be when, in a week or two, the last rails are laid on the Brandon-Regina line—3,345 miles. We have an equipment of 237 locomotives, 219 passenger cars, including 35 sleeping and dining cars, and about 8,500 freight cars of all kinds. These figures, of course, do not include the large number of locomotives and cars ordered and now in course of construction by the builders. The 20 men of 1897 have become 10,700 in 1907, with a payroll of over $5,000,000 a year. And these figures do not include the large construction forces, which at times run into thousands of men. The gross earnings are now on a basis of over $10,000,000 a year; the freight handled for the past fiscal year was 1,822,220 tons; and we carried 703,988 passengers.

Of his "last, best West," John T. Hall, commissioner of industries at Medicine Hat, had this to say, in February of 1908:

> During the recent municipal elections throughout the Province of Ontario it has struck me that the all-absorbing question was the question of electric power. You were told that you were going to get power for about $18.50 per h.p. per annum. We can develop power in the Alberta gas district for $2.40 per h.p. per annum for a 10-hour day. A great many people will hardly believe that, but it is a fact. In connection with this I will say that your Industrial Commissioner passed through Medicine Hat, and he dubbed it "The City of Eternal Light." It is the city where the gas is never turned out. It seems a waste of gas not to turn it out, but it is cheaper to keep it burning. Gas there is so cheap that the great expense in connection with the lighting is in the mantles. Breakage of the mantles takes place when the gas is lighted, and that is the reason that the gas is never turned out in Medicine Hat. . . .
>
> The next trip that I will take will be down in the middle States, telling the people of those States what advantages we have to offer in Alberta; that we have cheap power, and it was cheap power that made Hamilton what she is today, and it is cheap power that is going to make the West. . . . We had a visit recently in the gas region from Rudyard Kipling. He went up on one of the great Mogul engines operated by natural gas. They put a few inches of coal in the bottom of the grate, have a short pipe burner about six feet long attached to the end of the tube, they turn on the gas, it kindles the coal from above down, and at the same time makes steam in the boiler. Kipling is a man who wants to see everything. Afterwards his description of the gas belt was embodied in this statement: "You people in this district seem to have all Hell for a basement."

But the wheels of the West were oiled by the immigrants, whose qualifications were sometimes subtly, and often not so gently, called into question. In the spring of 1905, W. F. Cockshutt complained to the Club:

> We have almost every nation under Heaven in Canada today. Our Northwest is filling up to a large extent with foreign elements that in

some instances are not desirable. A Doukhobor or a Mennonite coming in there is in just as good a position as an alien that has lived in Great Britain 25 years and takes out his papers there and comes to Canada. . . .

Canadians had rioted in Vancouver in 1907, a critical year in the history of Japanese immigration, over what appeared to them an "invasion" of Orientals. *The Times* of London ridiculed the notion that a few thousand Japanese were likely to take over B.C., but anti-Oriental feelings were fueled by West Coast editorialists: "We are of the opinion that this province must be a white man's country. . . . We are an outpost of the Empire, and that outpost we have to hold against all comers," bleated the *Vancouver Daily Province*. The Government of Canada was shocked at the violent Vancouver confrontation, and so was Hamar Greenwood, Canadian M.P. for York in the British House of Commons. Greenwood, however, displaying the typical escalated British arrogance of his transplanted sort, ticked off the members of the Empire Club on quite other grounds:

You can deal as you like with the Chinaman for he is a patient fellow. He has no great Government behind him. You can deal as you will with the long-suffering Hindu. He has no nationality behind him and he is not viewed by the people of his own clan, class, or kingdom in the same way that a wandering Jap is viewed by the highly organized government of the Mikado. But, believe me, you cannot trifle with the Japanese, and whilst I say locally we must make a white Canada our ideal in the interests of our Dominion, and in the interests of posterity, and in the interests of the Empire, yet, unless we realize the delicacy of our foreign relations, especially with this Oriental power, and unless we realize the necessity of endorsing by patient loyalty the efforts of the Foreign Secretary of the time, we will do more to bring about unrest and possible war than we can possibly do in any other way.

That, gentlemen, is my message to you this afternoon. Your loyalty is undoubted, but the patience of the loyalty of some of our Canadian friends is certainly doubted, and I am one who believes that this riot in Vancouver has not helped, but has hindered, the solution of the Oriental immigration question in so far as it concerns

Japan, and I regret with a full heart that it is necessary, as it will be necessary, for the Foreign Secretary of this great Empire to make humble apology to the Mikado and to his Government for the reckless efforts of thoughtless people in the streets of Vancouver. . . .

Two thousand Sikhs from India had also entered B.C. in the months preceding the 1907 riot. By 1911, that number had doubled, and Dr. Sundar Singh appealed to Imperial sentiment for help in redressing his people's grievances:

Some few years ago a few troops of the Sikhs passed through Canada on their way to the jubilee of the late Queen Victoria, and the gentlemen who were in charge of them spoke very highly of them. These Sikhs went back home and they spoke of the vast prairies where they saw wheat growing the same as we grow wheat. The consequence was that a score of them came out in 1905—about forty of them came in that year and the next, and this went on till in 1909 there was quite a strong body of them, about 4,000 in all, engaged in agriculture; they were farmers in India, and of course they naturally took to farming when they came to this country.

They are British subjects; they have fought for the Empire; many of these men have war medals; but, in spite of this fact, they are not allowed to have their families with them when they come to this country; in spite of their being British subjects, they are not allowed to have their wives here. People talk about these Oriental races, and the phrase is understood to include not only the Chinese and the Japanese, but the Sikhs as well, which is absurd. Letters giving inaccurate statements are appearing in the press all the time. I do not know why all this objection should be directed against the Sikhs— against that people, more than against any other Oriental people.

These people are here legally; they have satisfied every process of law; they have been here over five years; they have been good to their employers—Colonel Davidson employs 350 of them in his mills in New Westminster—their work is equal to that of other labourers; their quarters are better, and they are making more wages now; they have fitted into the situation here; they have made good. [Applause] In spite of this, there are these letters going through the papers, and there are attacks upon these men; yet, although they are British subjects, nobody stands up for them. We appeal to you of the Empire Club, for we are only 4,000 in number, to help us in this matter, and to see that justice is done to these subjects of our King. . . .

Some people have spread the false statement that the Sikhs are polygamous: they are monogamous in India, and are not more polygamous than you are. They are strictly monogamous by their religion, and it is useless to spread these false stories. There are officers in India—perhaps some have come from Canada—and they can take their families to India to our people; are the laws made so invidious that it cannot work both ways? That law was meant to shut out the Japanese, yet, in the year 1908, 5,000 came from Honolulu, and they let them in. We do know that we are British subjects and we ask for our rights; if you can allow the alien to come over here, surely a British subject ought to have the same rights as an alien. . . .

The position cannot hold good; it is inevitable that it cannot hold good. These Sikhs are the pick of their villages, they are not out here like the Japanese and Chinese. The Japanese has to show only 50 cents when he arrives, but the Sikh has to show $200, and, if he cannot, he is sent away. Of course you can understand what the reflex action of this treatment might be in the present state of India. These people who are here, are here legally; if they were new people coming in, it would be a different matter; but as such they have rights, and I think those rights ought to be respected. . . . [Applause]

Enlightenment about subject races was not one of white humanity's strong points in the Empire Club's early years. Sir William Grey-Wilson, governor of the Bahamas; in 1911:

Now, the constitution of the Bahamas, like the other three B's of that portion of the Empire, is on a suffrage that is almost equivalent to yours in Canada. I have examined them separately and I think they are very much the same. That is to say, any member of a community who is in possession of a house of the value of $10 a year is entitled to vote. That, of course, is practically manhood suffrage. That vote is common to the blacks and to the whites. The inhabitants of the Bahamas are one quarter white and three quarters black. The result of our elections has been for many years past—and I would remind you that the Bahamas have a constitution almost as old as Newfoundland—that the black man almost invariably elects a white man to represent him. And why is that, gentlemen? You here are conversant with the horrors of the situation in the Southern States of America. In the Bahamas we have no such position. [Applause] I say that a white woman in the Bahamas, in the most isolated position, is as secure today as if she were in this room now. [Applause] I defy any one to say that about the Southern States of America. Now, gentlemen, why is that? It is not because we have treated the black man as the equal of the white; no. He admits himself—the most intelligent of them with whom I have spoken— he admits himself that he is the white man's inferior. He admits that he is of a child race, undeveloped; but it is because of being a child race we have extended to him, as we have to all the other races of the Empire, that universal unswerving British justice which is our common heritage.[Applause]

Gentlemen, I have spent a considerable part of my life in West Africa, where a handful of white men control the situation amidst hordes of blacks, and I say, unless that British justice, of which we are all so justly proud, was dispensed in an even-handed and absolutely righteous manner, we could never hold many of the possessions that we own today.

Right Honourable James Bryce, British Ambassador to the United States, brought similar self-satisfied tidings from another quarter in May, 1911:

There was nothing very remarkable about the British conquering India, because, after all, it was a conquest achieved by a civilized people, with civilized weapons, with civilized strategy, and by men of eminent ability, such as our Duke of Wellington. It was a conquest achieved by these men over a comparatively backward race, but what I am proud of is the way in which India has been ruled. . . . We have governed India for the sake of her people; we have governed it partly out of a desire which every intelligent, capable man would wish who wants to see things well done. We sent a great many able men to India with natural English instincts, civilized men, who wanted to do things the way a capable and efficient Government would desire. These men were imbued with the English ideals of justice and equality. They wanted to extend the full rights of citizenship to the natives of India; to protect them from unjust taxation; to improve the state to which the evil habits of the natives had brought them; to have cruelty discontinued; to establish good order; to police the country properly; to see that every one had the same kind of protection and security, as far as possible, that we have at home: and that has been achieved in an extraordinary degree, and an Englishman may now travel alone with perfect safety in almost every part of India.

I think all the sensible people in India know that, if by any possibility we were compelled to leave India, the result would be disorder, robbery, murder, anarchy, and destruction from one end of the country to the other. That is what existed before we came, and that is what would exist if we left.

Sir Clifford Sifton, Sir Wilfrid Laurier's energetic Minister of the Interior, had conducted the highly successful campaign to attract settlers to Canada in the early years of the twentieth century. He had raided the North of England and Scotland and commissioned booking agencies in Hamburg to sift applicants in favour of agriculturalists and peasants ("I think a stalwart peasant in a sheep-skin coat, whose forefathers have been farmers for ten generations, with a stout wife and a half-dozen children, is good quality"), paying the Hamburg agents $5 per head for the farmer and $2 per head for other members of the family. The newcomers by and large eschewed the East for the cheap lands of the West, cause for carping from C. C. James, Ontario deputy minister of agriculture in Tory James Pliny Whitney's government:

.... And when to the Dominion Immigration endeavours was added the campaign carried on by the Western land companies and the transportation companies, you will see that there was very little for the East to hope for from that movement. The result was that an extra effort was put forth to try and see if we could not attract immigrants directly to this Province from the Old Land. . . . Then was commenced, about 1907, a very active campaign in the Old Country to try and attract people to this Province. Out of that has come an organism, a fairly complete system in the Old Land, with head office of the management on the Strand, London. We located on the Strand, in London, because that street is the most important street in the whole world, I suppose. Now we come across people again and again who say: "Why, it is an easy matter, you ought to bring out people in tens of thousands to Ontario and the other provinces." Of course, people who talk in that way have had no experience in the matter as to what conditions we find in the Old Country. Here we have the rural parts of Ontario crying for men; have our manufacturers from one end of the country to the other crying out for more help; and we go to the Old Land in preference to any other country, because we think that stock is the best to introduce into this land. What do we meet with there? We meet with every other Colony competing for the same article. . . .

Although Canada in the first decade of the century was still primarily agricultural, the lucrative matter of industrial growth—especially in regard to the mineral resources of the country and of Ontario in particular—ran second only to the sentimental favourite of Empire as a Club theme. The subject was most often cause for rejoicing and self-congratulation but some sour notes were sounded. W. G. Miller, the Ontario provincial geologist, in 1910:

About mining booms and stock jobbing, I might say that technical men, mining men, and mineralogists always object to these booms, because the people get bitten and the industry gets blighted. For instance, after Cobalt was discovered in 1903, Toronto people having been pretty well singed in British Columbia mines, although we had as fine a collection of ore from the Cobalt district as one would wish to see, Toronto people were not interested. I had a fine collection at the King Edward Hotel myself, but you couldn't get a Toronto man to look at it scarcely. But the next year when the camp was paying handsomely, the people went to the other extreme, and now they have been bitten again, and are inclined to blame the mineral industry. But it is all caused by stock jobbing and bad advice.

If a man is physically ill he consults a physician—if he is spiritually ill he consults a spiritual adviser of one of the creeds. If he is in legal trouble he seeks advice from a graduate of a law school, but, if he contemplates going into the mining business (and this applies very specially to many of our business men) he takes advice from the first fakir he comes across who says he knows something about mines. Now if people would display the same discretion in this that they do in other matters the mineral industry would be on a much better plane, and it would be just as safe, and safer perhaps than many another business. Nine out of ten of the men who have written the most reports, and given the most advice, are the worst fakirs in Canada. Mining men know them. Of course, they are not all like this, but in many cases the greatest fakirs we have here had a reputation before they came to these camps.

The city of Toronto itself, the seat of the Empire Club, was not above criticism from speakers of the time, for example in matters of its attitudes to itself, its newspapers, and its citizens—including, of course, although sometimes belatedly, women. Hector Charlesworth, on daily journalism, *Toronto World*-style:

Now, the *Toronto World* was a curious illustration of the old financial methods, not merely in newspaper work but in business generally. I do not suppose it ever had an audit of its books. It never knew whether it was solvent or insolvent. [Laughter] It started on a shoe string. My future father-in-law loaned W. F. Maclean $400 and he started the *World,* and if the *World* had been conducted with proper accountancy methods, which I had been early trained to respect, it no doubt would have become solvent some time or other, but as a matter of fact it survived for 40 years, and was I think throughout that period insolvent. [Laughter] But it was a most interesting office in which to get a training, because it was run in this way: I may illustrate with a little story. One time I was sitting in a theatre with another member of the *World* staff, a fellow with a very loud voice. A couple of comedians started a dialogue on money matters, and one said to the other: "You see it's this way—you get it but you don't," and the other fellow said "Yes, you get it but you don't." The man beside me said "By God, that is like the *Toronto*

World.'' [Laughter] We had certain salaries named on the books, but it was doubtful whether you got it. Nevertheless, I do not think any publication had more loyal service or more industrious service than the *Toronto World.* A great many of the most celebrated men in this country worked there from time to time, and Mr. Maclean himself was a very hard worker. He never had a desk of his own, but would come and sit down at the corner of some one else's desk with a piece of paper and stub of lead pencil and write something. Then if he got restless he would get up and move around to another desk, but anything he wrote was pungent and something that everybody wanted to read. . . .

One of the historic cases with which I had connection, because I just happened to get the original tip, was the celebrated Hyams case and in connection with that case I may say that one of the murderers—and I have no hesitation in saying they were murderers—on the night before we were going to spring our big scoop, sent for me through his solicitor and offered me $5,000 to take to the *World* office and give to Mr. Maclean to prevent the publication of the story. I went back to my news editor, old Walter Wilkinson, and he said, "Is that right, Hector?" "Yes there is $5,000 down at the St. Charles Hotel," I replied. "For God's sake don't let them know it," he said. "We have to have that story in the morning paper." [Laughter] We were afraid that the necessities of the office would supersede any feeling for the public weal. However, it was our story and it got published.

J. J. Kelso:

You know it is almost a crime to laugh in Toronto, and one has to be very dignified and grave; although we are told that a good laugh is better than medicine any time. . . . In the United States the only place, so far, that has developed the festival idea to any extent is New Orleans, where the people have the delightful *mardi gras,* lasting for three days, but looked forward to with anticipation for months.

We made an attempt at something of that kind some years ago. We had a summer carnival—four days of solid enjoyment. That was a dismal failure. And why? Not because we did not want it to be a success, or that it was not a good thing, but because we were not educated up to the idea of enjoyment, of throwing business cares aside and going in for a pleasant sociable time, free from business cares and anxiety. . . .

With respect to sewage, Dr. Charles M. Sheard:

We need a supply of wholesome drinking water, and, with great scientific knowledge and foresight, we shove our pipe through the centre of the harbour and go just beyond the line of the sand limitation of the Island to draw our supply of wholesome drinking water. That is where we are, and that is where we have been for thirty years. As we have grown in population we have eradicated the pesthouse and the pit from our midst and we have turned them into our sewers, which, in turn, deliver the same filth down to our shore, and then we go along this beautiful waterfront and we pile it up with sand and gravel and old pipe and junk, and here and there a pile of coal, until, when we look at it as we come in on the deck of a steamboat, we say "Whither are we drifting?"

Dr. G. M. Milligan on women's rights:

Do the people sing here in their homes? What a great thing are the songs of the people. We used to sing when we were boys. "There is no luck about the house when the good man is away." I don't know that they would sing that in this day of women's rights! The father made them believe he was infallible. There were no divided councils; what father said was law. Now, that is a magnificent thing. . . .

That *was* a magnificent thing. Let Andrew Macphail of McGill University, on behalf of the women, have an enlightened last word:

This demand for the suffrage is in reality an attempt to arrive at a higher morality, to attain to consideration in virtue of goodness and not of charm. The real opponents are the women who master men by that easy device, and all men who find it so comfortable to succumb, because they find it so alluring. There is an active and a passive conspiracy working to the same end that women shall not be free.

There is no creature in the world so irritating to the woman who is merely good as the woman who is merely charming, and therefore in a condition of negative morality. . . .

Shut out from the world, the primitive woman was not free to develop an independent life. She adapted herself to the man. His views were her views; his dislikes were shared by her, and she adopted his opinions ready-made. She preferred to be dependent, and agreed that the man should continue to mould her mentality. This destruction of her personality and departure from her line of life became so permanent that she enjoyed it. Her sense of personal value was lost. It was found in external things, her beauty, her adornment, her children, or her husband. This lightness of regard for their own personality still persists, as we may see in the readiness with which a woman exchanges her own name for another, not once, but under certain circumstances—after a period of half-luxurious sorrow and self-conscious demureness—twice, or yet again, and each time with the greater alacrity. Without freedom there can be no free will, and without free will there can be no character. . . .

There is no middle station, half in and half out, exposing the evil and doing nothing for its amendment. This tentative standing-ground merely permits of a sudden release of the nature of the primitive woman in all its nakedness unchecked from within and uncontrolled from without. The spectacle is so revolting, I fear, that most women would turn back with grief and hatred of it to their old rule, rather than strive with a full purpose and endeavour after a new obedience. That is the essential difficulty with which those women have to contend, who would lead their sisters out of bondage. Their real enemies are of their own household, who hate to see this revelation that women make of themselves, which affords to vulgar satirists congenial exercise of their irony and scoff, for the torment or amusement of those who, like themselves, by continually regarding humanity as it is, have developed a capacity for analysis at the expense of a certain dryness and hardness of heart.

CHAPTER THREE

Patriotism versus Practicality

If a nation's state of mind may be determined by the sounds emanating from its lunchtime head tables, Canadians in the first part of this century were suspended between the most exalted patriotism toward the mother country, and a feeling that too often Mother treated them like poor second cousins. This dichotomy was supported on both sides by history. The patriotism side started back beyond the Plains of Abraham and forward from there through the United Empire Loyalists and the war of 1812 (which many saw as an attempt by the United States to annex Canada). This loyal British blood in the Canadian power structure produced those who at a moment's notice, or none at all, could make a speech about the Empire on which the sun never set, loyalty to the crown being a virtue to be equated only with godliness, without necessarily specifying which was No. 1 and which was No. 2.

But the same speakers, once the amenities had been observed, were much less cheerful about the other side of the British connection—trade. Long before, Canada's wheat had been protected in the British market. Britain's institution of a Free Trade policy in 1846 meant goodbye to all that, gave a big boost to the U.S. economy at the expense of Canada, and nearly broke up Canada then and there. Mr. Justice William Renwick Riddell, King's Bench division, High Court of Ontario, 1912, recalled the crisis of 1849:

Stagnation was universal in Canada, prosperity and progress in that part of the United States near her; many of the younger men lost faith in Canada and thought the only way out of the terrible position in which she found herself was annexation to the United States. Many men, some of them of great note and undoubted loyalty in after life, signed, in 1849, a manifesto in favour of union with the nation to the South—Sir John Rose, Sir John J.C. Abbott, Sir Francis Johnson, Sir David MacPherson, Sir Georges Cartier, Luther Holton, Sir Aimé A. Dorion, E. Goff Penny, the Molsons, the Redpaths, the Workmans—all names held in honour in Canada. It is to be borne in mind that no enmity against the Mother Land was expressed or intended. What was in view was a peaceful separation, gladly or at least cheerfully submitted to by the Old Land. The movement never seems to have laid hold upon the body of the people, and it speedily died out.

Well, not quite. Annexation to the United States still seemed to many the answer to Canadian commercial woes until, near the end of the century, the firmest supporters of the British connection, being also foes of annexation, independence, or reciprocity, suddenly saw some light: Joseph Chamberlain, newly-appointed British colonial secretary, proposed abandoning Britain's free trade system. His suggested alternative was Imperial preference—a tariff system that would give British possessions, including Canada, preferential treatment in British markets and vice versa.

George Eulas Foster, Finance Minister in Sir John A. Macdonald's Conservative government and its Conservative successors, was the first major politician to speak to the Empire Club, in December, 1903. He was for Imperial Preference:

One natural question is what will be the advantages to Canada? I want you to think of what the British market means. I want you to see that there are forty-two millions of people there, and that whereas the British producer of the food of that people grows a handful, he imports a whole armful. That about expresses the proportion between the two. Four million acres of wheat-lands were in cultivation 25 years ago in England; today less than 2,000,000.

What does it mean? Population is increasing; 30,000,000 then, 42,000,000 now, 50 or 60 millions in not many years hence . . . it is a market where there is a chronic deficit which is growing . . . and a market, rich, great, strong, wide now, which every year becomes richer and greater and stronger and wider for those who have entrance to it. Let the Canadian producer have entrance to that market, a favoured entrance over foreign competitors. Would not that be an immense benefit to the producer in Canada?

One word more, now, and that is this: You are asked (is it really a question now in Canada), you are asked to put Imperial Preference on one side and American Reciprocity on the other. Can the latter be galvanized into a question in Canada today? Depend upon it, there is a powerful effort being made to do so. But what have we been building for? What is this Grand Trunk Pacific for? To make great lines of railway which run east and west, and not north and south. Mr. Charlton [a Liberal supporter of reciprocity] goes down to Boston. What does he say? "Liverpool fixes the price of the Canadian product. You will simply have the exporting of it. Your millers will get the milling, your transportation routes will get the carrying of it. All the rich drops which come from those long and extensive transportation routes will fertilize your soil. Your business men will get all the peelings." In the name of Heaven what is Canada built for? Have we not ports of our own? Have we not railroads of our own? Have we not a canal system of our own? Have we not a merchant marine system of our own? Have not we a country up here which wants the droppings from its own transportation? Let Mr. Charlton come to the City of Toronto and put that argument here before this people and see how many favourable answers he will receive.

But the railways thus invoked were suspect themselves in some quarters, because of their obvious self-interest in trade and traffic of all varieties, whether it went north and south or east and west. Senator James McMullen in December, 1906:

I notice that "Jim" Hill [a famous Canadian-born U.S. railroad entrepreneur], who, by the way, happens to be a distant relation of my wife, was up in the North-West some time ago, and made a speech at Winnipeg, in which he talked very strongly in favour of better trade relations with the United States. He said that he should like to see the Americans take down the bars and promote better trade between Canada and the United States. Well, Hill has thirteen good sound reasons why he should talk in that way. He is building no less than thirteen branches from his main line into the Canadian North-West.

But railways were only part of the argument. Imperial Preference versus Reciprocity increasingly filled the air at meeting halls and the pages of newspapers reporting those meetings. One night in 1905 the Empire Club staged a debate in which two Canadians and two New-foundlanders [a separate British colony then] confronted a friendly, plausible American named Eugene Foss who had been talking up and down the United States on the virtues of Reciprocity. Mr. Foss had made a speech in Minneapolis, saying: "Our manufacturers have been too busy in recent years to give much effort or thought to the subject [of Reciprocity], but from now on, for a period, times will not be so flush, there will be less business and more time for thought, there will be fewer words and more time to think. This will turn attention to Reciprocity which promises to open foreign markets."

His Empire Club hosts were polite, but incisive. Dr. W. H. Montague, former dominion Minister of Agriculture:

In other words, Sir, the anxiety is for markets for your manufactures. This is not disguised, nor would it be possible to disguise the fact that that is why Reciprocity is being agitated here. I listened with a very great deal of pleasure to your Vice-President Elect. the Hon. Mr. Fairbanks, who delivered a splendid speech at the Home Market Club, and what did Mr. Fairbanks say upon the subject of Reciprocity? He said, in effect, that it was the desire of the Government of the United States to extend trade *wherever the extensions could be made without injury to American industries.*

Sir, we are anxious to extend trade in Canada, but we are anxious to extend it only by means which will not injure our Canadian industries, and we will not injure or destroy our Canadian industries, which have become such an important part of our national make-up, for the advantages of trade in any part of the world. Let me say to you and say unhesitatingly, that Canada does not dream of opening up her industries to the keen and destructive competition of the United States or of any other country.

Need I tell you that Reciprocity is incompatible with Canadian aspirations for a consolidated Empire on trade lines; as it now exists on lines of sentiment. Canada is anxious, and anxious with hope, that the grand scheme of colonial and preferential trade so ably being battled for by Mr. Chamberlain will succeed. We hold these views without hostility to you, but we hold them strongly and we look forward to the time when our products in the market of Great Britain will receive better terms than you do. . . .

May I say one word as to a certain opinion which was recently expressed in the Boston *Herald*. I do not believe that the opinion there expressed emanated from any responsible party, rather would I believe that it emanated from some one who was irresponsible and unthinking. The opinion is expressed in these words: "But the indications are that the awakening of American statesmen has come, the contest is on, and the grand prize is Canada, nominally commercial Canada, but actually the political Dominion." Sir, I should be less than a Canadian if I did not, for my own people, resent this expression of opinion. What would you think of Canadians, of their national pride, of their patriotism, if that did not stir them to the core? Supposing tomorrow a country 20 times the size of yours in population, in wealth, in strength, made any such proposal as the one I have quoted, what would be your answer? Sir, it would stir to intensity every fibre of your being. You would sing "My Country, 'tis of Thee" with still greater energy than you have sung it tonight. You would raise the Stars and Stripes, the flag you love, still higher and nearer to the blue. You would light the fires of patriotism upon every elevated spot from Bunker's Hill to the Golden Gate, and by the memory of all the great heroes whose fame is found recorded in the pages of your national history, from Washington to McKinley, you would swear anew allegiance to the flag you love. Sir, in the cheers with which you greet my words is to be found the answer of Canada, for Canada is British, her people are British, her hopes are British, and she believes it to be her duty to contribute her influence, be it great or be it small, towards the perpetuation for all time of British institutions upon the Continent of America.

One thought more. If tomorrow Canada were to consent to change all her plans, desert her claims of trade which have cost her so much to secure, give up her hold upon the markets which she now has, and join with you; what would you guarantee her in the way of permanency? When all our lines are down again, when the course of our commerce at your request has been changed, when we have deserted old friends for new ones, then some fine morning we should probably awaken to find that, as in 1866, our market with you had ceased; only it would be more serious now than then, because in the meantime our industries would have been ruined.

History repeats itself; I have to go back a good many years to get my illustration; but the older the wine the better, and the older the illustration the stronger. There was a time on the Continent of Europe when Greece and Rome were the dominant factors on that Continent, but, Sir, the dominant factors on the Continent of Europe today are the Northern people; and we are the northern people here. And we hope, though we may be hoping against fate, that history will repeat itself in this Continent; and I assure my friend Mr. Foss, that if that time ever comes, we shall treat the United States with the greatest generosity possible, as though they were still retaining their dominant position upon the Continent of America!

There is a story told of a gentleman who was absent from home and who received a telegram from one of his friends. "Your mother-in-law died this afternoon. Shall we embalm, cremate or bury?" And he answered that telegram, "Take no chances. Do all three." [Laughter] And so, Sir, I think I speak the sentiment of our Canadian people when I say, notwithstanding all the truths of philosophy, we have come to the conclusion at last that we will take no chances in dealing with our great national industry, but build it up in our own way, as our best contribution to Imperial strength and as our best contribution to the civilization of the globe.

That night a different tone came from Sir Edward Morris, Minister of Justice in Newfoundland. He did some diplomatic fence-sitting, because at the time Newfoundland was waiting for U.S. ratification of Newfoundland's own reciprocity treaty with the U.S.:

For me to be suddenly called upon to give a decision as to the merits of this case puts me almost in the position of the man in the story that I now recall who in life had two wives to whom he had been equally devoted and with whom he had lived for about the same number of years and on the most friendly terms. When he was dying himself, both of these ladies having predeceased him, he was asked where he would like to be buried. "Well," he said, "bury me between the two of them but a little on the side of Biddy!"

Now I think, Mr. Chairman, I am a little on the side of Biddy as put by Dr. Montague, and I think I must agree with what I have heard of the arguments. However, I think that the speech that has been made by Dr. Montague tonight, if delivered to various audiences in Newfoundland, would not to any very large extent help to bring about what the Chairman is so anxious for, namely, Confederation, because Newfoundlanders having heard of the disintegration of the Roman Empire and remembering that they are north of Canada, and with territory larger than England, and considering that Labrador is nearly as large as the Russian Empire, we too have great hopes of building a great nation.

[Dr. Montague:] That will make the United States third.

[Mr. Morris:] Dr. Montague has a little anticipated me because that is the point I was about to reach. When our population has increased to millions, when we are raising wheat down on Labrador, under glass if you will, and when we have short-line railways and fast steamers connecting with England, and our people have grown to an extensive population, millions if you like, when we have battleships and armies we will extend to Canada that same good fellowship and brotherhood that Canada no doubt will sometime before us be extending to the United States. But up to the present time, Mr. Chairman, in Newfoundland we have not been called upon really to decide the exact position Newfoundland should take. In reference to the great fiscal policy now being promulgated by Mr. Chamberlain, we are wooed on both sides. We have friends in England and friends in the United States, and in Canada, and it would be, as I say, risky for me to give expression here tonight to any very pronounced opinion. Newfoundland is on the very best terms with the United States; on the other hand she is on the very best terms with Canada. Newfoundland always remembers that when troubles and trials were upon the land, and upon the people, that they met with kindly response from Canada and especially from Toronto, and I say that good-fellowship and good feeling exists.

But at the same time Newfoundland looks to the United States for great advantages to flow from the ratification and adoption of the Treaty which has been signed on two occasions by two Secretaries of State for the United States. As you know, under that Treaty nearly all our products would go into the United States duty free. We look forward, I say, to that Reciprocity Treaty being sanctioned and ratified some day and we believe that great good will come to both countries from it. At the same time there is nothing in that Treaty in any way which affects Canada or any portion of the British Empire.

There's no doubt that some misunderstandings as to Canada's relationship with Britain helped give Americans the comfortable feeling that if commercial union led to political union, they would be doing us a favour.

Tory Senator James McMullen:

Sometime ago I was down in the State of Kansas, in Kansas City, and I was talking to an intelligent American gentleman, and he said, "You are from Canada?"

"Yes."

"Well, I am very glad to see you. Glad to have a little conversation with regard to Canada. Don't you think it would be better for your people to join us rather than to be paying taxes to England?"

I said, "We don't pay any taxes to England."

"What, no taxes to England!"

"No."

"Neither for army or navy or anything else?"

"No! we pay no taxes to England; all we do is to pay the salary of a Governor-General and the equipment of his mansion, which costs us about $110,000 a year. That is all it costs us; we pay no taxes."

In a very rough, gruff way, he said to me, "What the hell good are you to England?" [Laughter] He thought that tax-paying was the only possible good that we could render to the Empire.

Making light of American misinformation about Canada, poking fun at American ignorance of the Empire—wasn't it the kind of thing

Stephen Leacock could have handled to a T, leaving them rolling in the aisles? Wrong. The one thing Leacock didn't use as a basis of jokes in those days was the Empire. He wasn't very funny about Americans, either, in 1907:

Be it said without concealment and without bitterness. They have chosen their lot; we have chosen ours. Let us go our separate ways in peace. Let them still keep their perennial Independence Day, with its fulminating fireworks and its Yankee Doodle. We keep our Magna Charta and our rough-and-ready Rule Britannia, shouting as lustily as they! The propaganda of Annexation is dead. Citizens we want, indeed, but not the prophets of an alien gospel. To you who come across our western border we can offer a land fatter than your Kansas, a government better than Montana, a climate kinder than your Dakota. Take it, Good Sir, if you will; but if, in taking it, you still raise your little croak of annexation, then up with you by the belt and out with you, breeches first, through the air, to the land of your origin! This in all friendliness.

It wasn't always that friendly. Lt. Col. William Hamilton Merritt in 1909 saw Canada as a weak link in the Imperial chain, particularly open to attack from the U.S.:

What has been the history of the expansion of the United States? The original territory, under the Peace of Paris in 1783, covered the territory east of the Mississippi and north of Florida. Then the Province of Louisiana, the great Central West, was purchased from France in 1803 and Florida from Spain in 1819. Texas as a republic was admitted in 1845, Great Britain was euchred out of Oregon and Washington in 1846 and the remainder of the West wrested from Mexico by war in 1848, save a small piece purchased from them in 1853. Then Alaska was bought from Russia in 1867; Hawaii was absorbed in 1899; the Philippines taken from Spain in 1898, which might as well be said to include Cuba. A pretty good record of land grabbing—a ten-fold increase to the 326,378 square miles of the original 13 States. The question is, have they finished? Will history not repeat itself? Does the world appear to be breaking into small states, small trusts and combines, decreasing expansion?

Mr. L. S. Amery, the well-known British military expert, says: "I know that the average politician who hates all unpleasant facts will say 'the Americans are our cousins and friends; war with them is unthinkable!' " Unthinkable! There is no such word in international politics. We have been at war with the United States in the past. We have more than once since then been on the verge of war with them—the last time only 12 years ago, over Venezuela.

Mr. Amery, knowing the hopelessness of our military system and military position, goes on to say:

"We require a military system capable of putting, if it came to the worst, two million men into the field in Canada in the second year of war."

The humiliation of our impotence is made even more clear by Mr. Amery when he alludes to "the less critical case of India."

Therefore should we not wake up?

A British major general, C. W. Robinson, came up with a specific in 1911 that hadn't occurred to everybody—that the Number One priority in Canadian defence should be a fleet of warships on the Great Lakes, poised to handle any threat from guess who:

I know also that there are other portions of the Dominion requiring defence, such as the Pacific coast, British Columbia, and the West, Hudson Bay and Straits, and her extended land frontier of hundreds of miles. But I see nothing in all this to alter the fact that, if an enemy's vessels obtained supremacy upon the lake waters, they could bombard the cities upon their banks, destroy the railways running past them, and probably occupy those cities and Central

Canada; that the Dominion would be then cut in two; the West cut off from the East and communication of the Western Provinces with the Atlantic and Great Britain severed; and Canadian trade paralyzed. The Canadian lion would then be wounded, not in its tail, but in its body, and possibly mortally.

Most of the soul-searching, while it might touch upon U.S.-Canada relations, had a much broader scope—the future of Canada within the Empire. In 1907 Stephen Leacock got quite passionate in his arguments for a full partnership among Empire Countries, Imperial Union:

> Not Independence, then, not Annexation, not Stagnation; nor yet that doctrine of a little Canada that some conceive—half in, half out of the Empire, with a mimic navy of its own; a pretty navy this— poor two-penny collection, frolicking on its little way strictly within the Gulf of St. Lawrence, a sort of silly adjunct to the navy of the Empire, semi-detached, the better to be smashed at will. As well a Navy of the Province, or the Parish, home-made for use at home, docked every Saturday in Lake Nipigon! Yet this you say, you of the Provincial Rights, you Little Canada Man, is all we can afford!—we that have raised our public charge from forty up to eighty millions odd, within the ten years past, and scarce have felt the added strain of it. Nay, on the question of the cost, good gentlemen of the council, spare it not. Measure not the price. It is not a commercial benefit we buy. We are buying back our honour as Imperial citizens.
>
> That, gentlemen, is my political credo; there stands my article of faith. I do not care about the details of it, but I hope that maybe, sooner or later—I mean the sentimentality that inspires it—will be the fundamental article of faith of every man in the Dominion. I am one of those who believe that there is need now for an Imperial movement in this country. I believe the little Shibboleths of our political parties have worn themselves out and we must get behind them a new and stronger motive power, something that shall lift us out to a higher standing and higher inspiration in politics than we enjoy at present. We, the people of Canada, must get behind and shove, and of all people who should most advance the cause of Imperial Union, in whatever way we may complete it, I think those of us who are interested in education ought to be the most concerned. It is not usual to regard us, gentlemen, as leaders in political thought and leaders in political movement; we are generally regarded as a somewhat harmless and irresponsible class. Indeed we enjoy a sort of special license on account of our irresponsibility. I have found myself at gatherings similar to this prompted to say things which otherwise might have sounded recklessly irresponsible, merely on the ground that as a University Professor, I could not hope to understand what I was talking about. [Laughter]

Laurier was deposed by Robert Borden in 1911, in a bitterly fought campaign reflecting the problems and hopes of the country. Laurier had dissolved Parliament and gone to the people in the face of a Liberal party split and an Opposition filibuster over reciprocity in trade between Canada and the United States. The Conservative election cry, "No truck nor trade with the Yankees", spoke to a genuine concern on the part of Canadians.

At times this concern took the form of a superiority complex, as in the case of Rev. W. T. Herridge (husband of Mackenzie King's boon companion-to-come, Marjorie):

> We can well afford to share [U.S.] alertness, their enthusiasm, their strongly patriotic spirit, but I think we can do without . . . their yellow journalism, their grasping trusts—curious name—, their political wiles, their boastful superficiality.

The Empire Club's Castell Hopkins took aim at U.S. influence in Canada:

> Most people are now aware that through the Canadian-American Postal arrangement of 1895 a clear preference was and is given United States magazines and periodicals in this country—which, by the way, many are demanding that Great Britain should make good. Most people, however, are unaware how steadily the resulting influx of cheap United States periodical literature is moulding public thought along the lines of American military and navy traditions, American democracy and business methods, continental conditions and social unity—aided by the affiliation of Labour bodies and the assimilation of political methods. Added to this influence of current popular literature and the already-described power of daily cabled news is the curious effect upon the opinions of Canadian journalists which is exercised by the United States press itself.
>
> It is not an exaggeration to say that the average Canadian newspaper man rarely sees a British paper and still more rarely studies British politics or conditions from both sides and from authoritative sources. As a rule the Canadian journalist sees almost entirely the papers of the United States and Canada. When dealing with questions of sudden importance, such as the Jamaica question or the

EMPIRE
•BOOKS•

Phone Orders
Gladly Accepted!

CENTRE TOWN
240 Bank (at Lisgar)
236-2363
9-6 Mon-Wed, Sat
9-9 Thurs, Fri
12-5 Sundays

LINCOLN HEIGHTS
GALLERIA
2525 Carling Avenue
820-7023
9:30-6 Mon-Wed, Sat
9:30-9 Thurs, Fri

WE FEATURE MORE WAYS TO STRETCH YOUR BOOK-BUYING DOLLAR!

- *WE WILL NOT BE KNOWINGLY UNDERSOLD! IF A BOOK WE HAVE IN STOCK IS SELL-ING FOR LESS ANYWHERE ELSE IN TOWN, LET US KNOW AND WE'LL MATCH THE PRICE!*

- *DISCOUNT BESTSELLERS AT **25% OFF LIST PRICE!***

- *EMPIRE DOLLARS! RECEIVE **EMPIRE DOLLARS** WHENEVER YOU BUY **$25 or more.** THE MORE YOU BUY, THE MORE YOU RECEIVE!*

- *5% **Discount FOR Seniors** EVERY MONDAY*

- *CAN'T FIND WHAT YOU'RE LOOKING FOR? WE'LL GET IT FOR YOU WITH OUR STATE OF THE ART SPECIAL ORDER SERVICE AT NO ADDITIONAL CHARGE!*

- *ASK ABOUT OUR HANDY LAYAWAY SERVICE*

- ***GIFT CERTIFICATES** FOR ANY AMOUNT*

- *DISCOUNTS AVAILABLE TO LIBRARIES & INSTITUTIONS*

cabled decision of the Alaskan Boundary Tribunal, he is naturally and inevitably influenced by (1) the cabled, and, I repeat, the Americanized news in his own papers, and (2) by the clever editorials in New York, Chicago, or Washington journals. They are all before him, perhaps on the very day they are written; he has little from the British side of the case, either cabled or written; his opinion is formed or largely influenced by the piled-up masses of papers from a foreign country—and in these cases the country opposed to the national and natural view of his own Empire.

T. E. Champion of *The Telegram* took sarcastic objection:

I have been delighted with Mr. Castell Hopkins' remarks. I am not going to criticize them now, except to say that he is absolutely and entirely and wholly inaccurate about the newspaper press in this city and in the statement that newspaper men do not read British newspapers, and that they are wholly influenced by American sentiment. If he will have the kindness to step over to *The Telegram* as soon as he has listened to other comments, we will furnish him with all the English papers from January 1st. If he will come across to *The Globe* he will find the same or to *The Mail and Empire*. As regards Mr. Hopkins' address, taken altogether, it was interesting: it was true and very convincing; but as regards his remarks about the newspaper press, all I have to say is that Mr. Hopkins has relied upon his imagination for his facts.

Every once in a while the Empire Club resounded to speeches about royalty. These often were written in the form of sermons; not unusual, in that clergymen often were chosen to fill such onerous slots. Royalty was uncontroversial; other features of the Empire were not. No part of the debate on the British connection was so swept by tidal waves of talk, unmatched by deeds, as Canada's role, or lack of it, in Empire defence. All hands agreed that if Britain was at war, Canada was legally at war and theoretically liable to attack. The matter ended there, with a shrug. When Britain sent an expedition to the Sudan in 1885 and would have welcomed Canadian troops, Sir John A. Macdonald declined. "Why should we waste men and money in this wretched business," he wrote to Sir Charles Tupper. "Our men and money would be sacrificed to get Gladstone and Company out of the hole they have plunged themselves into by their own imbecility.'' In 1899 Sir Wilfrid Laurier steadfastly declined sending Canadians to South Africa for that war until serious British reverses so aroused English-Canadian public opinion that he was forced to agree to sending 2,000 men; public opinion being marshalled at least partly by a wildly energetic militia colonel and Conservative M.P. named Sam Hughes, who appealed in Canadian newspapers for South Africa volunteers and quickly got 1,200 replies. But as soon as that war was over and the heroes welcomed home, it was back to the status quo—meaning that Canadians both at home and abroad would have had to be superhuman to avoid developing an inferiority complex about being known for the next few years, up to the outbreak of war itself, as the cheapskates of the Western world. Richard C. Jebb of London, England, author of *Studies in Colonial Nationalism*, noted that not everyone in England thought the Empire, with its massive defence bill for British taxpayers, was a good idea:

> The anti-imperialists throw Canada into your teeth and ask you what signs you see in Canada of any disposition to share the burden of defence. I know in telling you this I am on delicate ground. However, I am merely relating to you how the thing is looked at in England and that is the objection to our Imperial idea that is always cropping up.

How small was Canada's contribution? Canada had no navy, no standing army, and a militia of about 49,000 all ranks when Lt. Col. James Mason gave the nuts and bolts of the situation to a glum audience in March, 1906:

> I do not raise the question, ''Should Canada contribute to the defence of the Empire?'' for that must be conceded. Canada could not protect herself, and only exists as a self-governing colony, or nation, by reason of her connection with the Empire; so that to contribute to the defence of the Empire should be regarded not only as a duty but as a necessity.
>
> The British Empire, with its vast possessions so widely scattered over the face of the globe, and its enormous business and trade

interests, requires now more than ever in these days of alliances of nations, a large and efficient navy and army to protect and to defend its possessions and trade. [This costs] . . . a grand total of over £64,000,000 or about $300,000,000. This gigantic sum is the levy for a single year only, and it has been frequently exceeded. Consider the heavy burden placed upon the shoulders of the forty-two millions of people who inhabit England, Ireland and Scotland. We, in Canada, contribute a little over $100,000 to all this expenditure of $300,000,000.

(As an Empire contributor to this sum, Canada gave about half as much as New Zealand, the Cape Colony, or Natal; about a tenth as much as Australia; about one-fortieth as much as India; and overall came second last in the Empire list, ahead of only one contributor: Newfoundland.) ·

Colonel Mason recommended increased emphasis on cadet and part-time naval and marine training, and donation of a battleship right away. A week later this flushed out Captain A. T. Hunter with his ability to find some fun in subjects that normally produced only long faces:

Imperial Defence hitherto enjoyed the privilege of being safe ground for the orator and flag-waver; no definite duties being undertaken and no definite money proposition being guaranteed. It was therefore very unfitting of Colonel Mason to deprive this subject of its vague and theoretic character and to propose so hard and inelastic a piece of collateral as a battleship, when we are all willing and ready at all times to put up, what we have always put up, a verbal undertaking to give our last man and last dollar. We are, I think, being put in the cold commercial position of having to put up or shut up. [Hear, hear]

Let us examine our obligations and then let us examine our means of settlement. As to our obligations there has been a good deal of confusion because by the use of metaphors we speak of the Mother-country as if she were a widow and we her sons earning ten dollars a week and asked to chip in for her support! Now, as a matter of fact,

51

an Englishman of my own age is not my mother and I am not under filial obligation to him. Ours is not the duty to give, ours is the duty of good comradeship to lend in the hour of necessity such things as we have or can get ready in the time of the hurly burly. I must therefore strongly oppose the idea of giving a battleship. I feel at the same time that we should start a constantly increasing collection of marine police and battleships or cruisers, of whatever type is considered most appropriate and that we should be ready to lend them on short notice and place them at the Empire's disposal without reserve. . . .The Maple Leaf as a land emblem is quite appropriate and correct but as a maritime nation at the present time ours should be the "sponge rampant." [Laughter]

Next as to money. Now there is no need of talking of money in this connection because we are always in the English money market. They are always lending and we are always steady borrowers, so we will pass on to the men. There are men to give or lend—it is a figurative speech, it is a metaphor, to speak of giving our last man. We will only lend him. We want him back when John Bull is through with him, even though he be maimed and blind, or eaten up with enteric. We want him back again because he is a Canadian, and in this connection I think there is considerable room for educating Canadians as to the appropriate and suitable sort of men that we should accumulate for Imperial loaning purposes. We must send men who will give other nations a formidable image of the Canadians. Now these erroneous images of nations do a great deal of good or harm. For instance there is the Chinese. The Chinaman has allowed others to think that he is unwarlike and servile with the result that we have fed him with kicks. On the other hand the notion we commonly have of the native of Kentucky is that every man is a Colonel and drinks raw whisky and that notion tends to make us respectful and hospitable. [Laughter] Now if we could only give the nations abroad the idea that it was not wise to have Canadians looking at them over the sights of the rifle that would start the idea that Canada was a lot of bad land for the invader, that it was lean in glory and rich in abusive words, and that the invader would likely come back, as they say on the Scotch borders, "Wi' a sark fu' o' sair banes."

Well, in selecting our men for the Imperial export trade I am afraid we shall have to look outside of our military organization. The only military organization in Canada is, as you are aware, the Militia—of whom the York Rangers [Capt. Hunter's own regiment] is undoubtedly the best Regiment [Hear, hear], and the Militia is, unfortunately for us, in its equipment and weapons, instruction, tactics and discipline, a very servile imitation of the British Regular Army. This involves the danger at any time of deterioration over which our public authorities have no control. Let me illustrate. During the South African war the Boers gave infinite annoyance by the discourteous manner in which they disregarded the rules of tactics laid down by the best European experts and it took six or seven times their number to convince those ignorant farmers of the error in their modes of fighting; and during that period the English officers, from Lord Roberts down, had the feeling that it was wise to adopt what are now called looser movements, more extended formations, and to allow what is known as individual initiative.

Now individual initiative, I may say to you who are not military men, is that degree of human reason which is allowed to a common soldier to enable him to come in out of a rain of bullets. The result was that during the South African period the British Army permitted, and consequently the Canadian Militia was allowed, a certain amount of initiative. But the lesson of the South African war has gone the way of the lesson of the American Revolution, and the British Army for the past year and more has been steadily retracing its steps, deliberately doing so, and the photograph of any military imbecility that is introduced in England is faithfully mimicked in Canada. For instance, a Japanese Infantry Officer is believed during the occurrence of a night attack to have struck a Russian with a sword—it is not well authenticated, but it is believed—and, accordingly, we Canadian Infantry Officers who during the South African war had been told to leave our swords in the tents—and they ought to be in museums—had them very much in evidence at the last Camp, and we practiced the drawing, carrying, saluting with and returning these lodge emblems and we did it to the rhythmic stamping of our own feet. Such are the horrors of war!

And it is going to be worse in the future. The highest military authority at present in England has very recently declared for precise drill as against loose movements. Accordingly it is inevitable that someone in the Militia Department at Ottawa will roar for precise drill . . . . Gentlemen, we Canadians cannot compete in precise drill with the professional Tommies and we will make a great mistake in selecting our next contribution to the Empire if we consider precise drill any qualification for selection. My proposition is, then, to select or to breed up in, or out, of the Militia, say one thousand Canadians with these qualifications:

(1) To be able to ride sufficiently well to get from one place to another.

(2) To shoot with the greatest possible accuracy at long ranges from 600 yards to 1,500 yards, the ranges at which the precisely drilled soldier of Europe never hits anything except by accident.

(3) That they should know the other use of a sandbag—I mean entrenchment.

(4) That they should have enough discipline not to be hung as bandits when taken prisoners.

A thousand Canadians with those qualifications, under an appreciative leader, could stall up a whole division of the best precisely-drilled troops in Europe. If we had them and sent them to the field, the next time the nations drew lots to see who should be invaded, Canada would get the "by."

Not that Canada was doing nothing at all. She had agreed in 1910, under Laurier, to take from Britain for training purposes two obsolete cruisers that the British didn't want any more. This didn't fool anybody.

Sir Richard McBride, Conservative Premier of B.C., in 1913:

I shall say not one word to offend a single individual in this room who may have at the moment strong faith in the political doctrines for which Sir Wilfrid Laurier must stand responsible, but you will permit me to go this length, and I do it, I hope, without causing the slightest feeling of criticism one way or the other, the navy that Sir Wilfrid Laurier gave to Canada three years ago was looked upon the world over as a screaming farce.

By that time, Sir Robert Borden had been Prime Minister of Canada for two years. He'd come into office with the naval issue in the foreground. At first he'd been in favour of Canada setting up her own

Navy, but a visit to England brought an urgent message from the British that there was no time. Money to build British battleships would help more. In 1912, Borden proposed an emergency contribution to Britain of $35,000,000 to build three battleships to be manned by the British. Stephen Leacock:

> If this measure becomes law, at the end of the war we may be able to erect a monument with the simple inscription: "To the glorious memory of thirty five million dollars, lost at sea."

Six months of fierce and emotional debate in the Commons followed before the naval bill was passed—only to be killed by the predominantly Liberal Senate. There the matter sat until war came.

CHAPTER FOUR

Brave Men and Butchery

1914. August 4: Britain, including (it went without saying at the time) all her Dominions and colonies, declares war on Germany.

October 16: First Canadian contingent of more than 33,000 troops, most of them civilians ten weeks before, land at Plymouth, England.

December 5: Prime Minister Sir Robert Borden at the Empire Club:

We offered them an expeditionary force on the 1st of August. On the 7th of August, the suggested composition of the force was received from the British authorities, and was immediately sanctioned by Order in Council. Recruiting in the meantime had already commenced, and within, I think, two or three weeks 35,000 men had been enlisted and gathered at Valcartier Camp, and within six weeks from the outbreak of war those men were ready to be transported across the Atlantic, fully armed and equipped for the war.

I went to Valcartier Camp four weeks after the day the sod was broken for it. The site consisted of a number of little farms, with farm-houses scattered over them. It had been taken for military purposes some time before, but nothing had been done by way of preparing it for use. I want to tell you what was accomplished by the time I saw it. A rifle range comprising a line of 1,500 targets, and extending more than three and a half miles, was completed within about ten days. A complete water supply, with necessary piping, pumps, tanks, and chlorinating plant, with about 200 taps fitted to ablution tables and 75 shower baths, was constructed. An electric light, power, and telephone system was installed. Streets were constructed, buildings and tents erected, and an effective sewerage system, comprising over 28,000 feet of drain pipe, was completed. Railway sidings with necessary loading platforms were constructed. Woods were cleared and elaborate sanitary arrangements prepared. Six large buildings for ordnance stores and for the Army Service Corps, buildings for medical stores, for pay and transport offices, hospital stables for sick horses, fumigating and other buildings were constructed and made ready for use within the same period. Thirty-five thousand men were assembled and put through a most systematic course of training in all branches of the service. Infantry, cavalry, artillery, engineering, Army Service Corps, Army Medical Corps, signalling and ammunition columns were organised, and all were trained in their respective duties. Sixteen thousand men were trained daily in musketry.

The force was ready for embarkation within six weeks from the outbreak of war, and could have been then despatched if arrangements for escort had been immediately possible.

Earnest men, with whose ideals I most deeply sympathise, from all over Canada have been asking me, "Why did not we send immediately 100,000 men across the Atlantic, why not send 150,000 or 200,000 men?" Do you realize what it would mean to send men untrained to fight against the most highly-trained troops in the world? I would not be responsible for it if all the people in Canada told me to do it. You might as well send a dozen or fifteen men from the street into a professional football club or lacrosse or hockey club and expect them to succeed, as to send untrained soldiers against highly-organized troops. We must train these men here and in Great Britain; they must be hardened, and brought into such physical condition that they can undergo the hardships of actual service under the conditions which must be present there without breaking down . . . .

Six weeks later another minister, Justice Minister and Attorney General Charles Doherty:

> Has it ever struck you that it is a long time since this terrible struggle began? Before the war is a very remote period indeed. When one looks back to things that used to be said and discussed in that period, it seems like looking back to a distant age. I remember, for instance, that people used to say—now I am not talking politics—that when England was at war, Canada was at war. Who says that now? Who thinks of this war as anything but our war?

For the next four years there was little but war. Matter-of-factness, deep emotion, human degradation, hatred and bombast, love and respect; it all came eventually to the comfortable podium.

Lt.-Col. W. N. Ponton near the end of February, 1915, talking about the First Canadian Contingent:

> Thirty-one transports gathered at Gaspé, having come down the river under small convoy. When the boys were on the decks wondering where was the fleet they had expected, they saw seven streaks of smoke on the broad expanse of ocean, and gradually the streaks of smoke assumed form and they saw that they were battleships and battle-cruisers of the Old Mother's navy, coming over to convoy them across the ocean. Gradually as they approached, they saw the Admiral's ship was leading, with the Admiral's flag flying. One of the captains of one of our Ontario battalions said, "What about 'Rule Britannia'?" No sooner suggested than done, and with greater volume than ever before the grand old song rang out from the *Cassandra* and spread to the other troopships, and the moment it reached the Admiral's ship the signal was given and the engines stopped, and the great fleet of battleships glided by instead of steaming by, so that they might take in every word and note of that welcome from the lusty sons of the Grand Old Mother, accorded in that great Imperial spectacle to the fleet that was to guide and guard them over. And when they came up to these Canadian men singing as they never did before, the Admiral's flag dipped, and the sailors manned the yards. One man said it later: "We suddenly stopped singing and something came up in our throats, and we think it was

our hearts.'' They never had such a greeting as they had on that memorable occasion when vibrant, virile young Canadians welcomed them in song.

Lieut. G. R. Forneret was in that convoy. By mid-January, 1916, he had both the memory of the crossing and the memories of the trenches. He read to the Empire Club a letter he had written on shipboard fourteen months earlier, then told how it was in action. The letter home:

We were convoyed by certain battleships. One was the Princess Royal, a magnificent ship, absolutely the last word. She had been keeping some distance to our left flank. One afternoon, about five o'clock, the cry went about the ship: "The Princess Royal is coming in.'' Sure enough she was. We crowded the rail to watch her as she lazily overtook us. She was paying us the compliment of an afternoon visit. On she came, looming larger and larger. Now we could make out the great guns in tiers protruding from the forward turrets; now we could see the crowded fighting tops; now the decks stripped to the steel plates for action. Now we saw the crew, hundreds of them, lining the decks. Now she was up to our stern. Her band was playing "O Canada.'' As she started to draw abreast there was a broadside of British cheers from her—crash—crash—crash—with a vibrant human note of patriotism and fellowship. Then we went clean mad. We scrambled to deck, breaking for points of vantage, and cheered and cheered until we were hoarse and dizzy. So she sailed past, proud, rugged, ugly, huge and magnificent. Our ensigns dipped, and the deep-throated greeting crashed and echoed from ship to ship till she passed on and we stood gazing devouringly after her. There wasn't anything to say. It was just British glory on the sea—and we were British. A senior officer clinging to the davit next me, kept repeating hoarsely to himself, his eyes shining through his tears, "My God—my God,'' like that.

He was a thoughtful man, Lieut. Forneret, and observant, as he turned from the emotion of the sea moment to what the war really turned out to be all about. For one, a general commanding a division found him and two platoons of men without rations one day and had rations delivered half an hour later. Days later Forneret was walking a muddy road when he had to step into a muddy ditch to get out of the way of the general's party. He saluted. The general stopped. "By the way," said the general, whose division had more muddy young lieutenants than most men could keep track of, "did you men get them rations I sent three days ago?"

Then came the trenches, the lieutenant's first trip in:

It was dark. I was told that I had to get my platoon into single file and to march very slowly and quietly. No one was to smoke or speak or allow anything to rattle, and we were to go along at slight intervals and not lose touch with each other. We had a sergeant of the Royal Irish Fusiliers to take us in. When we started up the road we were behind the shelter of a hill, and then we rounded a turn and moved parallel to both lines of trenches, Canadian and German. This sergeant kept talking to me in stage whispers. I did wish he would keep quiet because I was apprehensive. Presently we came towards a brick wall and were told that this was a target for German machine guns; that "they get the range in the daytime and spray it with bullets at night."

I asked the sergeant how long it was since the last spray. He replied that they had not done it for some time so it was about due.

The first thing we saw coming toward us out of the darkness was a stretcher party. Six men carried the stretcher on their shoulders, the wounded fellow covered with a blanket to his chin. Then a second stretcher party met us out of the darkness—and the figure on that stretcher was completely covered by a blanket. That was the first we saw of the ultimate price a man can pay to keep his country clean. Then we turned off the road and saw a poor Highlander, who had been hit, being looked after by a medical party. It was very upsetting. When we got about twenty-five yards further a bullet sang across, apparently close to my nose. Four of my men, coming behind me in single file, afterwards came and each told me confidentially that this particular bullet had gone between him and the man in front of him. It did not, of course, but it came close enough to be quite uncomfortable. No man who goes to the front is naturally fearless at first. If any man tells me he likes being shot at, I do not think he is brave—I think he is crazy. I was jolly well afraid. I

61

wanted to squat down behind something. I wanted to go home—anywhere where those haphazard bullets weren't. After the first two or three times you do really get more or less used to it.

Well, we kept on going, then I heard a muffled Irish voice—it was the Royal Irish Fusiliers' trench—and that muffled voice under my feet was saying "Who in hell got my pack?" So I knew we had arrived. I could just make out the outline of a man's cap against the dull light from a brazier. The cap wasn't military. The uniforms at the front are the most extraordinary conglomeration you ever saw in your life. A platoon going into the trenches looks more like a gang of railway labourers—some with Balaklava helmets, some with tuques, some with waterproof sheets about their shoulders, some wearing rubber boots, some wearing Strathconas, some wheeling barrows and others carrying bundles over their shoulders. It is about as distantly removed as one can imagine from the ordinary conception of a military performance. We had to stand behind the trench for a while, then we slithered down a sort of crazy bank and found ourselves in the trenches under cover, and very glad to be there. A trench is just a big ditch. In some places it is shored up. In other places it is built with sandbags and sheets of corrugated iron. There are sketchy floors in some trenches, which are blown up periodically. You work for a week making your trench dry and comfortable, then a shell comes along and blows the whole thing up. A dug-out is a hole scooped out of a mudbank. I have heard of dug-outs with furniture and pianos—but I have not seen them. As a rule they leak.

One fellow found a pair of German boots sticking through the wall, with toes turned up, and used them to hang his kit on—the place having been used as a cemetery. It is astonishing how men at the front can get used to what in civilian life would be most revolting. I found a new man most violently ill, who had been digging a dug-out and had come across a long defunct Hun. They are more of a nuisance dead than alive, for you are always running into them, and they won't move, so you must.

The most unreal sensation for a beginner in the trenches is when morning comes, you look through the periscope towards the enemy trench to see the source of danger—and none is visible. You see a field, perhaps a ruined building, see what looks like barbed wire fences with an earth bank behind them—but no sign of life. You are so apt to trust your eyes that one man always has to be the goat to prove to his comrades that there is danger. One of my men, after observing, went back to get his cap which was near a loop-hole that had been left open. I remonstrated with him, but he said nothing was going to happen to him. He took about three steps and crack! he was shot clean through the head from 200 or 300 yards distance through a loop-hole a foot wide.

The ultimate feeling back of every man's mind as he goes to the front is that he may be killed. Sometimes we talk about it—not very often—but that is the one thing that is above and beyond everything. Many of the good fellows of my battalion are now lying behind the trenches somewhere. There is a quiet spot behind the shoulder of a hill—one of the few quiet spots along the front. And as I stood there in the twilight of the pines, beside the grave of one of my men, I could not help thinking "What better end could a man want?" At home we are buried with all the dreadful panoply of death. Out there his own personal friends wrap a man in his blanket, and, quietly, at night, lay him beneath the open pines, and there he lies, while the guns and shells are playing the most magnificent requiem that it is possible for a man to have. His name ranks with the heroes and martyrs of all ages. And he was just a common man who was used to going to his office, to tea in the afternoon and to the theatre.

Major Wilfred Mavor, M.C., an infantry officer from Toronto, won his decoration at Festubert, where he was wounded. Here he speaks about the training of reinforcements:

We line the men up and have a look at them; tell them the Canadian corps is the best corps in France; tell them that they come to the best division in France; that they come to the best brigade, the best battalion, and they are going to be in the best company, and if it is not the best company it is their fault. Then we look them up and down, and tell them that soldiering in France is not the same as soldiering in England. You tell them there is no more barrack-room square—and you laugh up your sleeve because they are going to get it next day . . . . Then you categorize those men under different specialist headings. A baseball player is put in the bombing section;

he may be able to throw bombs pretty well. If he has been some sort of a machinist at some time, he is placed in the machine gun or Lewis gun section, as he will be more adept in fixing stoppages and that sort of thing in the Lewis gun. Then you put the husky fellows in the effective fighting section, and fellows that are good shots in the rifle section. You put all the boobs in the rifle grenade section. The reason for that, I think, is that we do not yet know the full value of the rifle grenade; it is the howitzer grenade of your platoon . . . .

After you have done collective training you will probably be getting towards the time when you have to do another little job . . . .

You call at Battalion headquarters, and the colonel tells you that your battalion is going to take a certain definite objective, and you are told all about it. The colonel tells you absolutely everything he knows, and you take down notes on the thing, study your map carefully with him, go through the whole thing, go back to your billet, get hold of a barn, get all your men in it, and tell them everything you know—don't care whether there are any German spies or not . . . .

After you have told them all about it, you will probably be told that in a certain place a little distance from the village in which you are located, there is a map laid out on the ground, with tapes showing the exact German trenches over which you are going to advance, and you go out and walk over those tapes, and wander around. They are set out by the real engineers, and they are all named; and you wander around and find your way in the country that you are going to go over. That is what you do the first day. Your men wander around, and you talk to them, show them on the map where they are on the ground, and then talk the thing over, answer any questions; they will all come up and ask you questions, some of which you cannot answer at all, and you will be greatly surprised how some men that you think have no brains at all, will come up and ask you ticklish questions about what you are going to do. One thing you always tell them—that is exactly how much artillery you have behind, so as to give them a great deal of confidence going over . . . .

In the night before you are going over you are not told the exact time; the zero hour is not given out for probably half an hour before you are going to jump off. On the night before you are going to jump off, you get your men thoroughly equipped with bombs, and lead them into their jumping-off trench, which in most cases is in front of your original front line . . . . Every man should know exactly where to go as we planned the thing out, and there should be no noise, no confusion at all; and about half an hour before zero hour every man is in his correct place, and what the infantry call aux-iliaries to the back come along, such as artillery observation of-ficers, and people who are going to dig the trench along No Man's Land, the Lewis gun people, the brigade machine gunners, and so on. As a matter of fact they are not accessory after the fact, because you are darned glad of them when you get to your objective.

Then you walk around the line. Your company commanders walk through the line and see that everybody has his extra drink of rum; tell them about the "show," and jolly them all along. Then you get your zero wire; pass the word along that zero hour is at such and such a time. Then zero hour arrives; hell breaks loose, and all the old iron in the world seems to be flying around, and you walk along behind the barrage, and walk in and occupy the trenches which the artillery have shelled. Then you either get killed, wounded, or you come back alive, and turn over the log-book and start in again.

Behind the lines, what? An answer from Rev. John Neil, moderator of the general assembly of the Presbyterian Church in Canada:

You may ask, what about the vices to which the men are subjected? Well, unfortunately there is a good deal of profanity amongst them, and I think there is a good deal of gambling too.

It would be wrong and foolish to minimize the great temptations to which those men are subjected, and if the British government could do anything to lessen or remove these, we Canadians will gratefully appreciate what they do; but we must remember that there never was a government in any age of the world that had heavier burdens than the British government has today, and we should be patient with them and try to understand their difficulties. Now, drunkenness is not the great vice, as far as I can learn. I know that people say, "You preachers don't know what you are talking about; you don't see the worst." Well, all the time I was in England and

France I did not see more than a dozen drunk Canadians. I am not saying they were not there; no doubt there were many more, but I did not see them.

I have official reports in regard to venereal diseases that are remarkably good, but you cannot always judge by official reports. Our boys who are brought in contact with those who are evil are no doubt in many cases led astray. But when I came in contact with our men and looked into their faces—men whom I knew, and some I did not, I could not and do not believe that the majority of those men who had been in the trenches one or two years and yet were so strong, had been led astray.

Speeches under the title, "My Experiences at the Front," eventually became commonplace, no less searing for that. But one was special: "Experiences of a Canadian Aviator in France." The speaker was Major W. A. (Billy) Bishop in January, 1918. He had shot down forty-five enemy aircraft in the summer of 1917 and wore the Victoria Cross, the D.S.O. and Bar, Military Cross (he'd served in the trenches before switching to the Royal Flying Corps), D.F.C., Legion D'Honneur, Croix de Guerre. Came from Owen Sound. He rose smiling after a cheer-filled introduction by the Club president:

I am not a speech maker, as you all know, but in the last ten minutes I have decided that if ever I go into a menagerie of any sort to exhibit myself, I know whom I will ask to be my manager. [Great laughter] I am going to leave behind me today more or less the set speech which I had on hand, and perhaps tell a few experiences of my own, to try to convey to you just what the life of a pilot is in a fighting squadron in France today. Of course, this varies a great deal with the squadron and the time of year and everything else, but I will just give you my own experiences, and you can get more or less of an idea of what we go through . . . .

The life we lead when not on duty is rather a light-hearted sort of life in which we try, when on the ground, to forget the work we have to carry out in the air, and keep it out of our minds. With this object in view the life of a fighting squadron is planned by the squadron commander. On all days there are sports of various kinds—horses to ride, tennis courts, and various other luxuries . . . . Meals are extraordinarily good, and at night we would have a four or five course dinner; breakfast in bed if you wanted it, or you could have it in the mess room; so that on the ground, life is not so bad . . . .

When it comes to the actual work in strenuous times such as when a battle is going on, or when there is any special call for a lot of fighting in the air, each pilot usually has two jobs a day, and sometimes three. These are regular jobs, and simply mean leaving the ground in formation with five or six others, and going out on a definite job of fighting, that is, to seek out and destroy the enemy, staying out for two hours, coming back, and then later in the day repeating this operation. Of course, it would never do to sit all day long, as soon as you come down from one job, and think of the awful time you had, and what in the world might happen on the next job. So pilots will come down and play tennis for an hour after they get on the ground, forgetting all about the events of the early morning; and then won't wait for the next job, but go up in their spare time, trying to sneak over to the line in hopes of having a little fight all on their own account. [Laughter]

The whole game of fighting in the air is not looked upon as work, and it is not really described as I call it here, a job. We speak more of going out for a fight, or, in the case of a man going alone, of going hunting. You will hear one pilot say to another at night, "How would you like to come out hunting tomorrow at ten o'clock?" The other fellow says, "Right you are." And there they go. In that way we have been able to develop a lot of pilots who would otherwise have come to France and done their regular jobs of work, and come down again, and been quite satisfied with that. Instead the pilot who has been a month in France will get keen and want to get a few Huns to his own credit, and will seek every possible opportunity to go out with some older man to learn his methods, and then later on, go off alone. Of course, it is a dangerous matter at first for an inexperienced man, and we forbid it until he has been out in company, then he gets the permission of his flight commander to go out. It has often happened that pilots who have been two or three days in France and are supposed to be up learning to fly a new machine, will slip over the lines and come back riddled with bullet holes. That is the spirit that has held for us the supremacy of the air up to the present. [Hear, hear and applause]

As to the actual fighting in the air, the most successful fighting has been done on single-seater machines, and we use no other (on our aerodrome) with the exception of one machine which carries two people. By single-seater machine I mean a machine carrying one man. This machine has two or more machine guns mounted straight in front of the pilot so that they will fire straight ahead, missing the blades of the propellor by a mechanical device as the blades revolve. The guns are fixed and cannot be moved, and to aim at a man you must aim the machine, and, of course, accurately. To do this we have a telescopic sight line along the top of the machine, which is in front of the pilot's hand, and as he sits back in the natural position of flying the machine, he can look through this sight, and of course aim that way. Shooting in the air is, of course, a difficult thing, because, although you are firing with two machine guns at the rate of 1,200 bullets a minute you are moving at the rate of over 120 miles an hour, while your opponent is moving at the same rate, and usually he seems to be moving about 50 miles an hour faster. [Laughter]

If a man is passing in front of you like this at say 120 miles an hour, you have to judge the speed and the range very accurately, and place your sights just ahead of him, so that when he reaches that spot the bullets will also reach it and get the man. To bring a machine down, it is not a matter of hitting it alone. I have seen a single-seater Newport machine come back with 116 bullet holes in it, and the pilot unwounded. Accurate shooting is the secret of the whole game, and now we are training our pilots, before they go to France, to shoot in all positions as well as to fly well. Some shots are favourites and much easier than others; for instance, when you are fighting another single-seater machine, if you are directly behind him you can fire straight at the pilot and he can't fire back at you, but, of course, it is a difficult place to stay, and no matter what he does you have to do the same thing. He may leap, turn on his back, twist around like lightning, or do any of the hundred little tricks we have, and you have to do the same thing in exactly the same time if you want to stay there; otherwise, you will find he is behind you in a second or two.

Fighting a two-seater machine is, of course, a different matter; it has its machine gun mounted in the front in the same way, but behind the pilot he has a gunner to fire one or two machine guns above or behind him. He has no protection above him, whereas in a single-seater you have a big engine in front of you. He cannot fire beneath him. He may be able to climb as fast as you, but he is never able to manoeuvre as quickly, so it becomes a question of manoeuvring, and, of course, judgment. You go into a range of three hundred yards and he opens fire on you. You watch his bullets; they are incendiary or tracer bullets, the path of which can be seen as they go through the air. You can see when his bullets are coming nearer you, and you turn to give what we call a "cross-shot"—a most difficult shot—and edge in a little nearer all the time, working from side to side to get underneath him. Even if you have to come straight at the man you have the advantage. You have two machine guns to his one, and in any case it is easier to shoot from a single-seater machine with fixed guns than it is for a man holding two guns and trying to get steady shots from them. He has the feeling—and this is the great thing—that the man in the single-seater is out for blood; and he does not want to fight—at least I have never yet struck a two-seater man who did, and that helps more than anything else . . .

He is getting nervous, and his shots are scattering all about. Of course, when you get into proper range, which is under 50 yards, you have him where you want him. [Laughter] If you can get underneath him you know that he can do nothing to shake you off, because, supposing he makes a turn to one side and has half finished that turning, in a single-seater machine you can catch up with him in half a second in that turn, remaining all the time out of his line of fire.

Another way of attacking two-seater machines that we use in formation is for three men to go out to try to get at a machine. One goes up on either side of him, about the same height; the other man goes down about 3,000 feet below, where he will not be seen. The two men beside him dash in on either side, just fire at random to worry the observer, while the man underneath steadily climbs up, and it is very seldom that he sees this third man coming at all. I have had a lot of luck this way, and although on one or two occasions the enemy has unfortunately seen me when I didn't think he did, the other times I managed to get up to 20 yards from him; then you take careful aim as if you were shooting at a target, and open fire, and about ten rounds is all you need—he is down.

To illustrate the different tactics we use, of course you will understand surprise is the greatest thing possible, but it is also the most difficult, and it requires more patience than anything else, consequently there are not many people surprised. You do it by using the sun and clouds, or mist, anything of that sort. For instance, if you dive at a man from the direction of the sun he very seldom sees you at all, as it is so nasty to look towards the sun that he hardly ever does so, even though he knows it is very dangerous not to do so.

One day, looking for machines to surprise, I passed about three groups which had seen me, and did not look good enough, so I let them go. [Laughter] Finally I saw this group of four, and managed to get about 6,000 feet above them. I stayed there for twenty minutes following them up and down. It is very difficult to see a machine of that type above you when you are at a height of about 17,000 feet, as I was then. The four enemy machines kept going up and down a certain beat, from Lens down to Cambrai, and back. I followed them up and down there for some time, and then started to come down. I wanted to get behind them, and they swirled off to one side, having seen another of our machines. I had to go up and wait again until they had cleared our machine, which was flying beneath them, and they resumed their former beat. Then, waiting until they were about to turn, I came down, judging my speed to be about 150 miles an hour, so that just as they were turning I would be about a quarter of a mile farther along their beat and behind them after they had turned. They were flying probably at 110. I was flying a slower machine than they were, so it meant that I had to have extra speed when I reached them, in case the surprise did not work and they turned on me. But they saw nothing. The rear machine, luckily for me, was slightly above the rest, and I came down, gliding along just about 10 feet underneath him, and then pulled my machine back so that the nose of it was probably a bare 10 feet from where he was. I could make out the smallest scratch on his machine, and waited until I had carefully got my sights in the exact spot where the pilot was sitting, and then pulled the trigger. The next moment, I was in danger of being hit as he fell, and I had to skid the machine out to the right, as he fell to the left and missed me. The other three had heard me shooting; they turned around, and rather luckily, the enemy machine I had brought down burst into flames as it was falling. They probably gazed at that a moment, and that was just time enough for me to get within 20 yards of the second machine to the rear, and get my sights on. The whole fight was probably over in 15 seconds at the very most, and the two machines were going down. The other two did not wait to realize that they were two to one, and in better machines than mine, or anything else; they saw two of their machines down, and off they went, and unfortunately I could not catch either of them. [Laughter]

I had occasion once, when flying alone, to see a two-seater machine above me and a mile away on our own side of the lines. It was such a rare thing. Probably only two fights out of five hundred would be on our side of the lines last spring and last summer. [Applause] This machine had been over taking photographs or something, and I commenced to climb up to it from directly underneath, hoping that he would not see me. My plan was that if he did see me when I was 200 or 300 yards underneath I would use the old trick of watching his machine gun. I might explain that the observer's machine gun can be seen as it sticks over the side of the machine, and you know from which side he is likely to fire. If his gun is sticking over the left hand side, you keep slightly to the right; if he suddenly switches his gun to the right and the machine banks over to get a shot at you, you skip back to the left. If he banks like that and keeps his machine gun on the left hand side, you know then that he is immediately going to turn back the other way. This is one of the little things you have to watch carefully. [Laughter] I was climbing along, not thinking much about that, and not intending to watch him in that way until I was within 200 or 300 yards, and I was still 2,000 feet underneath him—too far away even to hear his machine gun—when I noticed three or four holes in the wings of my machine about two feet away from me. The petrol tank and engine were both hit, and luckily for me they were both hit before I was, because the engine immediately stopped and I had to come down. That just illustrates that good fortune is not all one way. I should not call that good shooting; if one ever makes a hit at long range it is luck, and luck is a thing you can't help.

The same thing comes in with anti-aircraft firing. Sometimes a shell will burst so near to you that the smoke will pass all around your machine, the shell bursting, and not a single spot in your machine be touched. Another time a shell will burst several hundred yards away, and you are rather laughing at the man on the ground who is making such shooting. You come down to find that several pieces have passed through your machine.

Another job we have is to attack artillery observation balloons, and this is one of the nastiest. The balloons are captive balloons and held to the ground by a cable, at the end of which they have some means of pulling them down very rapidly. Our job comes before a bombardment or any small engagement on the ground; we must go over and settle those balloons in order to upset the enemy artillery. The problem of getting at them is the most difficult; that is, to catch them in the air, as they can be pulled down so rapidly, and the enemy watches machines coming across the lines with telescopes, and the moment these machines appear dangerous down the balloons go. But this disposal of them is of no use, because when you are a mile past them, up they pop again; so they must be destroyed, which means perhaps half a day's delay before the enemy can get another one up.

I can describe my second attack on a balloon, which was luckily successful. We all crossed the lines and headed towards our balloons. The day was very cloudy and misty, and the balloon was hard to find. I was new at the game, and very much worried for fear I would miss the balloon, so that on my whole trip over, six miles and back, I was looking for nothing else but a balloon, never for a moment thinking that there were naturally some Huns in the sky who would be looking for me. [Laughter] I found my balloon, and commenced to dive at it. I had gone down only a few thousand feet when I realized for several seconds that there had been the rattle of a number of machine guns right behind me. Remembering certain advice that had been given me, I pulled the machine back and began to dive again just as the Hun went beneath me, going in the direction I wanted to go. He was right in line with my sights, and although every bullet I had was precious for that balloon I could not resist it, and I let him have it. [Laughter] Although I was inexperienced, it was the best thing I could have done, and the Hun flew in exactly the place where he would have gone if I had asked him to. [Laughter] Of course I could not miss him, and he went down. It was next day before I heard the result. The anti-aircraft reported it the next day;

they had seen it, and I was so excited over the balloon, and so frightened, that I had lost it altogether. I did another turn. This time the balloon was sitting on the ground, and the people down there all waiting for me to come down. I came down 800 feet, and opened fire. As I was gliding past the balloon and firing at the people who had been scattered along the ground, I suddenly realized that my engine was not running at all, but had stopped absolutely. I worked as hard as I could with every adjustment I could find. Nothing happened. I was going at the tremendous pace of 200 miles an hour and glided straight ahead and picked out the place where I was going to land. Just at that moment, fifteen feet from the ground, one of the cylinders picked up, and then two, and then the whole lot went off with a roar, and I tore off. [Laughter and applause]

A return trip on these occasions is very exciting and very amusing. It is not as dangerous as it sounds, and I will explain why. We come back at a height of anywhere under 10 feet from the ground. Coming to a hedge or a clump of trees, we just duck up and over them, and down into the next field, and tear along, zigzagging all the way so that the enemy cannot warn their people ahead of you by telephone exactly where you are going, and just make in an approximate direction of home. You cannot pick out a landmark that low down, so you just keep tearing along till you are past the trenches, and you know you are all right. The reason you do that is that machine gun fire is not very dangerous, as you are passing at such a pace; they only see you the time you are in the field that they happen to be in, and you often come to groups of people around a battery of machine guns in a field looking around for somebody like you tearing along. I always imagined them very much pleased as they see you about two fields off, and get ready for you. You are travelling about 120 miles an hour. You dodge up over some trees and into their field. They are probably 200 or 300 yards away, and the only thing to do is to go straight at them, and, by the time you reach anywhere near that battery of machine guns, with your speed and a few bullets here and there, there is not a man within fifty miles of it, and everyone of them going hard. [Laughter]

Another job which we have been doing lately is to attack the infantry on the ground, and this is a little more dangerous because you have to do it from a height of about 500 feet, and then make your dive from there, because you have to pick out the place you want to fire at. You come down just above the enemy trenches, making certain that you are 200 or 300 yards behind, because the average man in a fighting squadron is not certain, to within 200 or 300 yards, exactly where our front line is and where the Huns are. You are using bullets which leave either a trail of smoke or a little spark of air as they pass, and as you come down you just scatter those around on the ground at random, even if you can't see a Hun anywhere, for they are all lying low by this time, and this has the greatest moral effect on them. In an attack of that kind you probably may not kill very many people, but the effect on the men on the ground is tremendous, and the effect on our infantry is correspondingly good, because the next day, if you happen to be near the ground, you will hear the story of the man who did it, coming down within 200 feet of the ground. The following day you will hear the story of a man who came down to 100 feet from the ground and fired on the trenches there. When you go back a week later you will find that a man came down to fifty feet—[Laughter]—and a little later, when they get out of the trenches altogether, you will hear that a man came down, and Heaven knows what he didn't do. [Laughter]

I think that covers, as far as I can remember it, all the little jobs we are called upon to do. Before I close I would like to speak of things in general as they are now. Germany has expanded at a tremendous rate in the air. The fighting now is no longer 6 to 10 miles back on the German side of the line, but it is over the lines, and the whole thing is uncertain, just like that—one day one side, next day the other, and it is anybody's battle. Now, that is serious enough; but France, whose Flying Corps has developed at a tremendous pace from the beginning of the War, has reached its limit, and in the coming year they have not planned any more growth in that branch; in fact they may have to contract a bit and disband several of their squadrons to fill up vacancies and keep up other squadrons. The United States is planning a tremendous programme, as you all know, 22,000 machines, but I doubt whether they will have 500 machines working on the 1st of April. The fact is this, that in the coming spring campaign, England will have to expand to meet the German force and to allow for the fact that France is not expanding any, and also for the fact that the United States will not be there in great numbers. It is an awful problem. We are up against it; this coming spring we have got to fight our hardest, fight as we never have fought before. [Loud and long continued applause]

For four years British Maj. Gen. J.E.B. Seely (who spoke in 1920) commanded cavalry, including the Fort Garry Horse, Lord Strathcona Horse and Royal Canadian Dragoons of the Canadian Cavalry Brigade. In the war's final year, when the last great German attack threatened to turn the tide against the allies, he was ordered to hold a vital area called the Moreau Ridge:

So into the open country, and away we went at as good a gallop as our horses could muster, and arrived at the village of Castile, which was just on the other side of the river from the Moreau Ridge. There I found a French general, cool and collected. I said to him, "What is the position?"

He said, "I am issuing orders to withdraw from Moreau."

I asked, "Why?"

He said, "Because the Germans have captured the ridge and this big Moreau Wood and soon will be behind me."

The position was that if we could not get possession of the ridge again, it was clear that the French and British armies would be divided, Amiens would fall, and with it probably—as I think all men now agree—the Allied cause.

"If we recapture the Moreau Ridge, can you advance and hold Moreau?" I asked.

"Yes, but you cannot do it."

"If we don't the Germans will be in Amiens to-night."

He said, "Yes, I fear so, and all will be lost; but can I possibly—I ask you—hold on out here with the enemy in my rear?"

"No, but we will recapture it." I said.

I gave the orders. Any man in my position, with such wonderful men, would have done the same. The Strathconas were to encircle the wood right around, a mile away; charge any Germans on the far side and establish themselves there—giving the impression, of course, that we must be a great host. The Dragoons were to establish a circle around the right of the wood. The Fort Garrys were for the moment to be in reserve and then with the rest of the Strathconas to go clean through the wood and join up with their comrades on the top of the ridge.

The leading commander of A Squadron was Lieut. Flowerdew; he received the Victoria Cross, but alas, it was a posthumous honour; if any man deserved it he did. I rode alongside of him myself as he went forward and explained to him what the idea was. I said, "It is a desperate chance, Flowerdew, but if it succeeds we will save the day." He said, "Yes, sir; yes, sir, we will succeed;" he gave me a glorious smile and swept on with his squadron. After a mile, we rounded the wood, met machine-gun fire and saw lines of German infantry in column advancing quietly into the wood as they had been doing for nine long days, marching steadily forward and driving us before them.

With a shout the squadron charged down upon those columns. Some of the Germans turned and ran, others turned and shot. As Flowerdew approached the first line he was shot from one side through both thighs, and of course the horse was shot too. As the horse fell, he waved his sword and shouted, "Carry on, boys, carry on," and on they went right through the Germans, sabering many. I, myself counted shortly afterwards seventy-five dead bodies killed by the sword.

Back again we came through them, and now were established on the far side of the wood crowning the ridge. One whole division of German infantry, believing that this was a great host, withered, retired, and fell back.

So the Dragoons made good on the ridge. The rest of the Fort Garrys made their way through the wood. These Germans were valiants; they would not surrender; a great many were killed, others were taken after desperate hand-to-hand fighting. I saw more Germans killed that day than in all the week; they would not surrender. As I passed one German near a tree, obviously with a wound in his throat, I said, I will send you a stretcher-bearer. He reached for his rifle but could not get it, and then he said, No, no, I will die and not be taken. Well, he did that, because the man behind him killed him. So the ridge was taken, and for twenty precious hours there, we held on, decimated, our men blanched but unbowed. [Loud applause]

On went the war that final summer, but the speakers now seemed overshadowed by the news—and the ones who told what happened in the last months of the war appeared mainly in the programs of 1919. Sir Arthur Pearson, who was blind, spoke in 1919 about St. Dunstan's, the generic name for a group of establishments at which blind soldiers were taught how to live with their condition: "first of all, we teach men to be blind." A blinded Toronto soldier, Bill Dies, a former star athlete, was in the audience as Sir Arthur told success story after success story of men who were making better incomes blinded than they had when they had sight. And of how they celebrated the end of the war on November 11, 1918:

No arrangements had been made. When the news came through about a quarter to eleven, every one threw down his tools or Braille book, or automatic typewriter, and stopped automatically; of course that was to be expected. In the afternoon the fire engine was brought out, and the motor-car was produced from the garage; the motor-car was harnessed to the fire engine; and St. Dunstan's Rag-time Band—a very good band, let me tell you—moved with fire engine and the men of St. Dunstan's and those fellows to the number of 600 marched through the streets of London, all through the principal streets, with the band playing in front. I don't mind telling you they had some reception. [Applause] A reporter on one of the London papers heard what was going on, and set out to chase them. He asked policemen, pedestrians and taxi-drivers and different people where the blind fellows were, and he said he always got the same reply— "All on their own"— and those are the words with which he ended his story that day. [Laughter]

General Sir Arthur Currie, commander in chief of the Canadian Corps, was a B.C. lawyer and businessman at the outbreak of war. His speech late in August, 1919, "The Last Hundred Days of the War," concluded:

On the first of last October we were counter-attacked by eight German divisions, two of which were fresh. That meant fifty or sixty thousand Germans, all quite willing to die, coming right at us determined to kill everyone if they could get through. And we were determined that we would kill every one of them rather than let them get through. On that day we fired seven thousand tons of ammunition into them. No wonder the ammunition factories of Canada were kept busy. It was fired to kill. If they got close to us and escaped the artillery we tried to shoot them with rifles, kill them with machine guns. If they came on, as they were quite willing to, we were ready to stick the bayonet into them. I want you to understand what war is and you cannot have war without the inevitable price.

We have fought on battlefields where it took our stretcher-bearers six hours to get out one wounded man. We fought over ground in which every inch was a shell hole, muddy and covered with unburied bodies. Now if you go to France, as many of you will, because your brave boys lie there, you will see a country, miles wide and hundreds of miles long, absolutely stripped of every form of human habitation. Where stood whole towns there is now not one brick on another. Everything is unspeakable desolation. There is nothing but shell holes and trenches and barbed wire where our men lived in dugouts with the rats and the lice. If they exposed themselves for a minute they were sniped and shelled night and day. When they came out to rest they were bombarded. That was the life that they lived and that to my mind indicates their endurance, the great outstanding quality of our soldiers.

Let me for a moment say something about war. We picture war as a business of banners flying, men smiling, full of animation, guns belching forth, and all that sort of thing. One, somehow or other, gets the impression that there is a great deal of glory and glamour about the battlefield. I never saw any of it. I want you to understand that war is simply the curse of butchery, and men who have gone through it, who have seen war stripped of all its trappings, are the last men that will want to see another war.

CHAPTER FIVE

Those Were the Days

The decennial census of 1921 recorded a balance—50.48 per cent rural, 49.52 per cent urban—in the population of Canada. The figures foreshadowed the fundamental conflict and the character of the twenties. Throughout the decade, the accepted doctrine of progress, the growth of cities and industry and of the working force (and coincident faint mutterings of a social welfare-oriented conscience) contended with old rural conservatism and habits of personal effort and self-reliance. In the circumstances, there was a broad market for nostalgia. Prime Minister Stanley Baldwin of Great Britain was quoted over coffee at the Empire Club—"To me England is the country and the country is England: the tinkle of the hammer on the anvil in the country smithy, the corncrake in the dewy morning, the sound of the scythe against the whetstone, and the sight of a plough team coming over the brow of a hill"—and B. K. Sandwell, then teaching English at Queen's University, contributed his own tongue-in-cheek recollections of the way it was, in Toronto:

What a change is this, gentlemen, from the days of my youth! I was brought up in this city in the noble nineties. Now, it is true that the nineties in England were beginning to develop this twentieth century pessimism of ours, but it had not reached this somewhat outlying portion of the British Empire before the end of the nineteenth century, and in those nineties we were cheerful, we were happy, we were contented. Why, I can remember a Toronto in which everything was for the best in the best of all possible worlds. I can remember a Toronto in which everything that Goldwin Smith said or believed was necessarily wrong—[Laughter]—because Goldwin Smith was always a pessimist, and it followed that the rest of Toronto was optimistic. I can remember a Toronto in which the rising spectre of Sir Wilfrid Laurier was perhaps the only fly in the ointment, the only cloud on the horizon; and it could always be reflected that Sir Wilfrid was only mortal and would eventually pass out. I can remember a Toronto in which the Toronto street-car franchise was the ultimate and final solution of all urban transportation problems . . . . [Laughter]

I can remember a Toronto in which the ravages of socialism were checked, stopped, walled off for good by the simple process of prohibiting public meetings in Queen's Park. [Laughter] I can remember a Toronto in which it was admitted that Europe had its problems, but Europe was a long way off, and was handicapped by age and the number of survivals of illogical institutions, and those problems would be solved in due course by a gradual migration of the population of Europe to the wide and fertile plains of Canada. [Laughter] I can remember a Toronto in which those immigrants who came from Europe, and settled in the wide and fertile plains of Canada, were expected to become perfectly good and satisfactory Canadian citizens just like ourselves after five years or so of Canadian education, and as the result of the gift of the Canadian ballot; and nobody dreamed of worrying that they would ever give us any trouble. They would learn in that short five years to buy our products, and, still more than that, to vote for our policies; and that was all that we expected of them. [Laughter]

Those were happy, confident, spacious days. I won't mention the names of the great financiers who were bringing into Canada the money that helped us to be so happy and so spacious and so confident, nor of the undertakings for the assistance of which they were bringing them in—very good undertakings, but some of them are now giving us some trouble. [Laughter]

Summoning up a rosy-coloured past, Sandwell went on, was one reaction to disappointment in the wake of expectations aroused during the war, when "We were told . . . we were having a war which was to end war, which was to wind up in a state of universal brotherhood, with everybody loving everybody else and every community falling upon the neck of all its sister communities."

Using an optimism-depression theory analogous to current inflation-deflation financial orthodoxy, he suggested the world was no worse than before, despite the editorialists. Or if it was, that was "only because the individuals in it are worse, less confident, less energetic, less self-reliant" in performing their tasks as individuals:

> What are some of the demands that we are presenting to government at the present time? We are demanding, for one thing, that the government shall stop wars and rumours of wars—that I have referred to already; that it shall stop banks from failing; that it shall stop people from getting divorces—or make it easier to get divorces, according to the way we think; that it shall stop churches from getting united, or get them united, according to the way we happen to think; that it shall stop the over-production or under-production of certain classes of goods; that it shall stop too high wages and too low wages; that it shall stop strikes. In Quebec the other day we demanded that it should stop cows from walking about on the road at night without lamps on. [Great laughter]
>
> Some of us are very energetically calling upon it to keep down forest fires. I never knew a government that started a forest fire; it is individuals that start forest fires. And so forth, and so on—that it shall regulate the morals of students in universities; we do not always appeal to the government for that, but we always appeal to somebody. The authorities of Queen's University are very busily occupied much of their time—which ought to be devoted to much more important things—in determining how much light or how little light should be tolerated at certain stages of undergraduate dances in the evening. [Laughter]
>
> Now, we seem to have adopted the attitude, in our dealings with governments, that the authority of government is something unlimited, something which can be invoked, turned on, fired in any direction to achieve any given end, simply as the result of the

81

pressure of bodies, the vote of the community, as if governmental authority were a sort of hydro-electric power, and all you had to do was to harness it and run a wire to the place where it is to be provided. Governmental authority is nothing of the kind. The exercise of governmental authority is one of the most expensive privileges that any community can enjoy. The more you ask the government to do, the more the government will have to collect out of your pockets for doing it; and if what you want it to do is something that you can do yourselves you will find that the government will charge you ten times what it would cost you to do it yourselves.

In the spacious nineties, although we were beginning to be a little reliant on authority, there was a good deal left to the individual in Canada. An example: I was a student in the University in the nineties; students were not compelled in those days to attend lectures. It was left to the individual student to determine whether a lecture was good enough for him to attend, or whether it was not. [Laughter] I do not believe there is an institution in Canada in which that is the case today. We have undertaken to apply regulation and compulsion to everybody, and personally I would far rather feel that the students who attend my lectures, or who do not attend them or who would not attend them, as the case might be, were coming or staying away in the exercise of their own more or less adult wisdom, and thereby developing their characters and their judgment, than to feel that they were herded in before me like a flock of sheep nine hours every week to sit passive, open-mouthed and open-eared, while I poured the true milk of the literary word into them. [Laughter]

It is very important to adopt the proper manner of looking at things. I hear people discussing the question of prohibition. It is astonishing how easy it is to hear people discussing prohibition, and I find that everybody is grieved about it. People who approve of drinking are grieved about prohibition because they say it prevents men from drinking. People who approve of not drinking are grieved because it does not prevent men from drinking. [Laughter] Surely that is all a matter of looking at it. If my friends who are in favour of drinking would only realize the beauty of the fact that prohibition, while it satisfies those who like a law against drinking, does not prevent men from drinking, then they would be perfectly satisfied [Laughter]; and if only my friends who approve of laws to prevent people from drinking would concentrate their attention on the fact that they have a law to prevent people from drinking, they, too, would be satisfied. [Laughter]

Other speakers chided Club members for wearing gloomy faces. Canada indeed had problems—"of debt, of taxation, of immigration, of labour, of provincial jealousy and misunderstanding, of exorbitant and unjust sectional demands"—admitted Sir Arthur Currie, but "were it not so, we would be the only Utopia on the globe." Advice is often incongruous, he continued, but the grumbling was getting out of hand:

The wail of our Jeremiahs over these problems is echoed from ocean to ocean. Luxury is rampant, they tell us. Extravagance is unprecedented. There is no thrift, no high seriousness. Nero-like, we fiddle while the Rome of our hopes is burning. Darkness has come upon us; the sun is hid, and the stars have withdrawn their shining. Only a sure and empty bankruptcy awaits us, and to that doom we are slowly drifting. But before that hour of our doom has finally struck we shall be broken as a united country. The Maritime Provinces will secede to independence! The Prairie Provinces will pass to the United States! Now, Gentlemen, I do not think I have over-coloured the picture or over-stated the facts. Speakers declare them nightly; newspapers print them daily, and every hour they are sent forth to the world as an expression of our people's thought.

Now, this continuous wail of fear has a most depressing and injurious effect upon our country. It is very much the fashion—and, I am sorry to say, often amongst those who pique themselves on their patriotism—to decry their own country. They are never tired of announcing that we are an enervated race; that Canada is a "played-out" country.

He, for one, Currie concluded, refused "to acquiesce in the accusations of inferiority." The conquest of national fear, he said, "rests, after all, on each individual."
Positive thinking and individual effort often seemed a thankless

gospel for the small businessmen, farmers and workers who were hit by the deflationary measures—tightened credit, and the shutting down of the government-controlled Wheat Board established in 1917 – applied in 1920 to counter the effects of the post-war boom. But the wounded were learning to walk: farmers were participating in politics, and labour was organizing. Employers, of course, were resistant. S. R. Parsons was a delegate to the International Labor Conference held in Washington in 1919 (Tom Moore was a member of the Canadian labour representation), where the question of the eight-hour day was paramount. Management's view, Parsons reported, was "spoken quite openly by the delegates of the European countries."

> This labour legislation, this whole programme, is being forced upon us and our governments, first of all by the workers themselves from inside, and then by outsiders, largely socialistic, who are pressing upon the workers. They said quite frankly, "Now we do not believe in much of this proposed legislation; we do not think it is good for the workers themselves and we do not think it is good for industry; we have been forced into it, however, and we feel compelled to support it." Quite a number of them were frank enough to say to me that if they were in our position, in the position of Canada, on this continent, they would certainly try to keep out of this programme of legislation as long as possible, as they did not believe it wise, especially in the interests of a new and rapidly developing country like Canada. However, as one delegate said, "being in the soup ourselves, we naturally like to get others into it, you know, and we would like to see the United States and Canada join in."

Many workers would side with employers, Parsons believed, citing the case of a conductor who had questioned him about the eight-hour day:

> I said, "Well, that was passed at the Conference." He said, "Well, I don't believe in it." I asked why, and he replied, "Now, take my case; I start out early in the morning; I finish my work early in the afternoon; and then I have just got to sit and look at myself for the rest of the day." [Laughter] And he went on to say, "Now, I cannot do that; what I do is take on extra work in the afternoon, for two

reasons, first because I cannot be idle, and next because I need the money." Is not that a sensible man?

An American, James Emery of Washington, D.C., deplored the "monopolistic, anti-social" nature of closed shops, but Samuel Gompers of the U.S. Federation of Labor ("its greatest organizer, its safest advisor and its wisest leader," glowed the introduction) castigated firms such as the U.S. Steel Corporation for the open shops they purported to run:

> Open shop—no one who declines to fool himself believes in the open shop. [Laughter] What the advocates of the so-called open shop mean is the shop closed to union membership. I know that there have been quite a number of specious presentations of that question as far as the open shop is concerned, but no one has persuaded himself other than at the end of that campaign he hopes to have the non-union shop, the workers rid of their slavery to their union.
>
> Perhaps my reading of history may have been all wrong, but I have never yet been able to find any evidence that the slave-owner was very seriously engaged in an effort for the abolition of slavery. I have not yet been able to observe either in reading history or the history of contemporary times that the masters are organized for the purpose of protecting the rights and interests of their servants. And it is a strange anomaly that in this year of grace, 1921, we find so many large employers of labour spending millions of dollars to protect the rights and the liberties and the freedom and the opportunities of their employees. I do not know whether you have seen these double-paged advertisements in the Canadian newspapers. I do not recall that I have any of them sent to me by friends for my information, but these double-paged advertisements appear week after week in which the employers' associations are advertising the arguments that they are standing with sword in one hand and shield in the other to protect their workmen from the slavery and the autocracy of the unions.
>
> Of course you know that the United States Steel Corporation declares it is an open shop concern, and you know also that the Bethlehem Steel Company has that as its slogan. Under investigations by a committee of the New York legislature it was proven, out

of the mouth of its chief executive officer, Mr. Grace, upon the witness stand, where he admitted that his company as well as the U.S. Steel Corporation when they declared for the open shop meant that they would not furnish iron or steel to any building contractor in New York State or elsewhere unless this contractor excluded any union workmen from that building. That is the open shop. And it was the sort of open shop that the late Mr. Bear, at the head of the great anthracite coal company—the gentleman has passed away and probably I would not mention his attitude other than that during the great miners' strike, a strike in protest against the further impoverishment and demoralization of the people there, he said that God in his infinite wisdom had constituted the employers of labour to be the trustees for the welfare of their employees, and he therefore desired no conference with the representatives of the coal miner. But justice to Mr. Bear's memory requires me to say that he lived at least long enough so that his actions stamped his former utterances as unworthy, for he sat in conference with the men of labour and brought about adjustments and improvements in the conditions of the people who worked, and their families, and brought about a better state of affairs in the coal mining industry.

But it is the Graces and the men occupying that same sort of position who are the Bourbons of 1921. They have not forgotten anything, because they have never learned anything. Industrially they are living in the twentieth century; mentally they are living in the fifteenth. The attitude of the master and servant, the baron and serf, that industrial and mental attitude won't do in 1921 and for the future. [Hear, hear]

Other attitudes died hard. The question of immigration, for example, continued to be debated along old lines of prejudice according to colour and kind. John S. Martin, Ontario Minister of Agriculture in 1928, saw immigration as a "link of Empire", but Charles Peterson of Calgary, echoing Clifford Sifton, fingered the settlement of Canada's marginal lands as the pressing concern:

A depressing number of Canadians, Britishers and Americans have failed, at great economic loss and to the everlasting detriment of

86

Canada, in establishing themselves permanently upon farms of that class in Western Canada.

"Flivvers," rural phones and mail delivery can play no conspicuous part in such a toilsome undertaking. It calls rather for the Spartanic life of the early backwoods settler of Old Canada, with something approaching the crude standard of living then in vogue.

Who is going to "mop up" this Herculean task for us? The greater part of this strenuous enterprise cannot be successfully accomplished by people accustomed to the high standard of living of most of the countries we are pleased to designate "preferred" in our present immigration policy.

Ontario, Nova Scotia, New Brunswick and British Columbia harbour this problem in an intensified form. Previous failures in colonizing these provinces have their roots in the fact that no special notice has been taken of the special character of the lands to be settled. The bush lands and enormous dry areas of the west come within this class.

We have insisted on focussing our propaganda on Great Britain and Northern Europe when a moment's thought should have convinced us of the futility of such an effort.

We cannot formulate intelligent immigration policies in Canada without reference to this situation. The obvious answer is a considerable influx of Central and East European peasants. No other class will successfully create permanent homes on land of that description.

W. C. Noxon, agent-general for Ontario in Great Britain, voiced some old fears:

All this brings us to a point as to how far it is safe for us to trust, to people of other races, British ideals and the fundamentals which underlie British life and society. I think it was never designed that every one should be born with the same degree of intelligence, nor educated to the same standard of worthiness, therefore we have a certain average degree of quality in our administration, or in the authority to administer. The standard of the governments in ideals and quality is no greater than the average in the voters. I would therefore suggest that, while we would welcome to our country all who are qualified under the immigration regulations, the vote should go only to those who will receive instruction, and qualify by examination. [Applause] By the adoption of some such course you immediately eliminate all the foreign-women vote; secondly, you eliminate all the foreign element which you do not really want to vote. On the other hand, you only give the vote to those who are willing to study and be instructed in the ideals and principles which underlie British Government; and to those we are quite willing to give it, after a period of instruction and the passing of a reasonable examination. It is not fair to me, as a citizen of this country, or to any other man who has raised a family, to bring his boy up to twenty-one years of age before he can vote, and then have all the ideals which he has had inculcated into him destroyed and negatived by one foreign vote. [Applause] I, for one, will do everything I can to see that the vote goes only to those who are properly instructed.

Across Canada, East Indians continued to complain about prejudice and restrictive immigration policies, often alluding to the vexing fact of the Orientals, who in their turn continued as the subjects of hard-hat paranoia on the part of West Coast politicians and publicists. And the Europeans complained, after their fashion. Rabbi Barnett R. Brickner, of Holy Blossom Temple, Toronto, on the policy of so-called "selection":

Let me give you an instance of some selection regulations which we have on the statute books in Canada today. We have several orders-in-council which are nightmares to our immigrants, for example an order-in-council known as "P.C. 23." This P.C. 23 was originally put on the statute books to operate against the Hindoos, to keep the Hindoos out of Canada. Friends, when I talk on the question of immigration today I am talking of immigration in terms of the white races of the world, not in terms of the yellow or the black or the brown, that is an entirely different question, and ought not to come under the policy of immigration at all. Now, this P.C. 23 was originally put on the statute books against Hindoos. It says that the immigrant coming into Canada must come over a continuous passage from the point where he leaves his native country to the time when he lands in Halifax or Quebec or Victoria. Until he lands here there must be no break in his journey. See how it is operating today, not against Hindoos at all. A man leaves Warsaw with his family; he sells all of his earthly possessions, and gets to Antwerp, and his wife or his children get sick. He stops for a period of a few weeks until they are well again to travel. They land in Halifax, and that father and immigrant cannot convince the immigration officials that he has come over a continuous passage; and, due to an order-in-council filled with red tape, that immigrant and his family are rejected and sent back. Is that selection, or is that exclusion?

Another order-in-council affected the Jews most particularly, Brickner went on:

It is working tremendous hardships on my own people. They don't have any difficulty with the show-money. They have a little difficulty with P.C. 23; but the real difficulty comes in this instance. A good many of my people live at present in places in Europe where there are no stable governments, for example, the Ukraine, where several millions of my people live, and only recently the Red Cross reported that over 300,000 of them were slaughtered in cold blood since 1919—over 300,000 Jews pogromed for no other reason than that they were regarded as counter-revolutionaries, as opposed to Bolshevism—massacred by both sides. Those who are fighting the Bolsheviks contend that the Jews are Bolsheviks; and the Bolsheviks, when they drive the other gangs out of power, maintain that the Jews are counter-Bolsheviks; and between the devil and the deep blue sea 300,000 have been massacred in cold blood, and not a word from the world.

Is the conscience of the world dead? A man escapes with his family from the Ukraine and gets into Poland; and he escapes from the Ukraine, why?—because he will not live under radical socialism and under Bolshevism; he is a conservative and a moderate man, unused to that kind of radical communism; and he gets into Poland. Poland will give him merely a passport—rather, a visa permitting him to pass through that country and to come to Canada. He has sold everything he had for passage. He gets to Halifax or to Quebec or to Montreal, and there is an order-in-council, P.C. 2669, which says that unless that man can show a passport from the country of his nativity he will not be admitted to this land. There is no stable government in the Ukraine; he cannot get a passport from anybody. Poland merely gives them permission to pass through the country, and when he is rejected because, perforce, he cannot fulfil this order-in-council, he has only one place to return to with his family, and that is to the bottom of the ocean, for Poland won't receive him, and he cannot go back to the Ukraine. Now, that is the sort of selective immigration we have on the statute books of Canada.

However, for many Canadians—new and otherwise—prosperity ran parallel with the problems of the decade. The mass-produced automobile put "democracy on wheels", as B. K. Sandwell phrased it. Touring became popular, and summer cottages—a Canadian institution—grew and multiplied. Hockey became the national sport, and the entertainment business—jazz, radio, motion pictures— boomed. The careers of American movie stars, American gangsters, American baseball players were eagerly followed by Canadians of the time. No translation needed.

The topic of sport fell to Dr. J. R. P. Sclater, a Toronto clergyman born in Scotland, who gave a discourse entitled "The Imperial Significance of Games."

Canada has produced two games that are the games of youth, which are an inestimable contribution to the athletic activities of the world. The first of these is ice hockey, the most beautiful game I have ever seen in my life—[Applause]—the fastest and most skilful. But it is not an Empire-binding force. Why? Because the Canadians are far too good. It is no earthly use trying to play against them. Even the most gallant of Britishers, engineering to stem the wave of some Canadian on skates, feels for about the first time in his life what it like to be a furry rabbit. Seeing the preponderance of Canadian skill, it cannot be a uniting force. But lacrosse can be. [Applause] I rejoice to see among the distinguished gentlemen immediately in front of this platform, one of the greatest exponents of that lovely game. It is a very great delight to see Dr. Hughes beginning to get the light of ancient battle in his eye; in a moment I expect we shall see him clutching an egg spoon, running around this hall, and scoring a goal at that end. He can take pride in being one of those who have developed a game which, so far as I know, is the only external game which has fairly rooted itself upon British soil . . . .

So let it be an interest for businessmen who can provide cups, and, what is more than cups, expenses; let it be even a matter for the benevolent interest of the government, that there shall be an interplay and intercourse of these best elements amongst all our peoples. Go over to the Old Country and beat them. Eat up England, intimidate Ireland, wallop Wales; subdue Scotland, if you can.

Tourism was growing: not only Canadians but Americans had taken to the Canadian woods. In 1939 Leo Dolan of the four-year-old Canadian Travel Bureau in Ottawa reported a call from an American who said: "I will be in Toronto on my honeymoon. Where can I fish?"

Dolan was all for promoting "the foreign British atmosphere" of Canada:

Let me read a letter from a young girl, written to me from Massachusetts, written, I may say, to me in my official capacity. She had visited the Province of Ontario and she puts the case in this letter far better than I could do it. Here is what she says, indicative, I think, of the thought in the mind of 95 per cent of the American tourists who come here:

"Wednesday morning we went bravely forth to make our first visit to a foreign country. Did we have difficulty getting through the Customs? No—a lot of fun. The official had an honest-to-goodness waxed moustache. Although he looked frightfully dignified, he forgot his dignity long enough to accept a Life Saver and kid us about the streets of Boston. Then we drove to a little place called Port Dalhousie. I had always lived on the Atlantic Ocean and I got another big thrill when I saw Lake Ontario. I could have almost believed that some magic had transported us back to Duxbury, Massachusetts, until I tasted that water, it was so difficult to believe that immense body of water could be fresh."

She goes on to tell of her experiences in the shops, the courteous treatment she received, and that she found the prices better than she had expected, far lower, and a better type of merchandise than she got in the United States.

She makes a reference, by the way, to a policeman who met her in St. Catharines, who was so handsome, and didn't seem to mind a bit because she laughed at his helmet and bicycle, but directed her to a good cafeteria.

But she closes with what I think should be of keen interest to every tourist organization in this country. She says: "If you want to make Ontario more interesting I suggest you scatter around a few more wax moustaches and helmets and bicycles. They are so darned interesting to unaccustomed American eyes."

There you have, as I see it, the tenet of a working programme for any tourist organization. Make this country darned interesting to unaccustomed American eyes. Then you maintain, as I say, that atmosphere of Canada, and that atmosphere of the British.

The Dionne quintuplets, born in 1934, caused an international stir, and a bulge in the U.S. tourist trade. Dr. Allan Roy Dafoe, the controversial custodian of the babies, talked about his wards at lunchtime:

Naturally, my chief interest in life for the past two years has been the quintuplets who were born in Callander and these babies we regard as the fairy princesses of Canada. And, without fear of contradiction, I can perhaps say I know more about the quintuplets than anybody in the world, but when they asked me in New York and other places how they make them, that is another matter. . . .

Now, there is no exploitation of these babies. I suppose in a mild way there is, we invite the tourists to see them and have contracts, but after all there is no exploitation and everything is under medical control. Everything is passed to Mr. Croll [Minister of Public Welfare] and the guardians meet regularly at North Bay once a month. They meet and pass all salary bills and keep the books and we know where everything is.

Now, as far as the tourists are concerned, we welcome the tourists as guests. We don't charge. We feel that is small stuff. True enough you would make some more money. The Americans can't understand that attitude. "Why don't you charge?" "Why don't you make more money?" "Put hotdog stands and everything around the place." We like to have things a little dignified. Besides, I have complete control. If at any time the children are sick, I am not going to show the children. If you invite tourists and make a charge and do not show the children they would say you were operating under false pretences.

Take the movie film. I only allowed them one hour. One day they only sat half an hour and all the filming was done in four or five minutes. The hour includes everything, but the babies come first, always. We welcome all the visitors. People all over the world have such an interest in these children. I think the world loves a baby. Multiply that by five and that is quite a bit and this interest, you know, is maintained even among men. Men go around hard-boiled and say that is all rubbish, but I get so much correspondence from men all over. One man, 78 years old, writes once a month to know how these babies are.

Now, the children, as I said before, look very much alike. My idea is that they are identical babies. I am not a scientist, so I want to make sure first or the scientists will want to pull me about. This is experimental stuff, anyhow. We have plans for any eventualities. Last year we showed the babies, one at a time on the porch. We had a large fence and at certain times during the day we allowed people inside the fence. Last year we had around 375,000 people there. That is a lot. Perhaps fifty per cent were Americans. Some days, perhaps some seven or eight thousand people were there. We showed first one baby and then another. The babies didn't mind it but toward the latter part of the season they began to get a little restless and didn't like it. They have to have some privacy. This year, we are hoping to have a plan whereby the public can pass through and see the children at play without being observed themselves. We want as much privacy as possible. We hope, in fact we know we are going to do that. We show them between certain hours. We expect to have a great many people, perhaps half a million there this summer. Think of the prosperity brought to the Province of Ontario. Think of the gas tax alone. They have to pass by way of Toronto or Montreal or the Soo. It takes a day to go and a day to come. They spend another day or two and they buy things to take away—souvenirs. After they get to the north country they are usually so pleased that they stay a couple of days more.

That north country was "the source of civilization, of business, and also of every form of attractive enterprise you have," boomed William Finlayson, Ontario Minister of Lands and Forests, and "the hope of the future of the province."

The forests of northern Ontario, an "incredibly rich" public asset, merited various kinds of attention, said Robson Black of the Canadian Forestry Association:

> Now, we know the casual view of a forest is that it is a patch of spruce, hemlock, pine, off somewhere in the great distance in the northern part of Ontario, alienated from all concern of ours, belonging to some so-called lumber baron; or else we conceive of it as a pleasant place to camp in, a good hunting ground, a group of spruces or balsams—always belonging to somebody else, and with perhaps a Royal Commission singing in the branches [Laughter] . . .
>
> But a newspaper, in its raw material, is just a flattened-out tree. Unless you can find a pile of pulpwood every year that runs 9,500 miles long, standing about so high and four feet wide, it is absolutely impossible to carry on the newspaper industry of this country. It is rather interesting to bring this back to terms of forestry. The *Chicago Tribune* in every Sunday's issue cleans off fifty-six acres of Canadian forest. A large New York newspaper does about forty to forty-five acres, also of Canadian forests.

Remarkably, the most important political question of the Twenties— that of the Governor-General's prerogative of dissolution, the central issue in the 1926 Constitutional Crisis—was side-stepped at the Club. While Mackenzie King made opportunistic political hay in the light of Lord Byng's need to grant to Conservative leader Arthur Meighen the dissolution of Parliament he had denied King, and a bitter Meighen withdrew from combat, there was silence at lunch-time—reflecting perhaps the political indecision that marked the decade. But if Ottawa impinged no more that Irkutsk on the rostrum, an increased flow of visiting Brits—1927 was Diamond Jubilee Year—filled head table. Several years later, then–Tory M. P. Harold Macmillan, who had been aide to the Duke of Devonshire when he was Governor-General of Canada, had some fun at the expense of the "peripatetic English politician":

How well accustomed you must all be to that type! The man who because he is regarded in the old Country as a bore or a crank, or both, who cannot collect an audience, as a last resort sets out upon a world tour. He begins the trail of desolation in the Mediterranean and there isn't a port or naval base from Gibraltar to Alexandria that doesn't echo with his platitudes. The Red Sea becomes the more oppressive for his presence. At Aden he spreads havoc and dismay. After a few weeks in India he explains to people who have spent a lifetime in that work the art of governing native people. Then, through Australia he pursues his chattering way. If he can find a corn anywhere he treads on it. If there is any kind of thin ice to be found he plunges bravely on to it. He comes across the Pacific to your hospitable shores. From west to east, from Vancouver to Halifax he goes, lecturing, talking, lunching, dining, always imparting information, never willing to listen to any. He blusters his way across three thousand miles, then, at last, having offended every sensibility and reopened every wound he gets back to the Old Country and the first thing he does is to add the Prime Minister to his list of victims and he besieges Downing Street and, finally, by a mixture of bullying, flattery and cajolery, he at last secures a K.C.M.G., for services to Empire.

In fairness, the members of the species were not always dull. Rt. Hon. J. W. Lowther, former speaker of the British House of Commons, Viscount Ullswater after his elevation to the peerage, and recipient of the Grand Cross of the Order of Bath for his services:

I suppose that amongst the worst things that the critics would say of the British people is that they are slow to move; that they do not advance very rapidly. Well, at the risk of repeating what I have said elsewhere, it seems to me that for people, just as for the individual, it is not haste which is so much required as direction. The rate per hour at which we are moving is not so important as the point of the compass to which we are moving. [Applause] In other words, there is no use in moving with rapidity towards a precipice; [Laughter] and I have quoted before and will quote again, a saying of Lowell's, I think, when speaking of change:

Change, just for change, is like them big hotels
Where they shift plates and let you live on smells.

[Laughter]

Well, with regard to our domestic legislation, upon my word, I don't think that we are so very much behind our children—if I may be allowed to call the Dominions children of the Mother Country. I don't think we are so much behind. Mothers are always rather behind their daughters. Our daughters are inclined to be a bit faster than their mothers, but even mothers now-a-days are trying to keep up. [Great laughter] We have shortened our skirts; we show our ankles a good deal; [Laughter] we have got what is practically universal suffrage. You have in one of your parliaments a lady member; we have got two. [Laughter] You have got a good-sized national debt; we have got a bigger one. [Laughter] Your state railways are in some considerable financial difficulty; so are ours. [Laughter] Your labouring population show a considerable disinclination to work; so do ours. [Laughter] You occasionally have strikes; we have plenty of them. [Laughter] You have a burden of taxes; good Heavens! we carry about three times as much as you; and as for divorce, well, you have plenty of them, and we have twice as many. So that, all together, we are not so very far behind you. [Laughter]

Not all travelling Brits were received as warmly—some quite waspishly. Two decades before Winston Churchill became the world's symbol for all that was gloriously brave and stubborn in the defence of freedom, he visited New York as First Lord of the Admiralty. J. K. Bangs, editor of *Harper's Weekly*, was not impressed:

Mr. Winston Spencer Churchill of London discovered that he carried in the back of his head all knowledge that ever has been in the world, all the knowledge there was in the world to come, with a few important things that had not yet occurred to the Creator himself, and he decided to come to the United States of America and lecture to the people of my benighted land upon such subjects as he felt, without his intervention on our behalf, we should know nothing of. His manager in New York, Major Pond, in order to give his first

1 *Stefansson, a visionary
astride a hobby-horse*

2 (Top) *"Canada does not dream of opening up her industries to the keen and destructive competition of the U.S. . . ."*

3 (Bottom) *Immigrants from Galicia: long lines of prejudice according to colour and kind*

4 (Top) *"A stalwart peasant in a sheep-skin coat is good quality"*

5 (Left) *"This is the grandest country on earth, and this is the finest town"*

6 (Top) *Prime Minister, Sir Robert Borden, reviews the troops in Ottawa, 1914*

7 (Bottom) *A Victoria Cross, D.S.O. and Bar, Military Cross, D.F.C., Legion d'Honneur and Croix de Guerre for the flyer from Owen Sound*

8 (Top) *Over the top: a raiding party sets forth*

9 (Top right) *Field Marshal Sir Douglas Haig with General Sir Arthur Currie, Canadian Corps Commander*

10 (Bottom) *The "curse of butchery": Canadians wounded at the Somme*

11 (Top) *Stephen Leacock: on the subject of Empire, a serious man*

12 (Bottom) *Mitch Hepburn, with Maurice Duplessis: co-conspirators against the rest of the Dominion?*

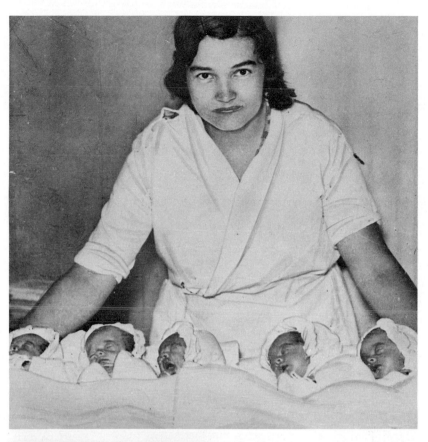

13 (Top) *Among the souvenirs, the babies*

14 (Left) *Dr. Dafoe: "Last year we had 375,000 people. . ."*

15 (Top) *In the cities, wage cuts and unemployment*

16 (Bottom) *In the Maritimes and drought-ridden Prairies, social devastation*

appearance greater distinction, invited all the notorious characters of New York, who were not at that time under indictment by the Grand Jury, to come and serve as a reception committee. There were just a hundred of us at that time, acting under the Major, Mark Twain, Andrew Carnegie and Bishop Potter. We all gathered at the Waldorf Astoria Hotel to see that Mr. Churchill was properly launched on the American waters.

On that occasion Churchill developed qualities as a hand-shaker that would have made him supreme inthe political parties we have had. He would seize the nearest New Yorker and pull him along and thrust him over on the other side; and so rapidly did he do this that, in seven and a half minutes, he had shaken hands with the whole hundred of us, and the reception, which was designed to last for an hour, was over in ten minutes. As I came on he grabbed my little finger and the fourth finger and the middle finger, and with Mr. Churchill's pressure I was projected like a bomb from a catapult, to land upon the form of Andrew Carnegie, who was cowering in one corner of the room. Major Pond came to me and said, "You are the youngest man in this room; can you do anything to break up this ice and save this situation for me?" I said, "Major, I am afraid I can't break any such ice as this; I am freezing myself; I feel very much as Dr. Cook must have felt when he discovered that he had not discovered the North Pole."

I said, "What do you want me to do?" He said, "Go up and meet Churchill." I said, "What, again?" He said, "Yes, you have been there once, and you will know how to go there and meet him the second time." So we came to where Churchill was studying the autographs on the wall, and he said, "What is it?" Major Pond said, "I want to introduce Mr. Bangs, Editor of *Harper's Weekly*." I stood forward and held out my hand, but recognizing me, Churchill withdrew his hand abruptly and said, very impertinently, "I have shaken hands with you once already." I said, "Well, Mr. Churchill, I have come back to get your thumb and forefinger." [Great laughter] But did I get them, Ladies and Gentlemen? I regret to say that I did not. Churchill turned away from me and began again to study those autographs on the wall; and I got as fine a view of a human back as living creature has had since the days when Adam and Eve went out from the Garden and left the serpent behind them.

Churchill himself addressed the Club in 1929 with the fine Imperial euphoria and ringing rhetoric endemic during the decade—touching on the subjects of British Imperial interests, the Navy, and the bad guys who

> would weaken or injure the enduring strength of the British Empire. [Hear, hear and applause] We must be careful that subversive movements do not effectually masquerade in the cause of pacificism and philanthropy. I dare say you have seen for yourselves how again and again certain classes of people go about to coax, cajole, cozen, and if they could, coerce the British Empire into giving up its rights, its interests and instruments of its vital security. [Applause] Our first security is the navy. [Applause] Our first security under Providence, and our righteous behaviour, is the Royal Navy. We have long enjoyed the naval supremacy of the world. We did not abuse that supremacy. We laid our ports open—those that were under the control of the central government—to the trade of all nations as well as of our own. We swept the seas of the slave trader, we used our influence for peace during the whole of the 19th century, and when the 20th century dawned it was the British Navy that proved the sure shield of freedom and civilization, and it was the British Navy that enabled the great republic of the United States to bring its influence to bear upon the closing phases of the war. [Applause]

Prime Minister Baldwin, in the summer of 1927, patted Empire Club pates:

> And one other aspect of your university life has given me intense pleasure. Lately some of the best graduates from Canada are beginning to play their part in looking after those parts of the Empire where the white man goes often alone to teach, to educate and to bring along the more backward races of the Empire. There is no more self-sacrificing work, there is no finer work; and you see Canadians in the Sudan and in the colonial services, medical men, highly educated men in the civil service helping to bear the white man's burden, and I am old-fashioned enough to believe that it is not enough for a country to concentrate solely on a lot of money for itself. The real spiritual force comes into it when its sons are ready,

as for generations Englishmen, Scotsmen and Irishmen have been ready, to give up the comforts of home life and go out on pioneer life and try to help people benefit from things that have benefitted others so much in the years past.

Baldwin's summation, "amidst a storm of enthusiasm":

The whole world today, with one or two exceptions, is singing loudly the praises of democracy. The whole world renders lip service to democracy. They have learned that cry from the English-speaking peoples. Our great task in the future is to show the world what democracy can mean. There have been democracies in the past; there are democracies today, but I like to think that no democracy today is even a shadow of the democracies that our children's children may see in years to come. Freedom, which you guard so well in Canada, freedom can only be maintained, as has often been said, by a constant vigilance. A democracy can only be maintained when every man, woman and child in that democracy means to do everything in their power to make that community better, stronger, freer. We need . . . educated people, educated not only in letters but educated in those deep, profound and moral truths on which our forefathers first of all built up the British Isles and went out to build up the Empire. You in Toronto, as much as in any place in the Empire, are the children of these men. From your position your influence on this great continent must be great, and must increase. Resolve, every one of you that you will all give your best thought, your best work, not only to the furthering of the interests of each individual among you, which, of course, is necessary, but to that greater community of which each of us is but a unit. Work for yourself, work for Canada, work for the whole Empire, and determine that so long as we speak the same tongue, obey the same God, obey the same laws, wherever we be situate, we remain to the end of time one people as the only hope of this world.

The balloon inflated with the sentiments of Baldwin and all was finally burst in the course of some common-sense observations by British-born Professor W. T. Waugh, of McGill, who admitted to concern over:

the superficial, confident talk that is going on now. We have had a lot of it in this country in the last two or three years. We have had visits from a number of British statesmen, Mr. Avery, Mr. Baldwin, Mr. Churchill, Mr. Thomas, Mr. Ramsay MacDonald, to mention only the more conspicuous, and on the occasion of every visit there have been great speeches extolling the Empire and pressing the harmony and unity that pervades it.

Relations hadn't improved within the Empire, and moreover, there were the conspicuous disruptions caused by "the attitudes of the whites in South Africa towards the natives and the attitude of the Australians towards the immigration of coloured peoples," and the fact that in many parts of the Empire the English were strongly disliked:

> They are notoriously unpopular in Australia, and in Canada—well, when I have been travelling about I have had some queer things said to me. [Laughter] There was a man in Saskatchewan, who was an exalted official in one of our great railways, I will not specify which, who within two minutes of being introduced to me said, "You know, we don't want Englishmen out here; what we like are Galicians and Lithuanians, and people like that." [Laughter] And I had other things said to me, not quite so sensational, but nearly so; and I asked myself, when people say that sort of thing to my face what are they saying about Englishmen behind my back? [Laughter]

The English themselves were indifferent, ignorant, and prone to make no distinction between Canada and United States:

> You might say that while the Empire people do not, as a rule, feel enthusiastic about the Empire they have still a cool and considered regard for its values. Their interest may not be emotional, but at any rate it is intelligent. Well, I very much doubt whether there is much interest at all, cool or enthusiastic. What strikes me most when I talk to English people about the Overseas Dominions is their utter ignorance. Of course I encounter it most in relation to Canada, because Canada is the usual subject of our conversation, but one

meets it in relation to other Dominions. My wife not long ago was talking to a lady in England who would be called, I suppose, an educated lady, and she knew that one of this lady's sons was somewhere abroad, and she asked the lady where he was, and the lady said, "Oh, he is in British Colombo." My wife looked rather astonished at this, and the lady hastened to add, "Yes, in British Colombo, in New Zealand, you know." [Laughter]

I fancy that the British know less about Canada than about any other Dominion, although it lies nearest. One gets some astonishing revelations. I remember when I was coming out here eight years ago, an educated lady, whom I knew very well, said she hoped I would not find the heat too trying; and not long ago I got a letter addressed to me, "McGill University, McGill, Ontario." [Laughter] The point of that story is that it came to me from an organization in England that existed to show hospitality and entertainment to young men, particularly University students, from the British Dominions overseas. [Laughter] A colleague of mine the other day got a letter from his Oxford College addressed to "McGill University, U.S.A." [Laughter] A student of mine who wants to enter one of the women's colleges in Oxford applied for admission, and a week or two ago she got a letter back saying that her application would be considered favourably, but it was not quite in order; it would have to be made through Washington. [Laughter] She had written from Montreal stating that she was an undergraduate of McGill.

In 1923, Ernest Lapointe had become the first Canadian to sign a treaty alone, the Halibut Fisheries Treaty with the United States. Diplomatic unity within the Empire was being broken, though many Canadians were of the mind that precedents set at Washington shouldn't be pressed too far. Prof. H. A. Smith, in 1926, a year before Canada appointed a resident minister to Washington:

How far are we prepared to go? Many suggestions are made, some of which are more worthy of attention than others.

The first suggestion I will not dwell upon very long. It is endorsed by one very well-known name—Mr. J. S. Ewart, of Ottawa—who considers that Canada ought to have a separate voice upon questions of war and peace. Now, I do not think I need take up your time in discussing that at length, because I gather that the name of your Club indicates that you would answer that suggestion in the negative.

Next suggestion is this—that we should maintain, so far as we can do so, separate diplomatic services of our own. That, again, seems to me to be open to objection. To begin with, there is the question of expense. I do not dwell upon that, because I imagine that if we thought it worth having we would be prepared to pay for it. But there is this further question: What is our diplomatic service at Ottawa and abroad to do? It must either agree with the British Ambassadors or it must disagree. There, again, you have the old dilemma. You know the old story of the burning of the library at Alexandria many centuries ago, when Caliph Omar laid down the rule that either the books agreed with the Koran, in which case they were superfluous, or they disagreed, in which case they should be destroyed. We are faced with a similar dilemma; if our representatives are only to say "Ditto" to the British Ambassador on every occasion they are superfluous. If, on the other hand, they disagreed, you get the question: are you prepared to push the disagreement to the point of independence, or are you prepared, after a certain amount of grumbling, to come in? . . .

But surely this is the most serious objection—that the Dominion should be called into continuous consultation; that they should have what Sir Robert Borden describes as an adequate voice in the moulding and control of British Foreign Policy. Sir Robert Borden's phrase was taken up by the Imperial Conference in 1917, which passed a resolution in favour of the Dominions having an adequate voice in foreign policy and foreign relations; and it has been left at that for nine years; nothing has been done to translate that generality into effect, the reason being that once you depart from the region of generalities and come down to facts you find it extremely difficult. The difficulty is not so much theoretical as practical. It lies in the nature of the practical work of diplomacy. Look at Lord Grey's recently published Memoirs, and you will find Lord Grey's office hours, when there was no crisis on and when Parliament was not sitting, were something like these:—he was in the foreign office usually from 11 in the morning till 7 in the evening; then he had two hours' work after dinner, and another hour and a half before breakfast in the morning. If the House of Commons was sitting, or there was anything special on, he had to work harder. Now, will you please try and imagine how, in the course of that day, Sir Edward Grey could have worked if he could not take a single step of importance without consulting all the representatives of the Dominions?

Suppose the French Ambassador or the American Ambassador comes into the Foreign Secretary's room—and these things happen not at long intervals, but every day—and says, "Upon this problem this is the view of my government; what is the view of yours?" The British Foreign Secretary would have to answer like this, "I am very much obliged to you for giving me such a clear and concise statement of the views of your government; and I will tell you the views of my government when I have consulted the representatives of Canada, Australia, India, New Zealand and South Africa." Obviously the thing cannot be done. . . .

In other parts of the Empire, Irishmen were rebelling, Egypt was treating for independence, and civil and political discontent rocked India. At Massey Hall in Toronto in March of 1921, a hostile crowd attempted to break up a meeting where Rustom Rustomjee, an unabashed apologist for Britain, was the speaker. Rustomjee ("the best introduction was given to me by that group of papers controlled and managed by that abominable liar, Hearst," which stated "Rustom Rustomjee, of Bombay, is a dirty British propagandist") returned to Toronto in October, to address the Empire Club:

It was my painful duty about two years ago to attend a meeting in Lexington called for the purpose of inaugurating a "League of Oppressed Nationalities." I naturally supposed that there would be speakers representing the coloured peoples of the United States of America, representatives from the Philippine Islands, from Haiti, from Liberia, from Africa, from French, Dutch as well as British colonies and dependencies. Among the speakers there was an American of Irish descent, a Sinn Feiner; an East Indian; an Egyptian; a Parsee; a Chinese; a Japanese; a Russian; and the burden of their song was the oppression of Great Britain in their respective countries. [Laughter] No love of Ireland or of India or Egypt actuates these men, because when the announcement was proclaimed of the strike in Great Britain at that meeting by Dudley Field Malone, the whole audience rose up and cheered, and cried out, "The British Empire is at an end." When the names of Lenin and Trotsky were mentioned, the very roof of the Lexington Opera House seemed to have come down. I say there was no love for Ireland or India or Egypt; it is their latent hatred of Great Britain; and when they shouted that the British Empire was at an end I, in my humble way, in the corner of the theatre, shouted—and I was thankful to say that I was allowed to shout, and shout loud—that the British Empire was not at an end, but on the contrary, as the days went by her duties seemed more clear, her work more majestic, her goal more sublime.

Britain would hold her Indian Empire, averred Rustomjee. J. L. Morison—a former teacher of history at Glasgow University, and a professor at Queen's since 1907—declared things would be settled there according to Greenwich time:

> We will give them step after step towards complete autonomy but we will not be hurried; we will not be terrorized into any rapid process of development; we will take our time which is also their time. That seems the proper thing. It means possibly the use of force. I am almost sorry, sometimes, that the Prussians have spoiled force as a moral thing, for there are times when force is a moral thing.

Royal Ontario Museum director Charles Currelly reported in 1923 on the uncertain conditions in Egypt, in the wake of a breakdown in British-Egyptian talks, giving the "master's side" of the situation:

> Geographical conditions often tend to make mental ones. Perhaps that very dependence upon the Government for their water, which means their food, has brought about the condition of mental depend-

ence on the part of the people. We very proudly say that Britons never will be slaves. I think it is quite right; I don't think any master could put up with us. Just imagine a real good Scotchman with a turn for argument as your own slave, for instance. [Laughter] I speak a little from the master's standpoint, because I have had slaves—rented ones—but still I know what the question is. . . .

I remember a case down in Suakin, a little out of Egypt, but under similar conditions, where a young lieutenant was sitting in front of his hut, and he saw a Bagara Arab passing with a sack on his shoulder. He thought he saw the sack move, and he said to his coolie, "Go and open that sack." Out rolled a small nigger whom he recognized as the son of one of his own soldiers. Now, those Bagara Arabs had been known to take boys and run them across to Yeddo, where they had been made into eunuchs, about one per cent of them, and if they could get one across in a year those fellows could live in very great comfort. There was a boy from the garrison stolen. The lieutenant asked his sergeant-major, "What will I do? If I shoot or hang that fellow there is not a particle of doubt I shall lose my commission; some Greek or Armenian or somebody will get the story through to the press and there will be talk of British brutality, and hanging without proper trial, and all this sort of thing; yet if I don't do it, and send him down, he will spend three months in jail, perhaps at Suez, and he will be better fed than ever in his life before, and he will sit in the sun and play tick-tack with a lot of other scoundrels, and he will be back to his old tricks again.

Well, the sergeant-major knew his own people, and he said, "Well, Sir, if I were you I would not do anything to him, but I would put a soldier on each side of him, and make him take the boy back to the women's quarters." The lieutenant said, "I didn't think of that; that will do splendidly." The fellow was marched back to the women's quarters, and it was announced that he had this boy in the sack, and it was told them what he intended to do with the boy; and those women flew at that fellow and they tore his flesh off his bones, and he died on the spot; he was dismembered by their fingers. That stopped the practice.

Irish M. P. William Coote attacked the Irish problem, and the nationalists, in 1920:

Easter Saturday was the day when the fatal hour arrived to strike, and the Germans sent their shiploads to Ireland; but the old British Navy had their tip in time, and they arrested the arms and sent the ships to the bottom of the sea, and the German submarine ran to Ireland with Sir Roger Casement, who was supposed to be the Ambassador at the Court of Berlin—we have a wonderful lot of ambassadors, but somehow they are living out of Ireland, a whole lot of them [Laughter] and they are remaining away for Ireland's good, and I trust that what will happen to poor De Valera is what happened to some men like Casement. The moment he touches Irish soil he is dumb. But don't you Canadians think that we in Ireland are downhearted; not the least. [Hear, hear] Don't think that the British Government has the slightest intention of listening to the idiotic nonsense of those men. I tell you that, when the old lion shakes his tail some day, there will be a rare walloping of those Irishmen. [Applause]

John A. Stewart, a New Yorker and founder of the SULGRAVE (friendship and good-will not only for the English-speaking world but for humanity) Institute also dismissed De Valera. The green peril, along with the so-called red peril and the yellow peril, were propaganda ploys of the directing minds behind a world-wide conspiracy against Anglo-American friendship:

We hear a great deal, particularly in political circles, about the red peril, and undoubtedly there is a red peril; but so far as Canada and the United States are concerned, the red peril can be dealt with so long as we have hempen rope and lamp posts. [Applause] I do not make that statement in any attempt to be humorous, but I am making a clear statement of fact. So long as we have Courts of Law, the justice of our cause lends might to our arms, and if the worst comes to the worst, lamp posts and hempen rope are always at our hand to be used. It is not that that is a peril to us. The red peril is only a part of the great reactionary movement that is abroad throughout the world. My distinguished friend, the Chairman, spoke of the yellow peril. The other day, in a speech in New York, I spoke of the yellow peril. I said that the red peril was not the danger to America or to Canada or to Great Britain, but it was the yellow peril; and I did not speak in terms of Asiatic nomenclature either. I spoke of the yellow men, the lily-livered men who are our citizens, who are so pacifist that they would lie down and let men walk over them, who would readily yield their rights in fear of danger of their own conjuring up. . . .

Now Mr. De Valera, so-called President of the so-called Irish Republic [Laughter]—I will refer to Mr. De Valera in passing because Mr. De Valera in himself is only an incident, only a symptom, only one of those evidences that, far underneath the surface, great forces are at work and are using all the De Valeras in the world as their tools—De Valera is nothing; he is the fictitious President of a fictitious Republic, and he has not been able to impress his own people in America to a sufficient degree to enable him to raise the $10,000,000 which so blithely he is speaking about raising, nor a half, or a half of that again. . . .

A few years later, however, the Club listened to Rt. Hon. Timothy A. Smiddy, a minister of the Irish Free State, discuss economic conditions and policies in his country in 1926. The real hope in the Republic was the ultimate reunion of Ireland, Smiddy said, but "we hope to achieve it by good example, by friendliness, by prosperity." And thank John Bull for that, said the American editor and publisher Arthur Wilson Page, in a speech on U.S. foreign policy:

I do not think that you can realize how grateful Americans are to the British Empire for finally settling the Irish question. [Great laughter] Not only have we most of the principles of our international policy in common with you, but when you have an internal pain it seems to be contagious with us. [Laughter] At every election, and between-times, the grievances of Ireland resounded from cart tail and soap box, and we could not elect a sheriff or a dog-catcher in any part of the United States without their being attended by the curse of Cromwell and the Battle of the Boyne. [Great laughter] A black-and-tan fight in the county of Kerry would lose a man votes in the Bronx; and the fact that an Irishman died in jail in Dublin had a powerful effect on the elections in Boston. Perhaps the British Empire does not feel that the Irish question is altogether settled, and we still have a few Irish twinges ourselves; but for the mitigation of its acuteness we give you our heartfelt thanks. [Laughter] The Irish pain, I hope, will gradually disappear, and as it does it will make it still easier to get the habit of working together.

The Irish, Egyptians, Indians, were largely distant trouble. In comparison, Canada was an unmarked page. At the end of the decade, the crash hit Wall Street and Bay Street, and only the idealists were left alive.

CHAPTER 6

"The whole world is against us"

For Canada, dependent on exports of farm produce and raw materials, the 1929 Wall Street crash that brought down the trading system of the Western World spelled economic disaster. (In 1929, Canadian domestic exports totalled $1,152,416,000 in value, in 1932, $489,883,000; by 1939, foreign trade had recovered only to $924,926,000.) Liberal heads—Mackenzie King's, notably—rolled in the wake of the stock market collapse. In the 1930 general election the new Tory leader, R. B. Bennett, a wealthy ebullient Calgary bachelor lawyer born in Hopewell Hill, N.B., preached a positive platform—positive in that it acknowledged the dire circumstances of the country—that delivered a 31-seat majority to the Conservatives. At the Empire Club, pundits were mustered for purposes of analysis and to propound remedies for the recession. Stephen Leacock:

> When you ask the ordinary person what has caused the depression, you get a great number of answers. In the current press and in the current speech, you read and hear, perhaps, that it is caused by the gold standard, by the currency, by the collapse of the monetary system. I don't think so. Some people say that Mackenzie King did it. [Laughter] Sir, I am a stout Conservative, but I do not believe that

it is among the sins for which Mackenzie King will some day have to answer. . . .

Now, Sir, turn your mind back and look over history. You know, professors invite you to look back into history and they never come to the surface again. The typical professor if you ask him to explain something, takes a deep dive underneath the waters of history and never comes up. You don't wait to see him emerge, but I propose a shorter retrospect than that. I only want to ask you in the very broadest way to look back a hundred years, if some of you can remember that long. Look back over a hundred years of our system. They call it now "the profit system." It's an awful thing. It is not the p-r-o-f-i-t-s system—I saw some of you prick up your ears when I said "profit"—I don't mean that. It is the profit system that has had a number of ugly words used for it—the system we have used ever since we came out of the Garden of Eden. After all, what do they mean?—that every man works for himself, that the economic interest of the individual is the basis of society; that you and I work first and foremost for ourselves and those near and dear to us and not for someone else's grandma is, and will continue to be the system—I take it and stand on it. I tell you that no other system has worked to knock out unfairness, modified if you like, to shorten the power of those who have too much. Fundamentally, my property is mine, my work is mine, and the fruits of my work, the result of the efforts of my brain and my industry—that is mine and there is no other system of running society and there never will be—none, none, none! [Applause]

W. C. Clark, of Queen's University, also defended the system:

In these days one accepts with certain misgivings an invitation to speak on current business conditions—lest one add unduly to the prevailing atmosphere of gloom. You will recall Eddie Cantor's recent predicament. He had just joined a society dedicated to the noble task of eliminating the word depression from every man's vocabulary. The next time he had occasion to speak he said: "Gentlemen, this is not a depression but candour compels me to admit that it is the smallest boom I have seen in several years." Candour compels me to go even farther. . . .

The problem before Canada and the world has been continuously underestimated in these last two years—and with disastrous results, as you know. It has also been exaggerated in some quarters. . . . To such people our economic machine has been broken into a thousand pieces and there is no one to claim the fragments. Surely that is an exaggerated, if not a wholly false, view. True it is that the machine is in trouble, that four or five of the sixteen cylinders are missing fire, that two or three of the tires are flat, that the speed has been slowed down to a snail's pace and that a good many of the passengers have had to get out and walk. But—if I may state a conclusion dogmatically without attempting proof at this time—the machine, in my opinion, is not incapable of repair. The engine needs to be overhauled, the battery recharged, the tires renewed, nuts tightened and moving parts re-lubricated. The brakes need relining and a powerful system of headlights needs to be installed if we are to drive again at the pace of 1929. Back-seat driving must be eliminated and more responsible, intelligent direction at the wheel is required. With such a thorough overhauling and such improvement in controls, it will probably be found that the "old bus" is still without an equal, superior to the only competitive model which has yet appeared, and capable of carrying us at record speed on to new peaks of prosperity.

Graham Towers, chief inspector of the Royal Bank of Canada in 1931, blamed a unique "efflux of credit": "During the five years ending in 1928 the United States loaned over $6,000,000,000 of new money to other countries—which means that during those five years the U.S. created sufficient credit to put $6,000,000,000 of purchasing power into the hands of other nations." There was no question, Towers said, that during the latter years of the period "the United States took the world on a credit spree."

The American statistician H. C. Baldwin, of Babson's, cited "super-salesmanship" as a major factor:

Industrial leaders had prided themselves on their policy of controlling production to fit demand, but in reality our mass producers were using every expedient known to sales and advertising men to inflate the visible demand to undue proportions. With unbelievable suc-

111

cess, consumers were taught to buy with money which they did not have. Much of this type of buying converged on semi-luxuries and luxuries. Salesmen and even bankers preached the doctrine. . . .

Stephen Leacock advocated the setting up of a rise in prices as a short-term measure, but plumped for a longer view:

There is a man abroad, called the Technocrat, many of whose speeches and sayings are foolish in the extreme. He has made what he calls "an energy survey of the world"—mostly seen from Greenwich villages and the speakeasies. [Laughter] The Technocrat has told us all kinds of silly things about abandoning our customary standard of values and substituting the scientific standard which is usually measured by an "erg" or an "umph." But like many false prophets, they may be showing the way to the true believer, and along side of the question of the power of humanity to produce and the capacity of humanity to organize lies the fundamental problem of our present organization and along that line will be found the ultimate solution some day. . . . We must set (our house) in order because there will never, never, never, be another depression after this one that would pass away of itself. This one, we trust, will go anyway—I hope so though we are not sure—but the next one, NO. After this one we are under irrevocable sentence of industrial death.

. . . We will have for that task a respite of perhaps a generation and in that time we will look forward to finding a means by which the production of goods and their consumption can be harmonized—not by the fool remedies of Socialism or the brute remedy of Communism, but by introducing new rules to the game. . . . The goal is that we will come out some day into an industrial commonwealth where we don't work as hard as we do now . . . where everyone will be doing a life work and never know he is working. We can imagine a commonwealth in which, as Julian Huxley says, two hours a day is enough for everybody to work.

The Technocrat is right. We work too much and we work too long. We even invent new things to work at. We don't need to do that. But life will come out somewhere. . . . Humanity is not licked yet. When I look around at this group of human beings, I feel that we in Canada, with the heritage that we have, can face this kind of task and we can win out and conquer it and achieve, not only the cure of this depression but the fundamental cure that will bring us to the real welfare of human society.

The Depression did not deal equally with the ten million Canadians of 1930. Bennett had promised to "blast a way into the markets that have been closed," but the main Tory thrust against the Depression was to increase the tariff by nearly 50 per cent, protecting profits and prices but ultimately limiting trade. Forget such "small and foolish notions," urged Sir George Paish, one of a vanguard of visitors who spoke before the much-heralded Imperial Economic Conference of 1932:

> If you buy freely and at low prices you will be able to reduce your costs of production; this enables you to sell freely and at low prices. You will agree with me, I am sure, that Great Britain's record is marvellous. From the end of the forties up till the war Great Britain presented no artificial obstacles to the trade of other countries. She invited every country—manufacturing countries as well as food countries—to send their products to Great Britain. She imported freely and what was the result? Did the foreign goods destroy British industries? Not one industry was destroyed! Every industry was fostered. In that time our export trade grew from £50,000,000 to £530,000,000; our wealth more than doubled; our income grew something like threefold; and during that period we sold to other nations nearly £4,000,000,000 worth of produce more than we bought. No other country in the world has such a record; and it is not possible to have such a record unless you have the courage to stand up and say, "We are prepared to face any country and have fair and reasonable competition." That is what Great Britain has been doing. You, her sons and daughters, will be proud of her as I am proud of her. . . .

At the Conference, held in Ottawa, Bennett did agree to preferential tariff-lowering within the Commonwealth, but the constriction within Canada offset any gains. The Depression deepened. Wage cuts and unemployment racked the burgeoning urban working class, and social devastation swept the Maritimes and the drought-ridden Prairies. "In the old days," said J. S. Woodsworth in a moving address in the

Commons, "we could send people from the cities to the country. If they went out today they would meet another army of unemployed coming back from the country to the city: that outlet is closed. What can these people do? They have been driven from our parks; they have been driven from our streets; they have been driven from our buildings and in this city [Ottawa] they actually took refuge on the garbage heaps."

Bennett, as soon as he was elected, had called a special session of Parliament, which voted $20-million for emergency relief work, and instigated a series of public works programs. At the time, the Tories were smug. "Public works," Federal Labour Minister G. D. Robertson told the Club in January, 1931, "have been approved to be carried on co-operatively by municipalities and provinces with the aid of the federal government, in 1,087 municipalities." Provincial undertakings, another co-operative effort, numbered 267, and there were "between 150,000 and 175,000" men at work "who would be unemployed were it not for this co-operative plan." But by 1933, in addition to the increasingly catastrophic situation of the farmers, 23 per cent of the labour force was unemployed. Declining conditions resulted in political discontent. Ontario dumped the long-time incumbent Tories in 1934, seduced by the populism and colourful personality of Mitchell Hepburn. Maurice Duplessis welded Quebec Conservatives and dissident Liberals into the Union Nationale, elected in 1936 as a reform party; radio evangelist William Aberhart, promising everyone $25 a month, led the Social Credit Party to victory in the 1935 provincial election; and the Co-operative Commonwealth Federation—a distinctively Canadian socialist party founded in Regina in 1933—formed the official Opposition in British Columbia and Saskatchewan.

At the Empire Club, Stephen Leacock poked fun at both the CCF party and the program, asking the rhetorical question:

Socialism? What do you mean by that? It is the government of impossible people by impossible leaders. It is an iridescent soap bubble floating in the air—a soap bubble of the good wishes of transcendental human beings, governing other good transcendental human beings. That is Socialism. And take it, if you like. We have a large party gathering now . . . and as I understand that new movement, all kinds of people—farmers, householders, lawyers, clerks and intellectuals—are all coming into it, but each one has the idea that he is going to socialize the other—not himself!

There are farmers in this movement. Do they mean to socialize their farms? Are they going to give over the management of their fifty acres in York Township to a pack of bosses sitting with their feet on the table and collecting their money as they do in Russia? Not on your life—they will drop dead in the furrows first. And then there are the householders. Do they mean that they will turn over their houses to a group of bosses to assign away their rooms to this one and that? No, they would die first! Then there are the young fellows—the bright intellectuals in your colleges and mine who are joining this new movement, and they own nothing except the pants they wear. [Laughter] Are they going to socialize their pants?

Members of the Club, not always demonstrably partisan, applauded as Robert Cromie blasted Bennett and King alike for dealing in "romance" rather than "reality"—and then strongly advised political, financial and business leaders to take lessons from Germany, Russia and Italy.

We read in the papers just yesterday that our political leaders at Ottawa, both Mackenzie King and Premier Bennett, instead of addressing themselves to the realistic things of Canada, are spending four hours and five hours in making speeches about titles and they are doing that while four or five hundred thousand of our Canadian boys and girls from 19 to 23, 24 and 25 years old, haven't got a thing to do! When you sit in your office as you and I do and a young fellow of nineteen or twenty comes in and asks for a job, you can't give him a job. You can't say, "Sonny, go next door: they will probably give you a job." You know you are lying. And you can't say that he will get a job tomorrow or the next day. If we had a shortage of foods and goods; if production was a problem with us, that would be something, but it isn't. We have a plentitude of foods and goods but lack the social attitude and financial technique to distribute them. Also we lack the psychology to adjust ourselves to the new era of plentitude we now find ourselves in. After all it is man's ability to adjust himself to new conditions which determines history, which determines man's progress and his growth. How will future generations regard our lack of ability to adjust our new machine world?

We come back to this continent with $23 worth of machinery per individual in North America. The next nearest is England with $11; Germany, $9; France, $4, reflecting the technology and soil productivity. . . . Go and see the evolution in relation to soil production. See Cyrus McCormick's old sickle, the reaper, the binder, the mower, and the thresher and see what man can do with machinery in one hour of field work that used to take him three days. Cannot you see from that an inkling of some adjustments that have to be made? . . .

Should we try to pay the same interest rate on our debt that applied when Calgary Oil stocks were worth twenty times what they are now, and every other stock accordingly? Or shall we trim interest notes down to an amount we can carry? . . .

Our social conception and ethical conceptions have to change because, after all, if you want to know and do things today, you don't hark back to old ritualism, and formalism and political theorism; you go to the new leadership of realism. And when you go and see what Mussolini is doing, you find that he has got a grip on the mind and the thought of the youth of Italy.

He is giving intelligent leadership. He couldn't help it because he would be edged out if he didn't.

When you go to Germany and see Hitler—and I had a close-up in Europe recently—you make some reappraisals. When you go to Russia and see what they have done even if on lower standards than ours, you see that if they hadn't organized, they would be heading toward the fate of disintegrated starving China. Organization beats disorganization; never forget that. When you come to Canada and the United States, you see that we don't have to go through the revolution that Russia went through, that Germany is now going through, if we address ourselves to the problem of our country, which is realism; to the most valuable asset we have which is our own living people, rather than dead debts or money theories.

If you want some conception of the possible standards of living on this continent, just think that in Canada and United States we are now only using about 60 per cent of our *present* plant. We are only using about 1/10 of our *potential producing energy and power*. With an economic set-up like this, you can see how rich we are just the minute we set our minds and plans to the task of not only using our present plant to capacity but tapping in and using at least a portion of our potential energy.

The earth's peoples are on the march. Radio and movies have now made it possible for the masses to look right into the Castle. This means that there will be no more government skulduggery behind castle doors. Radio means that youth no longer has to spend 20 years learning to read and write, and then spend another 10 years learning the significance of the thought and action behind that writing. The radio and movie, through the ear and eye, couple up the mind of the masses with the mind of government.

By the mid-thirties, Bennett was beset. In the 1935 general election, Canadian voters unseated the Tories and passed the buck back to Mackenzie King. A year later Charlotte Whitton, in a speech titled "Canada's Problems in Relief and Assistance," reported on "lights and shadows" in the government's social stewardship in rural areas:

All afternoon we drove through the dried out land: the Russian thistle grew so tall and dense that the road led through a tunnel of it, reaching to the top of the car and necessitating driving with the headlights on; everywhere the grey-brown desolation of the desert; here and there fence posts showing through the drifted soil; in odd places thin horses, poor lean cattle standing bewildered by the outbuildings: nearly everywhere good looking farm homes, "all on relief," the investigator told me. We drove up to one, and with what pride that woman told us she was "getting by." She took us to her cellar, with gopher canned in rows of sealers—"it's as clean a little animal as a rabbit when you come to think of it," she said, and explained that her boys had kept themselves in shoes and clothes for school through the bounty paid on the gophers' skins. She showed us, too, wheat ground for porridge, roasted and ground for coffee, wool shorn, cleaned, combed, carded, spun and made up herself. She was "getting by" and cheery in the getting.

Trekking out from the Makwa Lake area in far Northern Saskatchewan, I met a man, woman and child, with a wagon filled with brush, some bedding, a mule trailing the vehicle drawn by a thin and weary team. I asked them if they were trekking out for good. They

117

told me their home was South in the dry area: for three years, they had had no crop: this Spring they had put one in, then taken the grandfather, seventy years old, trekked North, thirty-eight days on the way they told me, staked a piece of land, cleared space for a garden, put in vegetables, potatoes and a few oats, had seen it well under way, had left the old grandfather there to "tend it," were trekking South to see whether they had any harvest there, and were coming North again to winter. "One way or other, we ought to have our keep, don't you think?" they said.

At another home in the country: a man forty-eight, his wife forty-five, three boys fourteen to nineteen, a girl sixteen year of age, a married son, twenty-two, with his wife and baby, living in the same house, another baby coming, and a little "slavey" given food and lodging and clothing for doing the work. All on relief. "These big boys and this young father don't want the risk of not getting on relief again, if they go, so they stay at home," said the older woman: a system that we have allowed to get out of hand subsidizes their idleness.

Up the Pacific Coast, on one of the islands, a man and his wife, university graduates, four children, in a poor log cabin, lent to them by a friend, growing tulip bulbs—they are light to ship so you lose little in postage: teaching the children themselves: hard and hopeless—yes, "but a great deal better," they said, "than the hopelessness of relief in a city attic."

In the cities:

A young artisan, thirty-five years of age, married to a girl who had worked in the office at the plant: a neat little home, furnished on their savings:—Short time, then shut down. "Out," four years ago. Everything saleable gone now from the little home, the home gone, crowded together in two rooms, three frightened, uncertain little children, his skill slipping through disuse, hope and confidence and outlook blurred.

Vary the story to take in the white collar worker, the ice man let out with the coming of the frigidaire, the clerk displaced for the young graduate, vary it to include, if you will, the "chiseller" and the exploiter, but remembering that suffering, need, idleness and despair play their own part in turning the man who cannot work into the man who will not work. Vary it for town and large city, for East and West, for foreign and British and Canadian families, and perhaps you will see some of the one hundred and seventy-five thousand families on relief in urban centres. . . .

The plight of youth:

Crossing on a ferry in British Columbia, where a kindly policeman was giving me a lift, we heard suddenly a "Hullo Sergeant" from the floor in the back of the car. "Don't you remember you had me in the jug back at Christmas for rod riding? Been waiting all day to take a chance on a car on this ferry." The lad later told me he was seventeen, had hiked from near St. Johns, Quebec, to the Coast, back as far as Sherbrooke, and was thus far West again. "Can't even make Victoria or Alaska though—the boat guys are too bright and tough." Oh! Yes! He could get work, a few weeks perhaps in the yards or mills, but if you were going to be broke anyway, might as well make a lark of it and see the country A darn good war though, that's what he'd like to see, something for a fellow to do then—the war yarns were the best in the hostels or jungles, he thought.

Twenty thousand men in relief camps, one hundred and twenty-six thousand young wage earners unemployed, two hundred and ninety thousand who have never worked at all—break them down into lives like this, and others, and others, and others, you begin to visualize the problem of idle youth, whether on relief or idle and dependent on their families. . . .

These are some of our problems, that leave us with one in six of our population at the best of times in these years and one in five in the winter, at the worst, drawing in whole or in part on social aid and sending the annual cost up to one hundred and fifteen million dollars for relief under our special legislation alone.

In 1935, Bennett had announced a startling New Deal for the Canadian people, a series of social reform measures passed in the pre-election Parliament. Mackenzie King, typically, referred the legislation to the Supreme Court for a constitutional judgment. The court ruled that the Depression did not justify wider federal jurisdiction, but appointed the

Rowell-Sirois Commission to review the whole matter of Dominion-provincial relations. The Report (issued in 1940) emphatically opted for more responsibility and revenue for Ottawa in accord, it stated, with the original intent of Confederation. Premier Hepburn of Ontario—dictatorial in his pretensions and by 1937 locked in combat with King and leagued with the power brokers in the province—led the anti-Commission forces during the research period, and thereafter. ''Present-Day Problems'' was the deceptively meek title of a speech he delivered in 1938 to the Club:

> I wonder if you gentlemen, who are leaders of thought in your own community, realize the inroads which are being made today upon the resources of this, the central Province, and the richest province? I wonder if you realize that at this moment you are paying subventions for coal from Alberta, approximately one-half the freight rates on feeder cattle coming from the West to Ontario, and you are paying subventions for wheat going to both seaboards? With respect to the Maritimes you are paying subsidies to the extent of $2.00 per ton on Maritime coal coming to Ontario, you are paying subsidies on fish, you are paying subsidies on potatoes.
>
> We have in Ontario a great industrial concern, located in Sault Ste. Marie, that is struggling along in competition with another great concern of a like nature, located in the Maritime Provinces, which concern derives approximately a million and a half dollars per year in the way of subsidies and our industry in Sault Ste. Marie has to compete, although, and this is the irony of it, it pays its share of taxation to subsidize a competitive industry in the Maritimes.
>
> Now, we have our railway problem which has been aggravated in no small measure by over-expansion. We agree that we suffer because of our very geography. But the great contributions we are making now toward railway deficits have to do with over-expansion in the West. We put up a million dollars a week, or at least we add that to our debt, as the result of trying to maintain railway service for those in the sparsely settled sections of the West. That is a tremendous thing. It is more than the entire budget of the Federal Government at the beginning of this century. . . . Then we built the Hudson Bay Railway, at great expense. . . .

Now, there has been a great deal said about national unity. I am just going to make this one observation with regard to my friend, William Lyon Mackenzie King, and I want it made very clear here that when I drank the Toast to the King, a few moments ago, it was to Our Majesty, the King. They said all around me, "The King." I wanted to make myself clear on that point. This gentleman at this moment is charging me with entering into a conspiracy to destroy Confederation. Now, I deny the allegation most emphatically. There isn't a more loyal Canadian in this great gathering than myself. Why shouldn't I be? I was born and raised here. Like the rest of you I love this Canada of ours and I am proud to know that this Canada of ours is a link in the great British Empire. I am not only a Canadian, I am an Imperialist, if you want to call me that. Naturally you expect that, since I am of Scottish descent—Scottish and Irish. As a matter of fact, there is quite a controversy between the two peoples in my country. The Scottish people insist that I am Irish, and the Irish insist that I am Scottish. I just want to make this observation about the gentleman at Ottawa. . . . He, who today is charging me with entering into conspiracy to destroy our Confederation is the same gentleman who, in 1930, and I was there in the Dominion Parliament at the time, sitting as one of his supporters, got up and enunciated a policy which I think did more, in the way of endeavour, at least, to destroy Confederation than anything else, when he said . . . "Not a five-cent piece for relief for any province with a Tory Government!" Just imagine, my friends, that man talking today about anyone else breaking up Confederation, and talking about leading a party, based on the policy of national unity. [Applause] My Gosh, I am glad there are some Tories in the audience. [Laughter] . . . .

What we want today is a better understanding as between the different provinces, and a better understanding will not be brought about by Federal Ministers going around and levelling charges that Quebec and Ontario are conspiring against the rest of the Dominion. We submit to all these drains upon us because we want to maintain our Confederation, and we are going to maintain our Confederation. It doesn't necessarily follow that we should be the goats of everybody, and I think I would be derelict in my duty if I did not, as your

Premier, put Ontario's case, as I did, fairly and squarely before the Rowell Commission.

Now, so far as I am concerned, I have washed my hands of the whole business, because the Dominion Government did something which I cannot forgive it for. There are many things it hasn't done, more than it has done, as a matter of fact. This Commission was set up for the purpose of studying facts and problems as between the Dominion and the Provinces, and before the Commission had a chance to report to the Federal Government, new taxation was levied by the Dominion which invaded a field of provincial taxation. Now, remember, my friends, Confederation was brought about as a result of an agreement between the Provinces. We created the central government, the central government did not create us. But before this Commission had a chance to report, the Federal Government, in the last session, invoked new taxation which invaded present provincial fields of taxation, and I refer particularly to the gift tax, which is a direct invasion of the field of succession duties.

I look with wonder in my eye at the many, many, millionaires I see around here. There is Jack Bickell, and Sam McLaughlin and all the rest of the fellows. I can't help but think when I see chaps like that around of how we are going to collect revenue for the province. I keep enquiring about their health. In fact, I think I will circularize a lot of the millionaires, day by day, to find how they are progressing, in the hope that some time or other I can excel last year's all time high record of collection of succession duties. . . .

The question arises, what are we going to do about it? Who is the Moses who is going to lead us out of the wilderness? The other night when I was talking to a gathering of people I said, "What would I do if I were King?" I didn't mean Mackenzie King, either. I would face the issues frankly and fairly. . . . The question of reducing overhead is one that has been cussed and discussed. I have done a few little things in the way of reducing overhead. I closed Ontario House in London, England. It was a miniature duplication of the service being maintained by the Federal authorities. But I got hell. . . .

Then, we closed this architectural monstrosity, known as Government House, and again I got a little slice of that other region—plenty of it, as a matter of fact. Well, gentlemen, it isn't any measure of disloyalty to close an institution of that kind. It was costing a lot of money and it was in need of repair. It would cost $100,000, at least, to put it in shape. Can this Canada of ours maintain provincial institutions like that? . . .

I speak as your Treasurer, and I know in the richest province of all, we can't go on indefinitely carrying this present burden of debt and this burden of taxation. There has got to be equality of sacrifice all along the line. We have got to take national stock and inventory. I hear somebody say, "Hear, Hear." It was a wee, small voice, nevertheless I think a lot of you gentlemen are quite in agreement with what I am saying at the present time. [Applause]

It is somewhat like the story of the fellow who had been frequenting one of my beer parlours. I am not looking at anybody in particular, so don't feel guilty. He staggered into a church while an Evangelist was conducting a service. He went to sleep. The Evangelist said, "All those who want to go to Heaven stand up." Everybody stood up but the drunken fellow. The gentleman said, "All those who want to go to the other place, stand." The noise awakened the sleepy chap and he stood up, and he said, "Parson, I don't know what in the world we are voting on, but I see you and I are in the darned small minority." [Laughter] . . .

Today I witness the demoralization of the morale of the people of this country because of inability of those in authority to settle our unemployment problems. You can't feed and clothe and house and shelter people indefinitely without breaking their morale. [Applause] That is what we are doing at the present time. We might as well realize that, too. [Applause] The most tragic thing I have witnessed at this moment is the demoralization of the young men of this country. My friends, just think, only a few weeks ago, we witnessed this terrible spectacle of physically fit, single, unemployed men, sheltered and clothed and fed and given medical care out of the pockets of the taxpayer, actually refusing to work seven hours a week beautifying their own city in the way of repayment. Now, years ago those men would have been ashamed to even accept charity but today the situation is changed so completely that these men are even prepared and did picket the City Hall, identifying themselves as those who wouldn't give back to you taxpayers seven hours of work in a whole week, for what you are doing for them. . . .

Another problem was pressing, Hepburn said in conclusion:

We are living in a new era. I was out on the Pacific Coast, not so very long ago, with my friend, Jack Bickell. You know, I get criticized for travelling with millionaires, but I was doing something for the province. I had two of them with me. If we had crashed, just think of the income you would have had. Two millionaires in an aeroplane with a tax collector! [Laughter] What a sacrifice for one's country! Out there, my friends, they are worrying about Pacific defence. The world is getting nearer together. Now, I say it is time for us to take stock and inventory, to put our house in order, because we are facing a new problem entirely, that of national defence, and the democracies of the world have got to stand together. There is no doubt in my mind, and I am not kidding myself about it, three nations have agreed upon the conquest of the world. . . .

George Foster, back in 1923, had broached the subject of Mussolini to members of the Club. Then, amusement greeted his analogies:

Did you ever think about it, really sit down and really think about what happened in Italy just a few months ago? The world seems to have swallowed the pill without thinking that it had swallowed anything unusual, but the pill was swallowed, and the effects are bound to be felt sometime. [Laughter] What happened? I don't know that I can put it more graphically than this. Imagine if you can that our genial friend Tom Moore, who is chief of the labour organizations of this country, should take into his head that, with only a fractional number of labour representatives in the parliament at Ottawa, he was going to govern the country, and so dressed his labour union men in black shirts, and drilled them in a semi-military way, and one fine day he hustled them all into line and marched up to Ottawa and said to Mr. Mackenzie King: "Get you gone!" and to the House of Commons, which is supposed to be a part of our constitutional government: "I have no favours to ask of you; I am going to control you;'' and said to the representatives of his Majesty: ''I want you to commission me to form a Government.'' On the question being put to him, ''Have you and your party been elected by the people?'', he would reply, ''No, I have dispensed with that formality, have elected myself and am here with my demand.''

Suppose Tom Moore and his friends had done just that, and ensconsed himself and them in the places of authority at Ottawa and Canada, and proceeded forthwith to rule this country by personal orders and had selected associates and made them ministers without election by constituents, wouldn't you think that a very grave question had been raised? [Laughter] In just that way Mussolini walked into Rome, established complete individual autocracy, over-turned all the results of the long struggle for constitutional govern-ment in Italy, and today reigns supreme dictator in Italy as in Rome. Where is the solid foundation of Government? On what does he base his claims? He has not been before the people for election. After he formed his government he has not gone back for an election. He simply sits there with his black shirts in the distance, and says, ''I am the master of this country, by direct force I am here, and by virtue of my black shirts, I am going to rule it.''

If that can be done in Italy it can be tried anywhere. The circum-stances were favourable, to his venture, or to put it better, were unfavourable to the cause of constitutional government in Italy, and so he was enabled to carry it off for the nonce. But the settlement has to come later, and it is either a question as to whether Italy is going to have an autocracy without any regard to the suffrages of the people, or to the constitutional conditions, or whether it is going to get back to constitutional government based upon the authority as expressed at the polls by the people of Italy. There is an action in reversal of constitutional government which, in all this hurly-burly, has not attracted much world attention, but it is there, and it has got to be solved. Already you have lesser Mussolinis starting here and there with their bands of red shirts or white shirts or no shirts at all, [Laughter] who are trying to play the same game in many parts of Europe today.

Italy was to be reckoned a minor matter at most in Empire Club annals.

There were those such as Robert Cromie, who admired Mussolini's firm grip in 1934, and the following remarkable dissertation was delivered the same year by Magistrate S. Alfred Jones, K.C.:

The study of Fascism is so absorbing, and its methods are so unique, that it demands investigation by any who are interested in the science of statecraft, particularly at this time when all are earnestly seeking a path which leads to the betterment of existing human conditions. Perhaps outside Italy today there is no question more frequently asked than "what is Fascism?" and there is certainly no creed which has been more misunderstood and so misrepresented—may I say, grossly misrepresented.

"Fascio" is Italian for "bundle." The Fascist emblem is a bundle of sticks bound together with an axe extending from the end denoting authority. Fascism is loyalty to an ideal. Perhaps the best definition of Fascism is insistence on co-operation. One will readily admit that co-operation is asked for by every government in every land as one of its basic principles. You will observe that the distinction Italy makes is in the word "insistence." Italy says "We want you to co-operate. We ask your voluntary co-operation. If you won't give it that way, then you must give it anyway." "You must co-operate" is the key-note. The inspiring ideal is that of working together and making sacrifices together of gain or leisure for the common good as comrades did in the Great War. As a matter of history, Fascism was born in the spirit of the trenches among returned men who would not allow politicians to throw away the fruits of their victory. Fascism came into being as a movement to smash the rich. This it eventually did, after years of battling, wounds and death, extending from March 1919 to October 1922, the date of the Fascist March on Rome. On this date more than 2,000 Fascists laid down their lives in order that Italy might live. You will see that Communism has something for which we should give it credit, viz: it was responsible for the birth of Fascism. Fascism was originally a patriotic movement to overcome Communism. It grew, developed and expanded and today Fascism is the spirit of a nation; today Fascism is Italy.

The criticism of the Fascist form of Government, which one hears most frequently, is that it is an uncontrolled dictatorship built around

126

Mussolini; that Mussolini is the keystone of the arch and that when he passes away the structure will crumble. Nothing, gentlemen, could be further from the truth. There is no Russian dictatorship in Italy. When parliament passes a law, Mussolini has no power to alter it. It is true that in Mussolini the Italians believe they have an outstanding statesman. They both respect and love him and almost invariably follow his advice. They delight to refer to him as "Our Leader" and, gentlemen, they accept his leadership. When Mussolini formed the opinion that it was proper and wise to change the law regarding elections to the legislature, he didn't issue a direction as to what should be the plan. What did he do? He had to go to both Houses of Parliament, gentlemen, and get their consent, and the Houses of Parliament sitting there have free and open discussion; opposition to Mussolini developed, but they made their decisions and the change was made. This savours of anything but dictatorship. The admirable system of Fascist education provides for training in statesmanship. Young men are continually being educated in the science of statecraft and are being brought along so that when the older statesmen pass along, they will be ready to take their place.

Commendatore Villari, whose cultured deliverances charmed us all so recently, tells of an incident regarding Mussolini. He says that on one occasion Mussolini was asked the question, "What will happen to Italy, sir, when you pass away?" Mussolini replied with a twinkle in his eye, "There will probably be a funeral. Possibly some choice flowers will be sent. Indeed, there may be some very fine speeches in which it will be said that the deceased was not such a bad fellow after all, and the next day the government of Italy will go on as usual."

The most recently installed European dictator, however, did not impress many speakers at gatherings in the early thirties. Willson Woodside had been in Germany "before, during and after the Hitler Revolution, with a return to Canada each time for mental re-adjustment." The situation in the summer of 1934 distressed him:

These are a people without a sense of humour, and good, plain common sense. They are the people who greeted each other in the morning, during the last war, with: "Gott strafe England!"; the

127

people who on any occasion would sing the Hymn of Hate. It could only have been in Germany, surely, that a person could be locked up for six months, as a feminine friend of mine was this summer, for replying to the common salutation of "Heil Hitler!" with "Heil drei Liter!" (which means "Heil! three glasses of beer," but rhymes very nicely!)

There was a little humour about Germany in this, but it was a grim sort of stuff. Someone told me, for instance, of two brothers, Hans and Karl, who had disappeared from home for three months. Finally a letter arrived—from a concentration camp. It was from Karl. "I like this place"; it went on briefly, "the food's fine. Hans complained about conditions here; he's dead now."

Then a Blackshirt friend told me that the day after the 30th June "Clean-up," when the Brown Shirt comrades were re-appearing, somewhat shaken, on the streets, the greeting between them was not the salute and "Heil Hitler!", but "What! You still alive!"

It was a summer with plenty of opportunity for adventure. Why! the second day I was in Germany I met a man who was carrying on the Communist underground propaganda work for North Germany. We were to go out for a paddle on the lagoon the next Sunday in his Peterborough canoe, but when I arrived at his lodgings I found he had been arrested the night before. I was told afterwards that I had just missed a second visit of the Secret Police by twenty minutes.

I met another Communist in a bookstore in Berlin—Berlin and Hamburg seemed to be full of them. We were talking together at the back of the store, pretending to thumb through some books, when a high police officer, stern-looking, with monocle in his eye and sword by his side, walked in. My companion's heart must have risen in his throat: "Oh! A visitor." He had to assume a calm air and go and ask the police officer what he could do for him. The officer only wanted a book on Bismarck!

That day I was to have lunch with three very high Storm Troop officers, in a fashionable Berlin hotel. When conversation had opened up properly, after lunch I told them the experience in the bookstore. It amused them heartily! Scarce a fortnight later two of these companions were shot dead, and the other placed in a concentration camp!

During this big "Clean-up" of June 30th I was living in one of the large German cities most affected by it, with a trooper of the Black Guards. He was the finest young German I had ever met, I think, and had actually once spent a year at college in America. On June 30th he was one of a party ordered to shoot three Brown Shirts, in a house only two doors removed.

I left this Germany of mass executions only to arrive in Vienna in time for the Nazi uprising there and the assassination of Chancellor Dolfuss. It was a mad time, with soldiers camped in the main squares, armoured cars patrolling the street, policemen with fixed bayonets, even the postmen and street car conductors carrying rifles. The curfew rang at 8 o'clock and everyone had to be off the streets, except those with a special police permit. It is a strange sight to see a great city utterly empty and dark at nine or ten on a summer's evening.

From Vienna I went to Salzburg, to the Music Festival. It wasn't very festive; music flourished indifferently in such an atmosphere of unrest. As soon as the guests had taken their places inside the Festival Theatre a cordon of police would be quietly moved up. Back and forth they would patrol, watching the neighbouring windows and roofs for bomb throwers. Then as the music-goers reappeared, they would quietly melt away. While Salzburg's guests watched "Everyman" in the Cathedral Square that afternoon, I had seen a group of Nazi rebels hustled into prison only 50 yards away!

I used to love Germany very much, but I am sure that as I crossed the border the next day I looked balefully at the patrol of Black Guards loafing about Freilassing station. Perhaps that is why I had several unpleasant experiences in Munich and was finally turned out of my hotel; I might have had a chip on my shoulder. One thing I know, I *would not* salute, and there seemed many memorials and celebrations in Munich which required saluting. However on my last evening I met a splendid German couple, had hours of good comradeship, and made two new friends for life. I had to set myself once more to distinguish between blustering, bullying Nazism and the Germany of friendly, hospitable people, of music and fairy tales, of the Rhine and Heidelberg. It was with very mixed feelings that I left the country.

My next stop was in the Saar. It was as if the clock could be turned back; you were once again in the Germany of pre-Hitler days. Here

129

was a German city, with German signs everywhere and German kiddies about—but never a Brown uniform in sight, no Dictatorship, no bullies. One thought: How lucky these Saarlanders are! But it is likely their German blood will triumph over everything else when the Plebiscite finally comes.

The little German man of 1934, Woodside opined, was a victim of government propaganda, "unremitting, dangerous and often vicious." Its slogan was simple, and borrowed from Bolshevism: The Whole World Is Against Us:

To the German people as a whole, who are taught to *believe* rather than to *think,* and to the young men in the Storm Troops especially, this seems plausible enough. Consider this sum of a lifetime's memories, related to me this summer by a Trooper of twenty-five, a fine, clean young boy with whom I have hiked and camped in better days: "My first memories, when I was five years old, are of my father marching off to war. Later, in the school, the teacher would tell us of how the whole world was united to kill little Germany. Then came those terrible years of hunger, when I was 8 and 9 and 10; it wasn't enough to fight the men in the trenches, now they were going to starve helpless women and children, too. How we hated the world then!

"I remember, when we would be out playing, seeing my little sister fall down in the street weak from lack of food. At school we could only have an hour's classes, and then half an hour's recess, because the children were so weak. At night we cried ourselves to sleep, we were so hungry.

"Then came the defeat. The soldiers straggled home dispirited, there was revolution and shooting, Germany seemed to be breaking to pieces. Now the French marched into the land, and brought coloured troops, to watch over German men and women. That is something we can never forget. Still we were hungry, but the Allies took away cattle and oxen and horses, our ships and our railway trains. They cut the Fatherland into two pieces, so that Germans had to go through enemy territory to get from one part of their country to the other.

"The Poles rushed in and tried to cut off the whole of Upper

Silesia, while we were disarmed, and prevented from defending ourselves. The French came in and occupied our Ruhr. Then came the Inflation—that awful time; we lost everything, everybody seemed to lose everything; the world had gone mad. It was worse than the War.

"For a few years afterwards we had a sort of prosperity, but it was not a happy time for good Germans. Morals became worse and worse, foreign money was buying out our industries, everyone was looking after himself, and no one seemed to care about Germany. Soon came the World Crisis, millions of Germans were thrown out of work, but still the Allies demanded reparations. The banks crashed, Communism grew rapidly, there was fighting in the streets every night . . . there was no hope for poor Germany. . . . Then Hitler came, and called on us young fellows to get together, to clean all this up, to develop new, fresh strength and make Germany a fine country again."

The driving force behind Hitlerism, Woodside said, was defiance of the world which caused the German people all this:

These are the feelings upon which Hitler and Goebbels play so easily with their incessant propaganda of the outside world which envies and hates them.

It is easy to understand how young people would be affected by such appeals to their emotions, but let me tell a story of how older people take it in too. A fortnight after the 30th June "Clean-up" I was in Upper Silesia making a study of the division of the territory under Versailles; I wrote an article entitled "The Crying Injustice Of Upper Silesia." One evening I was sitting in a sort of Y.M.C.A. restaurant, having dinner with half a dozen gentlemen whom I had met about the place. The talk drifted in a friendly way from Canada to the N.R.A. and finally ended up on the partition of their Upper Silesia. Just at this point Goebbels was announced on the radio, and began a poisoned attack on the foreign press "who come here, ingratiate themselves, enjoy our hospitality, then go away and write a mountain of lies." Before he had begun this attack it seemed that I had formed half a dozen new friends; now our little Entente was smashed. My "friends" shuffled uncomfortably in their chairs and busied themselves lighting up cigars, with not a word more to say. There was nothing for me to do but to excuse myself and go.

Germany was preparing a basis for rearmament, he warned. The Empire Club's George Drew was an energetic advocate of disarmament, and the force behind a series of prophetic speeches. "This is a very, very dry subject," Hon. Maurice Dupré began his, in 1933. "It is hard to crack jokes on disarmament and I am sorry that some of you didn't bring any pillows in order to sleep more comfortably"—a double-edged reference, one suspects. It was folly, Dupré said, to imagine that what was going on at the Geneva Conference was of no concern to Canada. There can be no security, he said, "while boundaries are fringed with bayonets."

At Geneva, political problems were posed by German resentment and the opposition between British ("disarmament before security") and French ("security before disarmament") attitudes, but there were also "technical difficulties," Dupré reported, posited on the prospect of chemical warfare and other dread armaments to come.

Another vexed question was that of the private manufacture of arms. The munitions makers were damned over more than one course at noon-time, but Senator F. Nye, at one time a member of a post-First World War U.S. Senate committee investigating arms deals, spoke best to the point, on Armistice Day, in 1934:

How are we going to account for our forgetting? How are we going to account for the brief moment we bestow now in memory of those who gave their lives to what they believed was the cause of ending war? I have before me a despatch taken from the *New York Herald Tribune* of November 12th, a despatch from London, and after I read that despatch I sat down, took my pencil and estimated that if it is true that there are sixty minutes in an hour and twenty-four hours in a day there are approximately five hundred and twenty-five thousand minutes in a year. Now, let me read this despatch from London: "Except for two minutes of silence in tribute to the war dead on Armistice Day today, the Sunday shift at Vickers Works at Crayford, Kent, worked all day long making machine guns, rifles and gas-projecting machines."

And I am not reflecting on Vickers, because what Vickers was doing the other munitions makers of the world were doing, engaged in an intense campaign of producing and selling the machinery of war, the machinery that is being sold to nations in preparation for no nation in particular, but in effect a programme of arming the world against itself, arming the world to a degree which is breaking the very back of every civilization upon the face of this earth.

How are we to account for it? How do we so easily forget the experience of only sixteen years ago? I think today the answer is more evident than it ever was before. The masses of people the world over know most emphatically that there is no such thing as profit for war for them, but there are a few in this world who have come to learn and whose books reveal the proof, that there can be and that there is profit in war and in preparation for war, profit to a point which finds profits flowing most freely when blood flows thickest upon the field of battle.

In my own country, I find the explanation for our short memories in the fact that during the four years of world war, in America alone there were created twenty-two thousand millionaires—men who couldn't have had that wealth except as men were giving and offering their all on the field of battle. Because there is profit in war and in preparation for war, we are constantly threatened by more of it. We are constantly being cautioned to beware of this country and to beware of that country. In my own country, our bugaboo is Japan and while our munitions makers in America are preaching to us the doctrine, "Look out for Japan," over in Japan the same identical munitions industry is preaching a doctrine to the people of Japan that has them saying, "Look out for Uncle Sam; look out for the United States," all of which is a very profitable foundation for those industries engaged in the manufacture and sale of munitions of war.

There was the historical case of J. P. Morgan's father:

I am going to suggest to you that the next time you come down to the States, down to New York, you go over and call on Mr. Morgan. If you find him in and find him with one of his honest days on his hands, he will reveal to you an experience which was his father's back in the early 1860s when he read that the American army was about to make an auction sale of 5,000 old and antiquated army muskets. Mr. Morgan sent his men to Washington and bought all those 5,000 muskets, paying for them $3.50 apiece. He asked if he couldn't keep those in the United States Arsenal until he called for them. That privilege was granted and they stayed in those arsenals for almost a year until Mr. Morgan read that General Freemont was trying to organize an army out in the neighbourhood of St. Louis. He had plenty of men but no guns and wouldn't get delivery of guns fast enough, so Mr. Morgan notified General Freemont as to what he had—five thousand rifles in fine condition. "If you want them, you can have them for $23.00 apiece." General Freemont wanted them. When they were despatched to him, he distributed them among his men and they were taken out on the range for practice and trial, where hundreds of men shot off their own thumbs and fingers, in such rotten state of repair was this artillery.

Freemont declined to recommend payment of the bill. A Board was appointed to arbitrate the claim and the Board finally said to Mr. Morgan, "You only paid $3.50 for those guns. They weren't in good repair as you said they were, and you aren't entitled to $23.00 apiece. We have made up our minds you should be content with our award of $13.00 apiece for those guns." And Mr. Morgan said, "Is that so? We will see about that." And to the courts Mr. Morgan went with his claim. After long litigation, the courts held there was a sacredness, a sanctity of contract involved here and Mr. Morgan should have $23.00 apiece for those guns.

A profit rundown of some U.S. corporations currently engaged in the production of armaments included:

Scoville Manufacturing Company, $655,000 profit annually during four years of peace; $7,678,000 each year during the war. Niles Bemert Powder Company $656,000 annually in peace time, as compared with $6,146,000 annually during the war years . . . General Motors, $6,000,000 in peace time, annually, and $21,000,000 annually during the war. . . . Bethlehem Steel . . . $6,000,000 profit during peace years as compared with $49,000,000 annual profit during the four years of war. Dupont, who rushed into the press last June, declaring that the purpose of this investigation authorized by the Senate was that of undermining the national defence of America, and was instigated by Reds and radicals and Communists—I expect if I had been in the Dupont shoes I would have seen red, too, if I saw anyone taking any steps which might in any way destroy the prospects in the future for such handsome returns as was theirs during four years of war—the Dupont annual average profit was $6,000,000 during peace years; during war years, it was $58,000,000. The Duponts enjoyed a return upon their investment, over the four years of war, of more than four hundred per cent, while men were giving their all or offering their all, at $30.00 a month and less out in the trenches.

The speakers' tone softened, however, as the European situation hardened, blowing with the wishful winds that prevailed at the end of the decade. Broadcaster Rex Frost ("From official circles in London, I received the assurance . . . that the fundamentals of European relations today are very much improved over those of six months ago") brought back a joke going the German rounds:

When I was in Germany the Third Reich was chuckling over an editorial which had been reprinted from an American periodical in which after making comparisons between the extraordinary similarity which existed in the physical appearance of Charlie Chaplin and Adolf Hitler, even to the little black moustache, the comment was made, "There's one great difference between the film comedian and the German Führer, however. Charlie Chaplin *knows* he's funny." Even Hitler is supposed to have chortled at that one . . . and when dictators smile . . . well, they say there's hope after all for the future of Europe.

Beverley Baxter, in 1939 a British M.P. and a supporter of Neville Chamberlain, in a report on "The World from Westminster":

Well, as we look around, gentlemen, we come to that land of sunny skies, Italy, and although I feel very little temptation today to think or speak except with absolute seriousness, I do feel that Italy is perhaps possibly a vital point in this whole situation, and certainly a point not without some humour. When Chamberlain went to Rome last January I decided to go as well. That is, I went the day before so as not to embarrass the Prime Minister by the two of us arriving together. [Laughter] So I took my faithful wife with me, and we went to the Grand Hotel in Rome the day before Chamberlain was due—and I would give you this advice, when travelling in Europe always go to the Grand Hotel wherever you are, because there is always something going on there, unexpected.

When we arrived I was a little disgruntled to see the foyer full of Swastika flags. It seemed an inappropriate beginning to British entry. Just then a little man walked in, with twelve officers marching behind him, and everybody making the Fascist salute. I said to the hotel proprietor, "Who is the gentleman in uniform?" "Oh," he said, "that is Dr. Funk, the German Trade Minister." So I sent word up to the Doctor enquiring if I might see him, and he said, with German courtesy, that nothing would make make him so happy, but he was just off. And out they marched again, this funny little man, with the officers behind him, all made the Fascist salute again, and Funk disappeared. And when I turned around, not a Swastika flag was to be seen in the hotel. Somehow, gentlemen, I think that is not without significance in the events which lie ahead.

The next day Chamberlain was due to arrive, and we went down to the station to see him come. The place was very crowded (and) I want to describe that scene for a moment because again I think it will have something to do with the events which are crowding upon us. There was an archway in the station and all the little Italian generals about five feet tall came in, not only covered with medals on both sides but with medals clinging to medals, clusters of them. There was an Oxford graduate—not an Oxford Grouper but an Oxford graduate—there and I said to him, "What are all these medals? I don't seem to be able to remember the battles for which they were bestowed." He said, "They are for the 100 yards, the 220 and the 440." [Laughter] All the little Italian generals came in swaggering around, and finally came Count Ciano looking very much like Prince Danilo of the "Merry Widow." Then came in the escort of 100 very fine troops and with the death skull and crossbones on their helmets. Then the rumour spread that Mussolini was not going to arrive, but suddenly the air grew tense, the very heart-beat of Italy stopped, Ciano went out, and in marched Ciano and Mussolini, with the Duce's chin a foot out looking like an avenging Thor, a very

136

broad man, extraordinarily broad with his waist pulled in by a rope, and marched down, turned right, marched down, turned to the Guard, kept on marching, inspected them, thrust his hand into his side—and of course the train should have come in. [Laughter] Italy, however, is still Italy and the train did not come in and Mussolini held his dramatic poise as long as he could, and then broke into a most agreeable grin that went right across his face. I swear he still sees the joke of being dictator.

Journalist Gregory Clark, who had covered the 1939 coronation of Pope Pius XII, returned to Canada "unable to shake off a profound intuition of peace":

The man who drove me through the lovely country up to Assisi was a young man, about twenty-four years of age. I asked him about war. He was very proud of his soldier's uniform, all complete with beautiful cape. He said, "Signor, young men can no longer look forward to war as an adventure, as a patriotic sacrifice. Today war means in our minds only death. I think perhaps in your time and older times war had some balance, some compensation, but now it means to my mind, death. I do not want to die. How terrible it would be to be away fighting in some far place, knowing that every hour of the day and night my mother, my sweetheart, maybe, some day, my little children are dying terribly. No, no," he says, "war has nothing for me or young men, ever any more". . . .

In Rome the Italian officials took me to the marvellous Exhibition where they are showing the Italian people the advances in self-sufficiency in Italy. They wanted most of all to show me the building where the arms and weapons of modern Italy were exhibited. They showed me monstrous bombs, shells, torpedoes, model planes of every description, engines of destruction. They told, with almost reverence, that Italy was strong, terrible in might; but when they took me to lunch I saw in the restaurants the Italian waiters serving, with a distaste so obvious that it was almost comic, the German tourists who now infest Italy these days in their great enthusiasm for the Rome-Berlin Axis. I saw in the same restaurant a long table, full of thirty Fascist Black Shirts, in their uniform of black shirt and gray trousers, entertaining about twelve members of the German Nazi

Party in their bright brown uniforms and red swastikas. The dark Italians and the bright blond Germans were all laughing heartily together but the Germans, fresh down from Germany, were casting curious, haughty and cold eyes around the restaurant at all us rag tag and bobtail. Before I left an official said to me, "Of course these Germans think they are God." . . . I did not go to Germany. . . . After all this past century of false prophets, what good to go and stare at Germany? I would see only what has been seen before, there, here and everywhere—nations like ours and theirs, fighting for a place in the sun. Maybe it all has no end.

CHAPTER 7

"In the logic of history, we shall win"

"Gentlemen," said the chairman to a combined meeting of the Empire and Canadian clubs about 1 p.m. on June 10, 1940, "the Honourable Norman Rogers is not here at the present moment, but we expect him. In the meantime I would like us to have a few words from Canon Cody, who will speak to us in connection with the serious situation that is developing at the present moment. Italy has declared war. Confirmation of this has just been received. I understand action is taking place already."

Dr. H.J. Cody spoke, as he put it, "just a word before Mr. Rogers comes." Glancing from time to time at the door where Defence Minister Norman Rogers was expected to enter, he spoke patriotic sentiments for a few minutes. Then the chairman, Empire Club president Dr. F.A. Gaby, rose to say, "We understand that the Honourable Mr. Rogers will land within two minutes (but) the word we have doesn't say whether he will land at the Island Airport or the Malton Airport. In the meantime, we have here a copy of his address, and if it is your wish we will ask Colonel Mess to read this to you."

. . . Rarely in the course of world affairs has there been such an extraordinary upheaval as has occurred since the 10th of May—just a month ago today. I think you will understand me when I say that in view of what has happened in the last month it was a matter of consideration whether I should be able to come here today or not. Being here, however, I should like to put before you as simply as possible, the position in which we find ourselves and the efforts that are being made to mobilize the resources of this country in the earnest and vigorous prosecution of the war.

Last September, together with Great Britain and France, we observed the progress of the Polish campaign. It was carried out and completed almost exactly in accordance with German plans. How far those plans were disarranged by Russia's action in Eastern Poland is a matter of no consequence at present. Various explanations were given of Poland's inability to offer more extended resistance. We were told that Poland relied too much on cavalry; that the expected rains did not occur; that the Poles were not a united people.

The average person was of the opinion, however, that things would be different when it came to an attack on the Maginot Line. And in expressing that faith the average person, consciously or otherwise, ranged himself on the side of some very eminent and highly trained military officers. We had read or had been told of the mighty Maginot Line. The Germans obviously thought it was formidable and they built the West Wall. The Dutch planned a system of flooding and the Belgians built extensive boundary fortifications and secondary water defences. A further defence line was prepared on the Franco-Belgian border. The general feeling was that, slow to start as the democracies might be, the French, British and Belgians could probably hold their lines long enough to complete the necessary preparations behind their protection.

Since then, however, we have seen the German army advance across Holland and Belgium and deep into France. Italy is threatening on the other side. The critical period has been advanced, and with it has come the necessity of advancing our own speed. The First Division and ancillary troops have been at the disposal of the United Kingdom for some time. Major-General McNaughton, as you know, with members of his staff, was at Calais and Dunkerque giving valuable aid to the Chief of the Imperial General Staff. Destroyers of the Royal Canadian Navy are operating in the battle area with the British Navy. The training and departure of the Second

Division are being hastened. A Third Division is being mobilized and the infantry units of a Fourth Division have been named and are being organized. The ancillary units of a Canadian Corps are being mobilized. The Veterans Home Guards are being recruited and plans are under way for the establishment of reserve Veterans Companies to be attached to the Non-Permanent Active Militia units. Equipment orders are being rushed to completion. Valuable stocks of war material have been sent to the United Kingdom and have arrived there. Canadian soldiers have been sent to the West Indies under the escort of units of the Royal Canadian Navy. The importance of that duty cannot be over-emphasized when you recall the amount of oil that is being shipped through the Caribbean Sea every twenty-four hours. Manufacturers of war equipment and supplies are putting on extra shifts to rush to completion the orders that are pending. New orders are being given at a more rapid rate than ever before. Citizens and associations of citizens are coming forward with suggestions, many of which are of the greatest assistance. Organized labour has responded wholeheartedly to the call.

But the final factor is the one which comes most nearly home to us today. I refer, of course, to the so-called fifth column activities. There can be no tolerance whatever for the alien who has come to Canada and who remains actively sympathetic toward Germany and the German Government. Internment of such people is a very mild form of punishment, for they are traitors to the land of their adoption. They must not be allowed at large. The Royal Canadian Mounted Police were sufficiently ready that on the outbreak of war all those who professed such active sympathy were at once interned. The same stricture applies to the alien who is admitted to Canadian citizenship and takes out naturalization papers with mental reservations as to the support he will offer this country in time of emergency. His good faith must be unquestioned and unquestionable if he is to continue to enjoy the privileges that are afforded to him here. Action has already been taken against certain Canadians, fortunately few in numbers, who would set themselves up as Leaders of Fascist or Communist groups and would cast aside forever all the essentials of democratic freedom.

We are all aware that German methods reach farther than that. We know that there may be German sympathizers among the naturalized

Canadians. We know that Germany will not hesitate to make use of those whose weakness or greed will allow themselves to be suborned to treachery. And we know that confusion in our own ranks is exactly what the enemy likes to see. I intend to be just as specific as I can be. . . . It has been suggested that the present emergency requires the internment of all naturalized Canadians of enemy alien origin. We shall never, I believe, subscribe to that policy of total proscription. There are thousands of naturalized Canadian citizens who are here among us because they have seen and experienced the horrors that accompany oppressive government in other lands. They expected freedom of thought and action when they came here and so far as it lies within us they should receive what they expected to secure. But they must not cross the line that divides loyalty from treason in this country. If they do, they forfeit the rights they have acquired, and will be dealt with accordingly.

There is another menace against which we must also stand on guard. I refer to the well-meaning citizen who spreads rumours without facts, whose imagination pictures trouble where there is no trouble, and who frightens his neighbour with fabulous stories of the Nazi meeting-house just around the corner in a cellar. That Canadian citizen, loyal to his very fingertips, will be indignant when I say that he is Hitler's best friend; but that is nothing more nor less than the truth. Let me make my meaning perfectly clear. If there is a weekly meeting of Nazi sympathizers, we want to know. They will be dealt with if we give the proper authorities the facts, and they will be dealt with as they deserve. It is true that it is not always easy to get facts, but if you have reasonable grounds for suspicion, please tell us, quickly. In many cases, you will find that the persons you suspect are already being watched by competent authorities.

There is need for increasing vigilance and caution. There is no need for undue alarm. The immediate demand is to hasten the help that we can bring to our allies. The fewer detours there are the better. . . . That which is wrong can never become right by virtue of conquest. Whether it is this month or this year, next year or later, so long as we hold fast to the faith that is in us and labour unceasingly for the ideals that are dear to us, sooner or later the world of reason and humanity will be restored. In this faith we will fight on, will endure and we will win. [Applause]

The speech completed, Dr. Gaby said, "We exceedingly regret that we have no word at the present moment of the Honourable Mr. Rogers." He closed the meeting. More than a 1,000 members of the two clubs trooped out into the summer afternoon, back to work. Some were not aware until they saw the big black headlines in late editions of the afternoon papers that at 1:25 p.m., while Defence Minister Rogers' speech was being read, the RCAF bomber that was bringing him to Toronto crashed about 50 miles east of the city. All on board were killed.

That summer the Germans, after invading Norway and Denmark, had outflanked the thought-to-be impregnable Maginot Line and knocked France out of the war.

Gregory Clark, then a buoyant man in his forties, had been to Europe twice since war began to report for the Toronto *Star*. Each time he returned he spoke to the Empire Club. August 15, 1940:

Only last spring I stood right here before some of you, fresh from France, and I told you about the Maginot Line. I told you no human power could penetrate it. I was right but there was a human power that went around it.

After telling you of the might of the French Army and of the readiness of the British Army and of the Maginot Line, I went back again to France and arrived two days after Holland and Belgium had been invaded. I was exactly in time to see that might brushed away as though it were dust. I arrived at half-past three in the afternoon at Calais, caught the half-past five for Arras, sat in a fine pullman coach and watched out the window to see the trainloads of refugees streaming past at every siding from Holland and Belgium. It was a lovely May afternoon. Paris had been all excited over the breaking of this boil of war.

It was nine o'clock in the evening when we drew into Arras station. It was almost deserted. Three days later it was so crowded, hour by hour, day and night, that you could not enter it. A week later it was in ashes, but there in the gloaming I got out and had a French porter carry my war bag across the station square to my hotel, the Commerce, where in the winter I had been a resident along with all the other correspondents.

The Commerce was deserted of correspondents and even of soldiers. Its sole guests were a rather well-to-do motoring lot of Belgians, the first of the refugees. Mademoiselle Odette, the manageress of the hotel, told me all my colleagues were up at Lille, nearer the blitzkrieg on Belgium. Mademoiselle Odette said that she had one room, that of an officer who hadn't come back. I got the stuff upstairs and went back out. It was a pleasant May night. An aeroplane crossed low—about five hundred feet. I said, with some anxiety, "That is a Hun." "Oh, no, that is not a Hun. If it were a Hun they would be firing at it." I said, "Well, I would have sworn that was a Hun." The plane crossed over again, he swung out and crossed again, and I said, "That is a Hun." He swung out and crossed a third time and completed that run. He dropped six bombs and missed the General Headquarters of the British Army, where I was heading, by one house, so accurately did he bomb.

From then on we had no rest. Inside of ten minutes Arras was in flames. In half an hour by the bright light the bombers came and were bombing the edges of the town, various army parks. That was the beginning of the blitzkrieg, as I know it. I had the curious fortune of arriving within half an hour of the beginning.

The following morning, very early, arrangements were made to join my colleagues in the line. We were put in our cars, two to a car, with a conducting officer who was a regular army officer, and scattered in various directions towards Brussels, where the main attack was taking place.

We left Arras at noon and we didn't get into Amiens until dusk. Amiens is a beautiful city—most of you remember it. It was now so crowded that there was not a place to sit down to eat. One or two of us, being old soldiers, remembered an old restaurant called the Coq d'Or. We found that it was functioning but by the time we got there, we met the proprietress coming out with some of the teapots and silver in her hands. Within a matter of an hour or an hour and a half, so quick did the destruction come, they too had joined the ever-increasing tide of refugees.

Amiens was under bombing all the time. They bombed the station, the aerodromes and the mechanized parks and military areas. Then also, there was the bombing of the civilians, wherever they took rest when they could go no further. You never saw parks so crowded. They were packed so you could see no turf. Then of course the Germans would bomb them. They would bomb them so they would move beyond the town and congest roads where our army traffic was trying to move. But most of the bombing on Amiens and Arras was on points of military importance, particularly the station at Amiens. It was filled with old men and women, and when the bombs did strike, the deaths could be counted in hundreds.

How easy it was now for the fifth column. I am perfectly convinced that in the hordes of refugees there were any number of German soldiers, German Intelligence men and advance men, trained for months to join these hordes and function in the interests of disorder.

The only actual death in our group of thirty was one of the drivers who was killed from a pistol shot from the crowd—a pistol shot that was completely untraceable but came from a fifth columnist. One of our conducting officers was later killed and two were wounded; but by a curious and possibly unjust circumstance, no newspapermen were either killed or wounded.

We got to bed in Amiens and by this time we knew that we were being of no service, either to our public, to our papers or to the Army. When we got to bed about eleven o'clock we were extremely exhausted and we had not been fed because I assure you it is difficult to eat when past you goes this endless throng of women and children, so obviously starving and hungry. You couldn't swallow a mouthful if you had to. It is a psychic confusion you get into in such times that only those who have suffered flood and disaster can understand. I was awakened about four o'clock in the morning by the captain who said to us, "Get up at once. They are on both sides of the town." We asked "What about our kits?" and he said, "Leave them in the courtyard of the hotel."

I came down to the courtyard with my haversack and such stuff as I could carry and left it there. We were taken to an adjoining hotel where the conducting officers were staying. Our cars were there, engines running, but we spent two hours waiting for orders. By this time they were bombing the station at the foot of the street. Finally orders came to move and as our convoy of cars worked its way past the foot of the street where our hotel had been we saw the street in flames. I don't know whether the Germans are wearing my shoes or whether the fire got them.

As you know, there were three evacuations. There was the evacuation of Boulogne; and when it fell, Calais was held for a day or so; and then Dunkerque, from which the main body of the army was evacuated.

We arrived at Boulogne about four o'clock on Saturday afternoon. Our cars were taken from us to be used for more important work. There we sat Sunday and Monday and Tuesday, until noon, under bomb fire, in the midst of this tremendous tide of refugees.

The Hotel Maurice, where we stayed, was a three-storey hotel, around a little courtyard with a glass roof. It was filled with refugees. We took the top floor. It was built of wall paper and laths. Edward Angley and I shared a room. I am addicted to one-half of my pyjamas, which half you will understand when I say I am addicted also to nightshirts. A bomber came very near and dropped a bomb at the farther end of the street. Angley leaped out of bed and said, ''Let us get out of here.'' I said, ''Get back to bed. Lightning never strikes twice in the same place.'' ''Very well,'' he said, ''I'll take your word for it, you know more about it than I do.'' I said, ''We must get some sleep. Tomorrow or the next day we may be in the water. We don't know where we will be. We must get rest.'' Angley lay raised on his elbow, cheek in hand, hating me, when a second bomber dropped a load on the far corner of the block our hotel was in. The women and children streamed out of the rooms of the hotel and we heard the thud of their feet and their screams and sobs along the halls down to the basement. This time we were lifted bodily a foot or two off our beds by the concussion that seemed to bulge out the walls of the edifice. I said, ''Let's get out of here.'' Angley said, ''Okay, you know more about it than I do, I'll take your word for it!''

We went downstairs and stood in an archway where there were a few people who couldn't stand the congestion and heat and stuffiness of the basement caves and dugouts. I had my dressing-gown and slippers. Mine was a kind of towelling bathrobe that I had bought in France when I lost my kit. We were trying to cheer the people up as we stood there. Across from us was a Belgian baby that had the tremors that affect small infants during bombings. The mother was past weeping and was making the strange sounds that a child makes when it has given up crying. Presently a French military nurse, in her blue uniform—a large imposing-looking woman—hearing the good humour of Angley and myself and sizing up my beautiful gown, came over and said very politely, "May I borrow your dressing-gown to wrap this little baby in?" Amid Angley's laughter that could be heard half-way to London, he said, "You cannot have this gentleman's dressing-gown, but you can have mine."

When it was finally decided to be rid of the thirty war correspondents, we left Boulogne at high noon, on a mine layer—a little ship smaller than a Niagara boat with over two thousand Air Force men on it.

One of the strangest things I heard during the retreat was from a French infantry officer that I shared the road with for a few miles. On his sector a German bomber had been shot down and of the crew, two, an officer and a non-commissioned officer, were uninjured and brought before him as prisoners of war. He was sitting at a table in the cottage that was his headquarters. The two Germans were marched in by a guard. The officer asked them their names and rank. That is all a soldier is supposed to give when captured. It is usually the prelude to some crafty conversation by which the victor hopes to acquire information. No sooner had the prisoners answered the questions than they launched immediately into a tirade. To the complete astonishment of the officer, the two took turn about and, with fury and eloquence, heaped scorn and contempt upon the French. They were a putrescent race whom the Germans had come to cleanse and destroy—pure Hitler, streaming out of these two youngsters in jeopardy.

The outraged French officer fingered the pistol at his belt and ordered them to be silent. They raved on. He shouted at them to be silent. They stood stiff and recited their piece breathlessly, in a sort of frenzy. "What did you do?" I asked. "I ordered the guard to throw them out," said the Frenchman, bleakly. "You must have felt like shooting them," I submitted. "I was tempted," agreed the French officer. You see, democratic people always feel humanity mastering them and that is why we must win. I think it is why, in

147

Matthew Halton's phrase, "in the logic of history, we shall win."
[Applause—prolonged]

The Battle of Britain, the blitz, made the whole world conscious of what the people of London were going through. Sir Evelyn Wrench, Sept. 19, 1940:

> We are a city of sandbags and forts and barbed wire. If you want to go from Buckingham Hall to the Admiralty you will see a fort of machine-guns. If you walk from the Admiralty across the Horse Guards Parade to the Foreign Office, you will pass two lines of barbed wire entanglements and show your identification card.
>
> You live with the bath full of water in case of an emergency in which the water supply breaks down. On the landing there are buckets of sand and water, and a stirrup pump is on every floor. We all have instructions as to how to detect different types of bombs.
>
> Each night we put out our clothes and all the things we want before going to bed, ready to dress in a few minutes and go off to the air-raid shelter. I dressed in three minutes once. And what a motley crew were there. There were some Canadian nurses, Australian soldiers, businessmen in pyjamas, but the camaraderie of the air shelter is really rather wonderful. You talk to everyone, and there is a feeling that all are in this together.
>
> The lack of sleep is really the chief danger that London is suffering from at the moment. The morale is splendid but lack of sleep is a terrible thing to face as they are facing it today, after what has happened in the last two or three weeks.

Eddie Johnson, London bureau chief for the Canadian Press news agency in London early in the war, had been bombed out of home and office:

> If Hitler hopes to shatter the morale of the civilian populace by these ruthless tactics, I can tell you he is doomed to failure. A trip into the ravaged areas of East London would convince him of that. The Government has done everything in its power to persuade these people to seek refuge in the country or in some other safer region. Some have gone but the majority have elected to stay.

They have adopted the attitude: "If we must be killed, let us all go together." But it hasn't always worked out that way. When a man sets off for work he often returns to a rubble heap that was once his home. His family may have been wiped out or he, himself, may have fallen victim to one of the raider's bombs. In such circumstances it is inevitable that many should have come to adopt a fatalistic attitude. Which reminds me of a little London evacuee.

On her first night in the country the youngster was asked if she didn't say her prayers before going to sleep.

"Oh yes," she replied.

"Well, kneel down and I will listen as your mother does," the lady of the house said.

The little girl repeated as usual: "Now I lay me down to sleep" and so on, and then improvised a postscript of her own—"And please God protect Daddy and Mummy from those German bombs, and do, dear God, take good care of yourself because if anything happens to you we are sunk."

One Canadian fighter pilot in the Battle of Britain was a 35-year-old wing commander, Mike MacNab. Beverley Baxter, on one of his annual Canadian tours:

He described to me the climax of the battle. He said that the fight had been so severe and the strain so great that none of his pilots could even take the risk of a single glass of beer—so swift was the battle, so necessary the nerve control and the quickness of the mind, that they did not dare even that. And he said, when this Sunday, September 15th, broke, with its sunshine and the menace of clear skies, he wondered how much longer he could go on. The strain had become so great, both to the Luftwaffe and the R.A.F., things were at such tension, that the question was, which would snap, which would break, because human nature could not endure much longer. On that Sunday the Germans came over, he said, like the Germans came in the infantry in 1914, almost shoulder to shoulder. They came in great massed waves and MacNab took his Canadians up. They saw one wave coming, and behind, higher, another wave, and still another wave, until the skies seemed absolutely black with Germans. The problem was really how to manoeuvre in the sky, because it was so full of fighting machines. The battle went on all day long, and then the Germans threw a great mass of over 500 bombers against London. Against London in the daytime—and towards the late afternoon. But the great formation of British fighters were working and shooting the Germans down like cattle. MacNab thinks that on that one day, taking the probable crashings and everything else, the Germans must have lost 500 machines.

When it was over, MacNab and his Canadians came down to the ground—not all of them, but those that had survived. Suddenly MacNab said, "Let's have a bottle of beer." The second in Command looked at him and said, "Mac, do you think the same as I do?" MacNab said, "Yes, this is the end. This cannot go on. They will not come tomorrow." And tomorrow dawned, the sun shone again, the skies were clear, and not one German machine crossed the channel. [Applause]

From then on, almost all German bombing in any numbers took place at night. Air raid story, from a touring air raid warden named A.E. Roberts:

[After the all-clear went a woman] rushed down to the cemetery close to her home, at five o'clock in the morning, when day was breaking. The air raid warden found her peering through the railing. She asked if there was any damage. He said: "No, they all look peaceful and safe in there." She said: "I am not so sure of that. My old man is in there and I am thinking of moving him to a safer place."

Another, same source:

Raid or no raid, two charwomen used to go to the City of London to clean offices in the early hours. On the bus, one said to the other, "Thank goodness, the bloomin' raid is over." The other said, "Yes, but it does take your mind off the war."

And one from British Army Captain Bernard Newman, author and broadcaster:

You remember hearing about the land mines that would come down

150

by parachute and would flatten a couple of blocks. Well, I was up in Manchester during a heavy raid. Eventually I took shelter in the cellar of the police station. At the height of the raid, a man rung up. He said, "There is a 'iciendiary' bomb in my backyard." They said, "You mean an incendiary bomb?" He said, "That would be it." "Oh, well," said the sergeant, "don't trouble us with things like that. Put the damn thing out. This is no souvenir business—we'll send round for it in the morning." They came around in the morning, and found the man lived in one of a row of small houses. There in the little back garden, instead of an incendiary bomb, dangling from a tree was the biggest land mine they ever saw. They said to him, "You didn't sleep at home last night, did you?" He said, "No damned fear. I slept next door."

Billy Bishop, the young fighter pilot of twenty-three years before, now was Air Marshal William A. Bishop, V.C., D.S.O. (with Bar), M.C., D.F.C. Just after the blitz he flew to England. One leg of the flight was from Newfoundland to Ireland, where he got the Irish anti-English view.

On landing in Ireland I went for a short walk through the country lanes to stretch my legs and came across a delightful Irish policeman. I asked him if he had heard any news of what happened in London the night before. "Sure," he said. "They bombed London all night long. There were some people killed but I don't think there was any harm done."

In London he had audiences with Prime Minister Winston Churchill, an old friend, and with King George VI. The King showed Bishop where bombs had straddled Buckingham Palace. When a bomb burst in front of the palace, the King hurried to a window to see what harm had been done. At that instant the second bomb burst in the inner courtyard behind him.

By autumn of 1940, something new had been added to the Toronto scene: a growing establishment of Norwegian fighting men, mostly airmen, who had escaped their country after the April invasion by Germany. Little Norway, Toronto called their base in the grounds of

151

the Canadian National Exhibition. Their commanding officer was Captain Hjalmar Riiser-Larsen, Royal Norwegian Navy. The Germans had not only invaded his country, but had done so, he felt, in an extremely ungentlemanly manner:

They based their plans on the presumption that Norway would not defend itself. They might have had certain reasons to believe that, when they looked upon the Norwegian defence, but the Germans are very bad psychologists and they didn't think about what was inside our hearts. We had a very little Navy which was mobilized in September last year; a very little Air Force, also mobilized; and the Army was not mobilized at all. There were just a few thousand troops in northern Norway, on account of the situation on the Finnish border.

On the night of the 8th of April they sent ships to attack all the strategic points of the coast. We got warning in the middle of the day on the 8th that a huge column of ships, transports and war-ships had passed the Danish Straits going north. We were alarmed, of course, but not perhaps as much as we should have been because on the 25th of December that very same fleet did the same thing and returned. We believed it to be some kind of manoeuvre. Anyway, to tell you how unprepared Norway, as well as Denmark was, I will tell you a little incident that happened in Copenhagen on the 8th. I happened to be there with my wife. We had attended a meeting when news came about the transport fleet. I was immediately called to Oslo where I was Chief of the Naval Air Staff. I had to take a plane at three o'clock in the afternoon. Our Danish friends begged me to let my wife stay back in Copenhagen. They said, "The Germans are going to attack Norway. Why not let your wife be here in Denmark? She will be perfectly safe here." I said, "Why?" They said, "Because we have a non-aggression treaty with Germany." Twenty-four hours later, Denmark was invaded.

I will tell you as briefly as possible what happened around the coast of Norway. In the Fjord of Oslo there is a very narrow part where we have an old fortress. The Germans sent several big ships with transports up the fjord in the middle of the night. It was a pitch black night, there were low clouds and poor visibility. The patrol boat at the outlet of the fjord was suddenly silent. Nothing was heard from it and another boat was sent out to find what had happened.

152

The patrol boat had been rammed in the darkness and had not been able to warn the place by radio. The German ships came up very close to this fortress and the fortress opened fire on the leading ship, the *Blücher*. She was hit by two shots from the 12-inch guns but she proceeded a few hundred yards farther and came abreast of our shore torpedo stations. They dropped two torpedoes into her and that was enough. One of the torpedoes tore open the fuel tank, and the fuel spread all over the water. When the ship turned over and went down the fuel was ignited. There were fourteen hundred men on board the *Blücher* and most of them were burned in the water. That was one thing which didn't make us Norwegians cry the next morning when we heard about it. On board the *Blücher* there were the three hundred Gestapo officers who were to have had control. The three hundred of them went down and none of us wept. There were direct hits on another of the big ships and they all turned around and retreated but sent the people ashore and took the fjord, both sides of it. Their plans had been that these ships should have passed the fortress without being shot at and go directly to Oslo, send the troops ashore, surround the place and take the King and Government prisoners—and then dictate the peace terms.

By this incident the King and the Government got time to get away from Norway into the north end of the country. The Germans then sent a cable to the garrison at the fortress, in Norwegian, saying that three French warships had permission to enter the port. Three warships came under the French flag and were permitted to enter the port. The Commander believed they were French ships that were coming to our assistance. When they had got past the range of the guns at the fortress they pulled down the French flag and hoisted the swastika instead.

In the Fjord of Trondhjem, which is quite a long fjord in the middle of the country on the west coast, the Germans got hold of all the Norwegian coast steamers they could lay their hands on during the night and lined them up along the sides of their ships, so that when they steamed past the fortress our gunners dared not shoot because they would hit Norwegians. Many would say they should have shot. I just want to remind you that Norway has had no war since 1814. For one hundred and twenty-six years no Norwegian soldier has lifted a gun to shoot another man.

At Narvik we had two old coast defence battleships of forty-two hundred tons. One was lying outside the port and one just at the entrance, when in the middle of the night German destroyers hove in sight—this is another trick of the German way of fighting. They sent an officer with a white flag in a boat to the Norwegian ship. The officer went on board and asked to see the Norwegian Commanding Officer and requested him to surrender. His answer was that "Our orders are to fight and go down." That is the standing order for the whole of the Navy. Well, nothing could be done and this German officer went down into his boat; but instead of going directly back to his ship—and the Norwegian ships couldn't open fire before this man got on board his own ship again—he went a few yards ahead with his motor launch and then fired a Very pistol, with a brilliant light and gave full speed, which gave the torpedo aimers on the destroyers a chance to aim their torpedoes, and the Norwegian ship was ten seconds later hit by one of the destroyer's torpedoes. In one minute the munitions magazine and the ship were blown in the air and only five or six men were saved. The second Norwegian battleship opened fire immediately following this attack and damaged, very badly, one of the destroyers and also damaged the second one before she was hit herself by two torpedoes. The first destroyer sank the next day. Two hundred and ninety-six good Norwegian sailors and officers went down. That is what happened around the coast in the middle of the first night. I should have liked very much to have had a chance to stand behind some curtains in Hitler's room around three o'clock in the morning when it was reported to him that the Norwegians were fighting . . . .

On land, the Norwegians had not mobilized, as I said, but [after paratroops had taken Oslo] young boys sneaked through the German lines with their skis and packsacks, and gathered into platoons where they met other boys, and the platoons gathered into companies and battalions. They procured officers and made what resistance they could. When this fighting took place the Germans understood at once that they had to get hold of the King. There is another thing they did which a decent mind could not conceive of. A diplomat is not supposed to take part in actual fighting, but the German Air Attaché was in Oslo and he got hold of the first German soldiers that came there. They took town buses and rushed after the King. Fortunately, the Norwegians had got some troops together, one hundred men or something like that, who made a stand against them just outside of the place where the King was, and the first man to fall was this German Attaché. They didn't get the King. From then on they were after him the whole time, trying to kill him when they couldn't get him alive.

Norway's Prince Olav escaped Oslo by train with his father the King and the Norwegian Parliament, hours after the Germans tried to force the Oslo fjord. In January, 1941, he told the Empire Club precisely how the Germans tried to kill the King:

We had settled down in a small village just east of Elverum where the Government met and discussed in what way we could best conduct the war and the administration of the country in this unprecedented calamity that had come over it.

While we were there the German Minister asked for an interview with His Majesty, with the Foreign Minister and with a small Committee of Members of the Parliament. This was granted and the King went back to Elverum by car. It is not very far. He met the German Minister, who again put forward exactly the same demands that had been made the day before, April 9, at 4 a.m. [when German ships were trying to force the Oslo fjord]. These demands for surrender having been rejected by the King and Parliament, were rejected again.

The German Minister went back to Oslo, and the next day a representative came up and asked to see the King again and was then brought up to this small village where we were staying. He came again with the same demands worded a little differently. There was one difference, that the King could choose his own Government, except that he had to have the Prime Minister that Mr. Hitler wanted. That, of course, again had to be rejected, but now they knew exactly where the King was.

That afternoon—this was the 11th of April—this little village, which consisted of I think about twenty houses in all, a general store or two, a school, a small hotel, a telephone exchange and a couple of farm buildings, quite close to a crossroads, this small place in which there were no services of any sort and in which the only military objective could be the King and his Government, was bombed by five, at least, possibly eight, German bombers, for one and a quarter hours. The first bombs were incendiaries, high explosive bombs, and afterwards the people were shot at by machine-guns. The population, the Government, the King and myself were then in the woods, taking the protection we could get, and we saw the planes quite plainly coming down over us, dropping their bombs and shooting their machine-guns against these small woods in which we were lying.

Later on there was shot down a plane in Northern Norway, and the airman's guide was found in which it was said he had written down his orders for a certain date and the instructions were "Go to Hamar, where the Norwegian King and Government are. Destroy everything."

Conscription was a touchy issue in Canada. A Canadian plebiscite on the conscription issue was still months away (April 27, 1942) and it would remain the single most contentious war issue in Canada, to the end. Late in 1941, without mentioning the bad word, George Drew came out in favour:

How has it been possible for Britain to do what she has done? What lesson can we Canadians draw from that inspiring scene? I think the lesson for us is that, when the safety of the nation is in jeopardy, the welfare of all the people of the nation must override the traditional, individual choice of action. [Applause] There the individual is called upon to recognize a social obligation to serve in whatever capacity will contribute most to ultimate victory.

Everyone to whom I spoke in Britain, men or women, recognized that this was not something the individual could decide for himself or herself, but that it was necessary to have compulsory selective service if they were to do their job. [Applause]

I am convinced, from what I have seen there, that the only fair and the only proper method is for the government to allocate tasks to our men and women, in the armed forces, in industry, and on the farm. The lives of all of us are at stake. This is such an emergency as we have never faced before. We need men, large numbers of men, in the armed forces. We need them immediately and we need them badly. We need men also on the farms and in the factories and we need women, too, in all these services. We also need women to relieve men for heavier jobs where that can be done.

We have no time to dodge cruel and inescapable facts any longer. [Applause] Surely we know now what we are up against.

Czechoslovakia's government-in-exile in London was headed by Jan Masaryk. December 3, 1941:

Hitler has tried to accomplish a mechanized Stone Age. In the old days the Stone Age was very crude, but it was then the order of the day. Nowadays he is pushing us two thousand years back, ten thousand years back, with the help of the great inventions, of the great intelligence, and of the great research work of two thousand years of what we call Christian or Western Civilization.

I have said more than once that Hitler has managed to generate more hate than any son of a deluded mother ever did in the history of humanity. I think I am not far off the mark when I say there are about two billion people who hate Hitler in different degrees. I never hated until I was away over fifty. It never occurred to me to hate. Some people bored me—when I saw them coming I went the other way. Others I liked; some I loved. But I have learned to hate actively, and that is a sin which Hitler committed to my soul, as he has committed it to untold millions of free souls to whom hate was not a word in their vocabulary. [Applause] And for no other reason, Hitler is doomed, just because so many people righteously hate him.

Bert Wemp, one time mayor of Toronto—a campaign he ran while city editor of the old *Telegram*—and a veteran of World War One, went to this one as a war correspondent:

We spent a day and a night with the Halifaxes and the Wellingtons. The Halifaxes are the large 4-engine machines, and the Wellingtons are the large 2-engine machines. They carry gigantic loads. When we reached the Halifaxes and the Wellington Squadron they said, "You are in luck. Ops tonight." We spent the afternoon looking over the equipment.

At 11 p.m. they were briefed. They went across to the airdrome to their machines and we followed them a few minutes later. We heard the sound of airplanes overhead circling around and around.

I said to the pilot of the first Halifax machine. "Have you any idea what machine is overhead?" We listened for a minute, and he said, "No, but it ain't one of ours."

A few minutes later the German bombers located their targets, dropped white and red flares and started to bomb. They set the place on fire. The whole sky was full of flak. Then, when the flak ceased and the fires were put out, the boys got into their machines and away they went for Duisberg in the Ruhr. We waited until the last one was off. Then we went back, tried to sleep, sat up a while, and then waited.

Just an hour or so before dawn we were back sitting in the control tower. The control tower is a square room and on one side there is a big black wall. The boys have their machines listed, A for Albert, D for Donald, G for George. After a while, out of the blackness: "G for George. G for George. Can you hear me? Can you hear me?"

And a little girl, of ninety pounds, with a fine voice, at the radio control—she had been sitting at the microphone all night and right back came, "G for George. G for George. We can hear you. We can hear you."

Then came a little later the roar of the engines and "G for George. G for George. May I land? May I land?" And the little voice, back into the microphone as fast as could be, "You may land. You may land."

And around the airdrome, one after another, the machines came in from that raid and landed. Then we waited, for D for Donald was still missing. Finally they said we had better go with the pilots to the Interrogation Room and hear the story of the raid. They had located the river, located the bridge, located their objectives, they had successfully bombed them and also had taken pictures.

We were eating breakfast when they said, "We think Donald is coming home." We rushed to the control tower again. Out on the balcony on the side we listened and over the radio came, "D for Donald. D for Donald. Can you hear me? Can you hear me?"

And the little voice, right back into the microphone, "D for Donald. D for Donald. We can hear you. We can hear you."

And then, a little closer, "D for Donald. D for Donald. May we land?" May we land?" And the answer, "Yes, you may land. You may land."

And back and forth the conversation went. "D for Donald. D for Donald. Can you hear us? Badly shot up. Two engines are out. Fuselage badly shot up. The crew is okay. Prepare for crash landing, if necessary."

They came in, and we stood waiting. Our hearts were hammering and we were watching that undercarriage to see whether there was an undercarriage there or not to come down. Finally, the undercarriage came down and he made a successful landing, and all the boys of the two Canadian Squadrons that night came back from Duisberg successfully. [Applause]

D for Donald had to take evasive action over Duisberg when he was caught in a terrific barrage of anti-aircraft fire. He was for an hour and a half in the Ruhr Valley and was finally driven east and got a bit to the left over Essen. When he was over Essen the anti-aircraft fire was so severe that he was blown upside down and he flew on his head until he was out of the barrage. Then he straightened out and came back on two engines.

It was even more difficult flying on one engine. Flying Officer D.T. Witt, D.F.C., D.F.M., R.A.F. Bomber Command:

On my 62nd trip, we had to do a night raid on Hanover. Having successfully completed our mission, we were leaving the target area, when a tremendous blast of anti-aircraft fire burst directly underneath us. We knew we had been hit, but not how badly.

Our troubles did not immediately show themselves. We got to the Dutch coast before the engineer discovered that our petrol pipelines had been damaged and we were steadily losing petrol. At that moment we had barely enough to make the English coast.

To conserve petrol, I stopped two of the four engines. It seemed that we would make it. Without warning, however, one of the operating engines cut dead. We swung around in circles, out of control. The other engine had to be throttled right back to enable us to keep the aircraft straight. Fortunately, we were at 14,000 feet and had plenty of time to look for the trouble. The engineer quickly made temporary repairs and the engine came to life again.

We continued on course. Suddenly I saw a flashing beacon ahead. I shouted, "England ahead." There was a lot of whooping and cheering. I thought of bacon and eggs waiting at base and started calculating how long it would be before I could get at them. That was a very pleasant moment. I scanned the sky and then I saw the moon ahead of me. It took a moment for the significance of that to sink in; the awful realization that the moon was in the wrong place for us to be heading for England. It should have been behind us. We were heading back toward the Dutch coast.

I swung the aircraft around. We were within five minutes of the English coast when one of the two remaining engines died on us. The next five minutes were like five years, but suddenly all our fears and worries vanished. We saw a challenging searchlight shoot up from the coast and we knew that we were over land, which, in itself, acted on us like a tonic. We had hardly finished congratulating ourselves when the last engine cut out. All the petrol had gone.

The machine was uncontrollable. We were at 9,000 feet and losing height rapidly. I immediately gave the order to abandon aircraft. I held the aircraft as steady as I could for the others to get out, then jumped myself.

Once in mid-war Bomber Command was threatened with the axe; extinction, disbanding. Air Commodore J.E. (Johnny) Fauquier: "In those days the equipment used by Bomber Command was such that only approximately three per cent of our bombs were hitting the aiming point. . . ." At the same time, enemy submarines were reaching peak efficiency. There were suggestions that "the time had come to split Bomber Command between Coastal Command (sub hunters) and other branches of the services."

But it didn't happen. The bombers became more efficient and the huge boost to public morale of the early 1,000-bomber raids helped the war effort, as well. Fauquier, on how it was done:

The actual planning of an air raid began with a special committee who chose all targets we were to attack and gave each one of them a priority. For example, when the submarine menace was at its peak, it was not only necessary for us to sink them at sea, we had to strike at the very source where they were manufactured. In this case we would be ordered to attack such towns as Hamburg, Kiel, Bremen, or some of the Ruhr cities, where the sub parts were made. The Commander-in-Chief, after consultation with the meteorological experts, decided what target was to be attacked and how many planes were necessary to do the job. The plan of attack was made out by his operational staff advisors and presented to him for his approval, after which it was passed to the various groups in Bomber Command. There were twelve groups in the Command—four were training groups, one a daylight bombing group, one a radio counter measure group, and six night-bombing groups, one of the largest of which was our own Royal Canadian Air Force Bomber Group. Of these six fighting groups, each one consisted of anywhere from 250 to 350 four-engine bombers; the population of each group was approximately 25,000 to 30,000, all ranks. Thus it can be seen that our Canadian Bomber Group was approximately the equivalent of two army divisions.

The six groups would be advised that they were to attack a certain city and the bomb load each was to carry. In addition a "Zero Hour" was chosen and each group given a different time on target, as it would be impossible to have over one thousand heavy bombers over one spot at one time and so if, for example, No. 6 Group was detailed for the attack, they might be given the middle part of the raid for their time of attack and if the raid was to last twenty minutes, they would be allotted a zero hour of Z plus 8 to Z plus 13—that would mean that all our bombers would have to drop their bombs and be off the target between eight and thirteen minutes after the attack opened. In addition, all groups would be advised of what method the Pathfinders would use to mark and illuminate the target. . . .

Approximately ten minutes before take-off you would hear engines come to life and roar up to full revolutions as the pilots gave them their final check. It used to shake the earth. Finally, the aircraft would start rolling. You couldn't taxi quickly because the aircraft weighed at that time before take-off somewhere between 60,000 and 70,000 pounds. They were difficult to handle when they were that heavy, so we had to be very careful. You drove slowly up to the end of the runway and when it was your turn to take off you turned slowly into wind on the runway and on receipt of a green light flashed at you by the Aerodrome Control Pilot or starter, you pushed your throttles forward and were away. From that time until you returned you were entirely on your own. Unlike fighting on the ground or daylight bombing, when you could see what your pals are doing, at night you are entirely alone.

Then began the long haul, climbing as fast as possible in order to be at the correct height as ordered at briefing by the time you reached the enemy coast. The enemy coast will gradually appear before you and you would see searchlights snapped on very much as a flashlight would appear to you across a field at night, except that the silver and blue beams, as thin as pencils, reached up far above your height. At the same time orange bursts fired from heavy aircraft shells at approximately your height would tell you the battle was about to commence. You would watch the searchlights very closely and avoid large concentrations of them if it was at all possible. To be caught in their beams and coned was to ask for trouble, as the German wisely considered a bird in the hand worth two in the bush and would throw everything within range at the illuminated aircraft. Unless you got out of this cone fairly soon, in approximately 30 to 40 seconds, your chances of survival were rapidly approaching the zero mark. To be illuminated by a large number of searchlights at night gives one the most conspicuous feeling imaginable. In fact you could not feel more conspicuous if you were to walk down Yonge Street without your trousers. It makes you feel as if every German in Germany were looking at you personally, and rubbing his hands and saying, "We've got you this time, Boy."

However, by altering course slightly and diving and gathering a little speed it was usually easy enough to get out of the view of the coastal defences and start again your long trip to the target. From the moment the enemy coast was sighted every eye in the aircraft was straining and searching for enemy night fighters—and that meant seven pairs of very alert eyes. You probably know that a bomber crew consisted of pilot, navigator, bomb aimer, flight engineer, wireless operator, mid-upper gunner and tail gunner.

If you saw the fighter in time, you took avoiding action. If not, you were usually listed as "Missing," as things happened pretty quickly in the air and especially at night, so very little warning was ever given of the approach of this type of danger. From time to time before reaching your target it was necessary to pass over or near ground defences which never failed to salute you with a barrage of heavy flak. This would continue until you neared your goal, when far ahead, sometimes 40 or 50 miles, you would see that the Pathfinders were on their job by the target markers which they would drop toimark the main point in the target that you were about to attack. Immediately after, hundreds of flares would be dropped also by the Pathfinders to illuminate the city beneath. We were usually then about 20,000 feet in the air. Of course, the enemy defences here were more concentrated and the display of fireworks would put your Toronto Exhibition to shame—searchlights by the thousands, guns both heavy and light, firing different coloured shells, the burst of heavy anti-aircraft shells all around you and, unfortunately, too often you would see the exchange of tracer bullets followed by a long thin stream of fire hurtling vertically towards the earth. This would be one of our own bombers on fire. It would be followed by a crash, by a large red fiery mushroom shaped explosion which seemed to blossom out and stay exposed for two or three seconds, then die out leaving a few glowing embers. Occasionally, you would see a tremendous mid-air explosion which would light the sky for many miles around. That would be one of the poor chaps who received a direct hit, usually in a petrol tank, and exploded in mid-air.

Various forms of anti-aircraft shells were used by the enemy. Some of the more spectacular ones would rocket into the air, leaving a trail of sparks behind them and on bursting, three other rockets would shoot out at different angles until they, too, exploded.

On the ground was a bubbling mass of brilliant white light, which looked exactly like boiling solder in a plumber's fire pot. These white lights were the incendiaries fiercely burning, and when they set buildings on fire the white light would turn into a deep orange. Occasionally, when we raided towns where there were chemical factories we would see flames of every colour of the rainbow—blue, green, yellow and pink. All the time, the flashes from the gun muzzles of heavy flak batteries could be seen as the guns fired—then came the wait of a few seconds, approximately 12 to 17 seconds, and finally the thud and blast of air as the shell exploded near you. Often you could smell the fumes from the shell explosions as you flew through the spot where the explosion took place a second before.

It is very hard to explain all the details but it was rather a pretty sight, even if we were playing for keeps. Throughout all that time only the gunners were able to keep a lookout for enemy fighters as the rest of the crew had a special job to do. The bombing run was usually a tense few moments, when the bomb aimer guided you to your aiming point. Eventually the time would come when he would yell "bombs gone," and you could feel the aircraft jump as each heavy bomb left its station. You usually kept on a steady course for approximately thirty seconds, in order to allow the camera to take a picture of the actual spot where your bombs landed. Immediately after this you set a course for home and I can assure you it was a really wonderful feeling.

However, all danger was not yet over, as all the way back you had to be on the lookout for night fighters, as you were on the way in. If you saw one a running fight would ensue, until he either got you or you lost him. Sooner or later, however, the English coast would appear, and then your own aerodrome. You then wait your turn to land and after landing be interrogated.

Sometimes these trips took as much as nine or twelve hours. That, with the relaxation of the tension after landing, brought on extreme fatigue and that is why most air crews received such liberal leave. . . .

Few people today are aware of the price that the Bomber crews paid for this. In killed and missing alone, not wounded, the casualties amounted to fifty per cent of Air Crews engaged on operations.

Commander Rowland H. Stokes-Rees, R.N. (nicknamed Rosie), was a submariner. He told an evasive action trick that submarines liked to use: get directly under the destroyer that is searching for you. But one should not follow this up, he noted, by doing what a friend of his had done. Becoming curious as to the exact position of the destroyer above him, because he no longer could hear its engines, he

came up to see exactly where she was and gazed into the frozen face of an engine room artificer. He had put his periscope through the bottom of the destroyer. I did see the periscope when the submarine came back into harbour. It looked more like a saxophone than anything else, but I don't know quite how true the story is that when he took it away again and dived and slipped out of his predicament he very nearly sank the destroyer by the hole he left in her bottom. . . . .

That brings an important point to light, the morale of our submarine crews, which is superb. They are picked men from general service naval volunteers and they go through a really good training. They have infinite faith in their C.O. and First Lieutenant and they wait for orders, quietly but on their toes. One submarine was saved the other day, according to the official report of her Commanding Officer, by this morale factor. After they had attacked and had gone deep during the counter attack they were very badly shaken by a pattern of depth charges, which only just missed being lethal. Their lights were all out, the propeller shafts were running untrue in their bearings, the hydroplanes were jammed, and worst of all, the battery tanks were cracked and starting to give off chlorine gas. In other words they were out of control and on their last legs.

At that particular moment the coxswain came up to the C.O. with a signal pad in his hand and held it out and said, "Most urgent request, Sir." The C.O. shone his torch on it in surprise. It said, "Able Seaman Jones, such and such a number, requests to revert to general service immediately." In his report the Captain said that he at once passed the signal pad round the boat and the crew laughed so much that, to use your expression, they "snapped out of it" and got away by sheer optimism.

Well, I don't think I could end without telling you this little anecdote. We always used to have a "Show the Flag" visit from foreign flotillas. One particular year we had one of the regular visits from a French flotilla.

We gave them the usual dinner; we played some odd games. It was arranged that one of the training submarines should go out and give all their officers a dip. We took them out to the usual practice area, four miles outside, and gave them the most beautiful dive. We then sat on the bottom, as only a real expert crew can do it, without anyone knowing that she is there, then we stopped everything, opened a bottle, toasted "Vive la France!" and then went back to harbour.

So the next day arrived. They said, "You will go to sea with us." But they had set out to have a jolly leg-pull and somehow we sensed it. I remember my skipper saying, "Rosie, we are in for it." I little knew how right he was.

We went out to precisely the same place for diving. We were put in the Control Room. The Captain came down and, with a stony glare at the First Lieutenant, said "Tout prêt?" "Tout prêt, mon Capitaine," he replied. "C'est bien. Plongez vite!" That I think was "Crash Dive" in French. Well we did "Plongez vite." We went full speed ahead. Everybody opened everything he could find and we assumed the most alarming angle. Being visitors, we had nothing to hold on to and we slid across the Control Room plates. As it was very shallow we hit the bottom with a resounding crash, which of course was part of the joke to them as they had something to hold on to. But, unfortunately, the bottom was very muddy and nothing would get us out even with a good deal of "siffling." "Siffler" is a very good word, meaning to whistle, because when you blow with high pressure air it does "whistle." A good deal of "siffling" and a good deal of going full speed "en arrier," and so on, but nothing happened.

So we had to have a little conference. It had happened before in training classes and we all knew what to do. The only thing to do is to put everybody unemployed forward. Then when the First Lieutenant's whistle goes you again blow and go full speed astern while at the same time everybody runs uphill from forward to aft through the water-tight doors to bring the stern down. But whereas our water-tight doors are more or less egg-shaped, theirs were round and one fat chap got stuck in the first doorway. Progression naturally ceased very suddenly and the runners came to a dead halt.

So we stopped "siffling" and going astern and had another conference, and decided that the "fat party" would have to be weeded out and put at the after end, where he would just have to jump up and down when the whistle went. So he jumped and the rest ran, the air "siffled" and the motors went astern; and we came out beautifully, so beautifully that we went straight over and put the stern deeper in the mud than the bow had been. That jammed the propellers and burned out the main motor fuses, so we now had no motive power for the moment either. There was nothing for it but to move the fat party up the bow and repeat the whole thing a second time when what with the jumping and "siffling" and running we finally shot to the surface, whereupon the French Captain calmly turned around to us, and said, without a smile, "Voila!" My skipper, who did not speak a word of French but was ever polite, looked at him and most rightfully said, "Mercy."

Byng Whitteker, a Canadian from the Ottawa Valley, had been in London as script writer and narrator for the North American edition of the BBC's Radio News Reel—taking BBC reports from all over the world and choosing what would be of most interest in Canada and the United States. He was proud of the BBC's worldwide reputation for truth; that short-wave radios the world over were turned on, sometimes at the peril of the owners, to hear what really was happening in the war. He also had a sense of humour about the wide variety of news services the BBC broadcast, tailored for different audiences:

I'm reminded here of a very humorous cartoon which appeared in a London paper, humorous at least to a person working in the BBC. Shortly before D-Day an official spokesman from General Eisenhower's headquarters broadcast detailed instructions to the underground forces in the occupied countries. You may have heard some of the instructions on "Radio News Reel" as we rebroadcast most of them to North America. Now this cartoon shows an announcer sitting at a microphone, with a frantic, harassed individual dashing into the studio while the announcer is reading, "Now: tonight every able-bodied man should destroy all bridges, set fire to army installations, barricade the roads, blow up the factories, hamper troop movements." And the frantic individual is shouting, "No! No! Not here—this is the Home Service."

Matthew Halton was an eloquent war correspondent, first with the Toronto *Star* and then with the CBC. He had been with the Canadians in Italy, through the stubborn winter battles of Christmas, 1943, at

Ortona and later at Cassino. Before summer he was back in Britain for what the world had been waiting for, the main event, D-Day in Normandy:

I was with the formation that General Keller commanded—the Third Canadian Division—in the assault landing on D-Day. I remember him talking to these troops and he said, "Gentlemen, if you want to die, when you get on shore, stay on the beaches. If you want to live get off the beaches." "But," he said, "at the risk of sounding like a 'blood and guts' General, I want to say to you, it doesn't matter whether you live or die so long as you do this job. The important thing is this enterprise. Please remember you have an individual responsibility. Please remember, the whole fate of the invasion may depend on you. Your division may be overwhelmed. Your brigade may be overwhelmed. Your whole company may be overrun, but you must take cover in your slit trench or wherever you are and fight on."

And on the night of D-Day, one Canadian brigade—it happened to be a Western Canada brigade—had reached its objective.

On D-Day plus one, two and three—true enough it happened by an accident of war that Rommel chose this point to attack with his tactical reserves of Panzer and Tiger tanks—the division was not overrun. The Brigade Headquarters was overrun and Regimental Headquarters were overrun and it looked for a time as if that invasion were going to fail but these men fought on. Battalions were gone, companies gone, and at such a time men by all the rules of war have the right to surrender. But these men fought on and when two German tanks came into the little courtyard which was headquarters of the Regina Rifles, the Italian cook came out with a Piat mortar that he had never used before and knocked out the two of them.

The fight went on from the beaches of Normandy to Caen. Carpiquet, on the way to Caen, was a tiny village with an airdrome. A brigade had to take the place—the North Shore, the Queen's Own of Toronto, the Chaudière. They decided they needed another brigade and they borrowed the Winnipeg Rifles, four regiments, plus a regiment of tanks. You know how they operate—one squadron of tanks with each regiment during an attack.

The Commanding Officer, the Brigadier, said to them before the attack: "To win the Battle of France we have got to win the Battle of Normandy. To win the Battle of Normandy we have got to take Caen. To take Caen we have got to take Carpiquet."

In the morning the attack began. They had a barrage of 450 guns, for the initial stages. When the smoke cleared I could see the men. It is a sight one has seen before and one will see again, I suppose, but which always fascinates—men advancing through a wheat field. Those of you who have not been to war may think of attack as charging and running. They can't do that. They seem to be advancing very slowly—eight or ten men here behind a tank, and eight or nine there, and the enemy mortar fire coming down on them. A mortar shell falls, a cloud of smoke and dirt, and you are watching from the pig-pen at the end of the Carpiquet airdrome.

The smoke clears. You see two or three going to their knees and falling over. You see the rest going on. Two of them come to a slit trench where there is one German. These men threw two hand grenades and the German caught them in his hand and threw them back. The third hand grenade blew the German's right arm off. He caught the fourth and fifth in his left hand and threw them back. The sixth killed him.

That is the kind of opposition they were up against as they fought their way through the wheat field, the Chaudière and the North Shore — English-speaking and French-speaking.

One would have no realization in that pig-pen at Carpiquet that Canada is now facing the most serious political crisis since Confederation began [the conscription crisis of late 1944]. One would have thought that the English-speaking Canadians and the French-speaking Canadians were going almost hand in hand across that wheat field.

I am not going into the political crisis at all just now. One thing I would say. No matter what one may think, no matter what one's opinions about French Canada, no matter what one's opinions about this worst political crisis since 1867—that is, in 77 years—whatever the rights or wrongs about the conscription situation, nobody can say that the French-Canadians are taking their present attitude because of lack of guts or physical courage on the battlefield.

And so these men, these Canadians, against what one British General called the worst odds they had ever met in Normandy until

169

that date, took Carpiquet. The Chaudière and the North Shore taking the north hangars of the village and the Queen's Own of Toronto taking the south hangars. The control buildings were taken and as a result of that battle that day, with atrocious losses, we got Caen.

The fighting in Europe went on that winter, inexorably moving north. It was halted for a few anxious weeks by the Battle of the Bulge, then moved on again. President Franklin Roosevelt died on April 13; the presidency (and legend) of Harry Truman began. In Holland that month Charles Foulkes commanded the Canadian Corps (peace in Europe was less than two weeks away) and later reported:

About the 27th of April the 1st Canadian Division picked up on the air a wireless message from the 25th German Army suggesting that they would like to have a parley to discuss putting food into Holland. This had previously been discussed on a high level. Field Marshal Montgomery gave authority and on the 28th of April a conference was held at Achterveld between the two lines.

The German delegation arrived outside of our line. We called a truce. The delegates were met, blindfolded, and brought in. General Bedell Smith represented General Eisenhower; General Sir Francis de Guingand, General Montgomery.

The head of the German delegation, a Dr. Schwebel, who had a portwine nose which must have cost him a couple of bottles a day to keep in bloom, arrived blindfolded. Across the table from him was a Russian representative, who was about 6 ft. 6 in. in height, and about as wide, with the ugliest face I have ever seen. As the handkerchief was removed from Dr. Schwebel's eyes, he broke into a cold sweat and was of very little use during the whole conference.

During this conference the Boche were very difficult to deal with, and the only satisfactory result we had was arranging a further conference, in which it was insisted that Seyss-Inquart, who was the Reichskommissar, should come to the Conference himself. When Seyss-Inquart and his entourage were brought in, and it was really quite amusing, Prince Bernhardt had just acquired Seyss-Inquart's car, which was a very nice Mercedes and still had the Reichskommissar's number on the front. We brought Seyss-Inquart in a jeep. As he got out of the car he was faced with Prince Bernhardt driving his own car, which he apparently did not relish.

During this conference Seyss-Inquart would not agree to anything. General Bedell Smith lost his patience, and pointed out that after all, we were going to shoot Seyss-Inquart some day. He said, "That leaves me cold," to which General Bedell Smith responded: "We will see you are cold."

The only outcome of that conference was that the Germans agreed that they would not interfere with the food being taken by the Swedish Red Cross, and the Swedish Red Cross guaranteed that they would look after the distribution of food. So it was agreed that the 1st Canadian Corps would take the food inside the German lines and dump it down. 240 vehicles were given to the Dutch Red Cross to cart it away. We had anticipated this, and that day we put in the first hundred tons of food.

We had considerable difficulty with the Germans because they did not want to continue the truce. I was very anxious to continue the truce because I felt if I once got the German Army to stop fighting, the Commanders would not get it started again. The Germans would not agree to a complete truce. They wanted a corridor to bring the food in. I pointed out I was not able to carry on a battle between 4 and 6, and carry on peace the other time. I pointed out I would not carry on any fighting, but if the Germans created an incident, we would reply tenfold.

We had no difficulty with the Germans putting the food in. Our main difficulty was that the Dutch civilians, who were to unload the vehicles, were in such a poor state of health and malnutrition, that after working for twenty minutes, they had to stop. It was very difficult to get the vehicles unloaded.

After these initial food talks, we had several more talks to try and get a better arrangement with the Boche to put the food in.

It was after one of these talks that we persuaded the German Army to surrender.

We were discussing ways and means of not creating any incidents, and I had suggested it would be much easier if we had a telephone line between my quarters and those of General Blaskowitz, so that if he decided to surrender we could accomplish it much quicker. He agreed and a telephone line was laid.

During the conference on the 3rd of May—it had been suggested by the Higher Command that perhaps General Blaskowitz did not understand what the real situation was—I produced from my pocket

171

a map of Europe in which I had marked the small areas which were still in the hands of the Boche. I pointed out the ridiculousness of the 25th German Army in Holland and the few Huns hanging on in Denmark. They were rather impressed with the map. I told them to take it away with them, and I suggested now was the time to surrender. Then General Reichelt made a very impassioned speech, in which he said they were ready to blow the dikes, destroy the country and fight to the last man, rather than be made prisoners and sent to Russia as slave labour.

This annoyed me. I told them there was no intention of putting the German army into Russia; that we had already reserved a place for them north of the Elbe. That I considered if they flooded Holland they would be war criminals, and I pointed out if, after my warning, they blew the dikes and flooded Holland, I would see that their names were inscribed on the roll of war criminals, and they would be punished accordingly. This rather shook the Germans and they agreed to surrender, provided I would give them an undertaking that they would not be sent to Russia.

I pointed out that my instructions were "Unconditional Surrender."

That night we got instructions from Field Marshal Montgomery that he was having negotiations with the German High Command for surrender, and he sent down a copy of the terms of surrender. I got on the telephone and ordered General Reichelt to come at 11 the next morning to Wageningen and receive the terms of surrender. I dictated the surrender terms to him, and set him back to bring Blaskowitz and Seyss-Inquart to sign. He was very truculent. However, after some argument he agreed, and on the 5th of May these terms were signed and the German Army came under our control.

That created a great problem. Blaskowitz had under his command about 125,000 soldiers, I had some 25,000 Canadian soldiers. The Germans had removed every Dutchman who was not a collaborator from office, so that every Burgomeister and engineer was a Nazi or had sworn allegiance to the Nazis. Therefore the problem I had to face was to take these 130,000 and disarm them, to continue to feed the Dutch population, and to make sure that the essential services did not break down during this period.

I was also particularly anxious that now that we had ended the war that not one Canadian soldier should lose his life.

Now the alternatives with which I was faced—the first one was to take the Boche as prisoners-of-war, and if we did take them as prisoners-of-war it meant we were tied by the Geneva Convention, which meant we would have to feed them at a scale about ten times more than we could bring in for the Dutch population. So I decided to deal with them as capitulated troops: that is, have them stay with their own Commanders, force them to feed themselves, so that if there was any shortage of food, the Germans went short.

This plan seemed to work all right. I immediately placed all the Germans, soldiers, sailors, air men and civilians under the command of General Blaskowitz. We dispensed with all civil authority. With every German Corps Commander I placed a Canadian Divisional Commander, and with every German Divisional Commander, I placed a Canadian Brigadier, to see that my orders were carried. Blaskowitz issued those orders to his subordinates, and my subordinates were there to see it was carried out. In the main it worked out all right.

However, Blaskowitz pointed out he was not in a position to get orders through to all his Commanders within twenty-four hours, and I was afraid we might have an incident. For that reason I delayed the march into Holland by the Canadian troops for 24 hours. I have been severely criticized by some members of the press for the delay. However, if I had to do it again, I would take the same procedure; I would not risk one Canadian soldier's life to please all the press in the world.

Now the next problem. The Germans had laid 2,000,000 mines in Holland, and these mines were laid all along the Coastal belt and along the rivers. I decided that those who laid them must pick them up. So the German engineers, some 4,000 of them, were given the task of picking up their mines. It was unfortunate. We used to have 14 or 15 casualties a day. However, there were still plenty of Germans to do it.

That was the smallest part of the problem. We now had to feed the whole of Holland, get the Boche disarmed and march him from his positions in Holland up to the north, across the Zuider Zee, across Northern Holland into Germany, and I decided that they would all march—officers and men, and they would march with the minimum of transport, and only the sick and wounded would be transported. We had some difficulty with this, but we put the Boche on five horse-drawn vehicles, and anyone of you mixed up with the war would know that that is a minimum, to carry the food. And during this trip they were searched for loot, and as you all know, the German is the best looter in the world. They had systematically looted the whole of Holland. Hardly a thing was left with the German Army when we finished. To give you some idea of the booty which we took from the Boche, and returned to the Dutch— 20,000 Radios; 30,000 Bicycles, 259 Barges and Boats; 400 tons of Food; 5,000 Cars and Motor Vehicles; 800 tons of Medical Supplies; 5,000 horses, 2 Million Cigars, and 60,000 Litres of Spirits. . . .

Now, as a former commander of men, I want to say one or two things about what we can do for the returned soldier. The task has been well done. No soldier has been found wanting: they have all gone through hardship, suffering, and above everything, lived a generally unnatural life. They have been away from their relatives and friends for five years. I believe the schemes the Government has for rehabilitation are quite satisfactory, but that does not go far enough. What I want to appeal to you now for, is to be long-suffering, to be tolerant toward these men. You want to remember that it was Crerar, Simonds, myself and many others who, for the past five years, have been teaching these men to be tough, to be blood-thirsty, grafting, vicious, to kill in cold blood, to scheme and deceive the enemy, and you cannot change that over night by an Order-in-Council. I hope the majority of these men will settle down; I am sure they will. But there will be break-ups in family relations, there will be untoward incidents which none of us will condone. But I do appeal to you to be patient, to be tolerant and helpful, remembering it was these men who risked, and some of them lost, their lives in order that you and I can be here today.

CHAPTER EIGHT

The Cold War

Remarkably little time passed between the real war and cold war, a development to which Canadians awoke a little faster than was their wont in major international issues. In September, 1945, a defecting Soviet cypher clerk in Ottawa, Igor Gouzenko, blew the whistle on his comrades. The military intelligence networks Gouzenko exposed had been getting information on the atomic bomb, anti-submarine devices, radar, and other war "secrets"—their informants all Canadians except for Allan Nunn May, a scientist who had come from the United Kingdom in 1944.

Pundit Willson Woodside described the affair as "the greatest treason scandal ever uncovered in an English-speaking country," and went on to reflect the nation's hurt feelings:

> Unfortunately, the trouble isn't quite as simple as just *selling* information. Worse was the fact that so many were willing to give it away, having come, through a long and insidious process of indoctrination in university and press, and from some pulpits, to hold what they considered a "higher patriotism" to Soviet Russia, than to their own country and the ideals it stands for.

There are disturbing implications when one considers *why* the

Soviet Government should have established such spying and fifth column activity in our country, which was friendly to them during the war, which freely handed over to them many of our most valuable war secrets, carried on clothing and relief drives, founded societies of friendship, and held so many public demonstrations, patronized by our highest dignitaries right up to the Prime Minister. An insistent question is whether the Soviets ever felt so friendly towards us.

Churchill's Tories were out of power in Britain. Anthony Eden, his foreign secretary and later to be (briefly) Britain's prime minister, voiced a lament to the Empire Club in 1946 that didn't require much updating in the next few decades:

Sometimes when one reads the international discussions and the sharp polemics which support them on either side, it almost seems as though the world had forgotten that just a short while ago, Britishers and Canadians, Russians and Americans, Frenchmen and Chinese, and so many others of the United Nations were laying down their lives in the hope that when victory was won, peace could finally be established on the basis of respect for international engagements and acceptance of the rule of law.

In the face of these disappointments, what should we do?

George Drew, Premier of Ontario, by background and inclination seemed cut out for even bigger game. He made regular fact-finding trips to Europe during the war. With the national Tory leadership within (it turned out) his reach, his outlook on international issues had a wide audience. Berlin, divided into four parts under Russian, French, British and American control, was the main cold war background of the time between the old allies—East and West, Communism and Democracy. Drew, early June, 1947:

When I flew to Berlin less than two weeks ago, I had the good fortune to arrive on a brilliantly clear day. As we circled very low over what had been the third largest city in the world before the war, it was evident that with the exceptions I will mention later, there is not a single building in Berlin proper which has not been destroyed by bombing or completely gutted by fire. It is one thing to read about it—it is another thing to see it. The outlying suburbs which are separated from the city itself by green stretches have not suffered so badly and some houses in that outer perimeter are still intact. Those are the ones mostly that are used by the Military Missions which are there today. Inside the city, however, is a scene of destruction and desolation on a scale which has never been known in the world's history. It is almost like Pompeii, multiplied a thousandfold.

That shattered city is symbolic of the tremendous problems with which the victorious powers are confronted. In a city where four and a half million people lived before the war there are still three million people living in all that indescribable wreckage. Where they live it is hard to imagine, even when you walk through the streets and are right beside them. Some of them have rigged up small huts by creating some sort of a covering in the corner of two standing walls and then closing this in with stones, bricks or rubble. Others in great numbers are living in what remains of the basements of the buildings in the city. Others are living in what are merely caves in the rubble itself—nothing more than primitive caves. It is true that they have restored the sewerage system and the water system to a considerable extent, but little imagination is required to realize that in both cases very limited opportunities are available to make use of either of these systems. Some lines of the underground have been opened and are operating with the few cars that are available. Surface trams without any glass are also moving along those tracks which it has been possible to repair. It is only the skeleton of a city in which human beings are living under conditions which can only increase month by month the utter hopelessness which hangs like a dark and oppressive cloud over all of them.

No matter how much we may hate what they have done, it is not a pleasant thing to see human beings on the verge of starvation and far beyond the verge, and living under conditions in which human beings have seldom lived before. It is not a good thing for the rest of Europe that people should continue to live under conditions in which some measure of decency and self-respect cannot possibly survive.

No building has been done in Berlin. It would be hard to imagine where that would start. Before any new buildings could be erected it would be necessary to pull down the shattered walls of those which still stand in their gaunt desolation.

My own feeling is, and it is only a passing individual opinion, that Berlin should never be rebuilt, but should stand in its present shattered form through all the centuries as a reminder to other dictators and those who support them, of what happens to rulers and to nations which seek to achieve world domination under any name.

Commander Rowland H. Stokes-Rees, Royal Navy, chimed in (June, 1948) with a rather devastating analysis of the old ally, Russia, as having

that terrific art of falsity of statement—almost as strongly developed as some of the North American press. Also they extol the basest treachery, exploit with Machiavellian cunning every situation as it occurs and pour out promises that defy description—the right promise at the right time. A powerful combination for evil.

Their character can be summed up in one word—*SINISTER*. In the first place, they are 100% suspicious—not without justification because every time the bell strikes, to use a naval expression, some foe overruns their most cultivated areas which must get awfully boring. This is most unhealthy. Then they are very childish—amazingly so, which, when coupled with oriental craving to save face, is equally disturbing.

One incident in London during the late War might illustrate this point. It was my duty to give their mission within reason all possible help on weapons. The first thing that struck me was that my opposite number in that mission—a Russian naval captain—was never able to see me alone. Secondly, that both he and his "witness" comrade, another captain, never vouchsafed any return information, but told most unconvincing lies. One said he wasn't in Russia at the relevant time and the other said he spoke no English. Both untrue and childish enough to be pathetic. Added to this, they always placed a bottle of sherry on the middle of the table—a drink which in my opinion would give one cirrhosis of the liver easier than looseness of the tongue—and poured continuous and copious draughts for their victim.

What worried them was our 4″ Mk XIX gun, fitted in all merchant vessels—a feeble weapon of misguided conception known from its simplicity as the "Woolworth" gun, which was mistakenly expected to make a bang loud enough to sustain the morale of the merchant seaman whilst, at a ridiculously short range, producing a splash big enough to make the submarine dive. Neither was the case. This was obvious and yet, for lack of any available alternative, so many of these guns were in use that our suspicious comrades were certain that this was Churchill's secret weapon. For two days they kept coming around to this weapon and its dark secrets. Their sherry bill must have been enormous. I had nothing to tell them. Finally, however, the brain box worked. I looked furtively over each shoulder, took one more draught to the detriment of the liver and beckoned them closer. "The secret of the gun is that the cartridge case ejects faster to the rear than the shell leaves the muzzle," I confided and blushed shamefacedly. Their sigh of relief bespoke their feelings—their work was accomplished. They did report this stupendous nonsense back to Kremlin. What I have never been able to discover is whether later they were executed for impertinence or incompetence.

On June 26, 1950, the Republic of Korea—a member of the United Nations—was invaded by North Korean forces that were believed to include Russians and Chinese. U.S. President Harry Truman reacted almost as quickly as if the attack had been on the U.S. itself. Canada was not far behind. Within sixteen days, three Canadian destroyers were in Pearl Harbor en route to join the fighting. The Canadian aircraft industry geared up rapidly to produce jet fighters. Canadian troops made ready. Rumours of Soviet submarines in the Gulf of St. Lawrence swept Ottawa. The *New York Times* man in Ottawa, Percy Philip, recalled that Churchill, in his memoirs, said that often Hitler helped the Allies win, by doing the wrong thing:

And the Moscow boys in North Korea, it is clear, have done us all the same kind of service. They tipped Moscow's hand and in doing so warned and scared everybody. If it had not been for their attack on South Korea, which was a member of the United Nations, we would probably have gone on talking for years about what we were going to do to implement the North Atlantic Treaty and doing nothing much. But the Korean incident showed the pattern of Moscow's tactics. It

179

called the dangerous situation in artificially divided Germany to everyone's attention. And perhaps most important of all it touched the United States in a vital spot.

We have heard a lot in these past months about the sacredness of the U.N. Charter, international honour, and government morality. That's all very pretty but I should like you to look at the contrast between this incident and those that preceded it.

The United States, the United Nations and all the rest of us allowed the Communists to overrun China, to threaten Burma and to carry on a guerrilla war in Malaya without doing a thing about it. Let us be frank. In spite of all our mouthings we did not really care about preventing the spread of Communism until it threatened us where we live.

What was different in Korea was that Korea is as essential to any nation which wishes to control Asia and the Pacific Ocean as is control of the Straits of Dover and the Dardanelles to anyone who wishes to control Europe and the Mediterranean.

In England we take a common-sense view of these things. We may give other official reasons why we fight—the protection of Belgian neutrality in 1914, the preservation of Polish and Rumanian independence in 1939—one must always have a high sounding moral excuse for public consumption, but if you look closely you will find the Straits of Dover and the Dardanelles just round the corner every time. . . .

It was a piece of good fortune that South Korea had been recognized by the United Nations as a self-governing country and even although its government was a minority government—for the last election gave some strange results—it could appeal to the United Nations for protection.

When one considers how American presidents have hesitated and fiddled around when even graver situations have arisen in the past, the amazing decision and quickness with which President Truman acted in these last days of June stands out as something almost beyond understanding. Suddenly, overnight, last June, the whole country, and in a measure the whole world, swung into action for a cause which superficially at least, seemed far more remote from U.S. interests and much less a moral issue than the invasion of Belgium in 1914 or of Poland in 1939.

This is a phenomenon which in itself deserves close and separate study. In the United Nations and in the North Atlantic Treaty the great ebullient country of the United States has become our partner, a supposedly equal partner. Before that partnership was formed, the problem for the rest of us has always been how to get her into war. But it looks now as if we were going to be made to look the laggards—and our friends and neighbours will, I fear, be much less delicate in reproaching us with being slow than we were on other occasions. Let us hope they do not try to hurry us too quickly along the road we are travelling together.

If one looks at the case of Canada alone what a difference there is between the thinking and action of your government and people in these past few months and the simpleton beliefs that marked the years after 1918, the years before 1939, and seemed to be creeping over us again. Some may think your government has not gone far enough even now. That is none of my business. What I find amazing and comforting is that you Canadians have shouldered your knapsacks and started out in good spirit along the road away from illusion and make-believe. You have decided to defend what you believe to be right against what you feel to be evil.

There was something of an opposite tone, however, when External Affairs Minister Lester B. (Mike) Pearson came to the Empire Club on April 10, 1951. He said much about Canada's place in the world but obviously felt Canada's role in Korea required defending:

We must convince the United States by action rather than merely by word that we are, in fact, pulling our weight in this international team. On their side, they should not attempt to tell us that until we do one-twelfth or one-sixteenth, or some other fraction as much as they are doing in any particular enterprise, we are defaulting.

It would also help if the United States took more notice of what we *do* do, and indeed, occasionally of what we say.

It is disconcerting, for instance, that about the only time the American people seem to be aware of our existence, in contrast say to the existence of a Latin American republic, is when we do something that they do not like, or do not do something which they would like.

181

I can explain what I mean, by illustration. The United States would certainly have resented it, and rightly so, if we in Canada had called her a reluctant contributor to reconstruction in 1946 because her loan to the United Kingdom was only three times as large as ours, while her national income was seventeen or eighteen times as large. In our turn, most of us resent being called, by certain people in the United States, a reluctant friend because Canada, a smaller power with special problems of her own, ten years at war out of the last thirty, on the threshold of a great and essential pioneer development, and with half a continent to administer, was not able to match, even proportionately, the steps taken by the United States last June and subsequently, which were required by United Nations decisions about Korea.

The leadership then given by the United States rightly won our admiration, and the steps that she has taken to implement them since, deserve our deep gratitude. The rest of the world naturally, however, took some time to adjust itself to a somewhat unexpected state of affairs. Canada, in my view at least, in not making the adjustment more quickly, should surely not be criticized more than, say Argentina or Egypt, or Sweden.

From the big picture, the official political or military situation report, it is a long way to the front lines. Bill Boss, a thoughtful veteran (as a correspondent) of the war in Europe, went to Korea in November, 1950, with the Princess Patricias to join the 1st British Commonwealth division. He was back in early September of 1951. The fighting was going well enough. Canadian troops had spent a boring summer, "perhaps one or two days of real soldiering a week," at raids designed to pinpoint Chinese positions. He had seen killing "at the rate of 2,000 corpses to a battlefield," so he assured his listeners that stories they read of such slaughter probably were not exaggerated, the way the enemy threw troops at the United Nations lines. But something else bothered him:

Korea conveys certain impressions on first sight. These impressions last with the soldier. Living the life he leads, he has no opportunity to go out and discover what he can about the country's culture, its history, its traditions, to make the sort of friendships that cement

182

impressions, and help to build that international bridge which we have succeeded in doing in Europe, and now that we are oriented to the East, it would seem that the opportunity was open to do. The country stinks and smells; it is dusty, dirty, filthy. You can't imagine the impact these have on the senses.

Also, Korea is an unbroken succession of hill after hill, mountain after mountain: you climb one to find the prospect of the next one—climb it in turn to see the next. To the soldier this means work, and hard work, with 75 pounds on his back to carry.

Under these conditions it is not surprising that the Canadian soldier has developed an unfortunate attitude to the Korean civilian. There may be something in this that is a challenge to us right here in Canada.

Look at it from the point of view of the Koreans. The war has meant the destruction of their country on a massive scale. From Taegu north as far as you want to go to the Manchurian border you will find the sites of what were homes and clusters of dwellings— mere piles of ash—the ash of rice straw burnt. At first it is gray, then it turns into a sort of pink violet. And this ash is the thing, which to my mind, connotes Korea today, not necessarily the hills. Korea has become levelled. Its buildings, the public ones—most of them modern—destroyed, or made shells, its intellectual life pillaged by the abduction last year of its leaders, the professors, the teachers, the professional men taken prisoners by the Communists and marched north. God only knows what happened to them. Its libraries destroyed or taken away—destruction on a scale estimated by the Korean government at three billion dollars, in a poor country, and on a scale which the United Nations Rehabilitation Agency estimates at two billion 500 million dollars. We plan, incidentally, to help Korea to the tune of 250 million dollars.

I think it is pretty evident that the Koreans have a stake, are entitled to some consideration. But in point of fact, the attitude worked in our troops by the various factors that have been operative in them since they arrived, is a feeling of superiority, an arrogance, a condescension, that can lead only to resentment by the Korean civilian. They do not yet, but they can come to hate us. Such things, for instance, as the elbowing of civilians off the road. The shaving of an oxcart by a jeep going by just to see how close you can come, and give the Korean leading his oxen a bit of a scare. Snarling when Koreans approach Company areas. I was driving along the road to Uijongbu two weeks ago last Saturday, and reached a military checkpoint, where military police from the three powers represented among the troops in that area were stationed. As I was about 300 yards short of that checkpoint, I saw one of the military policemen kick a Korean civilian across the road. Having kicked that civilian, he went across the road and kicked him again. I drove up and stopped the jeep, and I called to the Canadian corporal who was with the other two policemen, and I asked him to have the man who had been so active to come to my jeep. I still remember my upper lip quivering as I spoke to that man. I said "Soldier, I don't like United Nations policemen kicking the Korean civilians around." And he said, "Well, what do you expect me to do when they get in my way?" I said a few crisp things about the conduct that we expect from military policemen.

There are two things which I remember about this. One is that a soldier found it possible to behave in this way. The second is that another soldier, one of our boys, found it possible to see a man do this and not register some protest. I said to the Canadian corporal, "Corporal, if you had been half a man you would have done that for me."

This lack of concern for the Koreans can be dangerous. Our friends are few in the East. We need every one we can get. If our troops—and I am not speaking exclusively of our Canadian troops—but of our Western troops, if our troops can behave this way, have this attitude, and yet back home, back here in Canada be to all appearances good, law-abiding in every way, respected citizens, is it not possible that any one of us transplanted there might react the same way, have the same attitude?

Now that perhaps being the case, the answer, it seems to me, is in education. These boys are the products of our Canadian homes and Canadian schools, our Canadian society. It is not the Army's business to teach religion, to teach philosophy. The Army's job is to take the men we give it and make soldiers of them. To make better soldiers of them in Korea requires education in the things Korea stands for.

To back up this contention, Boss told of exceptions—a company sergeant major with the Royal 22nd of Montreal who, coming across dreadful conditions in a Korean hospital, organized food and clothing donations; and the way the Princess Pats avoided the hazard entirely:

> They had their first impressions, as everyone does. Then they went into the training period in the south and had some time before finding themselves committed to battle to interest themselves a little bit in what was going on. Their Padre, Capt. Roger Nunn, had been a missionary in Korea. He was able to do some explaining. By the time the Patricias reached the line they had acquired some understanding, some appreciation of the Koreans. This was fed by the assistance, work and devotion of labourers our boys called "rice burners," who worked with them. The rice burners soon grew from the 75 originally detailed to us, to 185. They brought in their friends and relatives because they were well treated. These have stuck with the Patricias through thick and thin.

Early in 1953 a meeting was held in Massey Hall, Toronto, at which the so-called Red Dean of Canterbury was the star turn. A Toronto businessman, Farley Faulkner, became embroiled in an argument there. After a story in a Toronto newspaper about him, he was asked to tell the Empire Club about it:

> Now the hand of the Kremlin succeeded in reaching into Massey Hall and grabbing hold of my body when I stood up to defend England against accusations being made by the Dean of the Church of England, who was describing Russia as the "architect of the future," and referring to England in a very bad light. My reward for that was that I was seized by what they call a "goon" squad and escorted out of Massey Hall. Now that is the physical hand of the Kremlin, and it can reach into the heart of this loyal city and into Massey Hall in such a manner.

The cold war background by the mid-1950s included joint U.S.-Canadian construction of radar lines across Canada's North because, as Defence Minister Ralph Campney put it, "we can hope that because the invader is being closely watched for, he may never come." Meanwhile, anyone who spoke even a moderate word about the Soviet Union did so at his peril. I. Norman Smith, associate editor of the

185

Ottawa *Journal,* travelled to Russia with the then External Affairs
Minister Lester B. Pearson. Mr. Smith spoke March 5, 1956:

> Since coming home I have learned that what I saw with my own eyes
> I didn't see with my own eyes.
>
> Many who read my Russian articles here or in other Canadian
> papers just smiled knowingly and put them aside. "Smith's been
> taken in," they declared. They gave my reports and Mr. Pearson's
> trip to Russia scarcely another thought.
>
> Gentlemen, I would like to talk to you about this today. I refer not
> to any personal pique that I am not accepted as a poet or prophet. I
> speak of the fact that since returning I have found from phone calls
> and personal conversations with friends and strangers, that Canada
> is full of people who know infinitely more about Russia than I do.
> Almost without exception none of them has been there. . . .
>
> Before I go on perhaps I should summarize here, in not more than
> two or three paragraphs, what I reported from Russia.
>
> I found a country where the State is all and the individual nothing,
> where freedom is almost exclusively the freedom to do what you are
> told in the interest of the State. I attended a pathetic service in a
> Roman Catholic Church that testified grimly to the persecution of
> religion. I was dealt with by an officialdom which though "correct"
> was machine-like, and whose arrogance to the underprivileged
> citizen could easily be, though revoltingly, imagined.
>
> I told of the uncivilized "hospitality" of Messrs. Khrushchev and
> Bulganin when they so very crudely determined to make the Cana-
> dian foreign minister and his party become ill from the forced
> repetition of 20 Vodka toasts; and I depicted Khrushchev as a man
> who perhaps from fear, ignorance and arrogance combined, might
> easily misinterpret some Western move and in what he thought was
> self defence crush the push buttons at his elbow and send the world
> to atoms. I wrote that I despised Communism with heart, mind and
> soul, and that there could be no mistaking that Soviet Russia and
> Soviet Communism aimed to rule the world, even as *Pravda* re-
> minds us every day with its abiding slogan: "Workers of the world,
> unite."
>
> But I also reported that I hadn't seen many underfed people in the
> crowded cities, nor inadequately clad people, nor shriven, beaten

apathetic people. I had been amazed at the busy cities as I strolled around freely by myself, at the TV, at the book stores, at the signs all around of vitality and alertness, of pride in country and in work, and a longing for education. Train travel had been comfortable, shops had been full of goods and full of people freely buying, markets had been crowded, parks showed carefree gaiety, opera, ballet and theatre revealed exquisite, matchless beauty and artistry. I hinted at the dynamics of Communism, at production and development running at full spate, at cleverness in propaganda and skill in mass psychology. I said I believed—and regretted—that Soviet Russia under communism was a *going concern*.

Now then, by some process or habit of thought it seems that the majority of readers ignored my criticism of Russian life and my indictment of Russian intent. Instead, they fastened exclusively and resentfully on everything I said about power and progress, about health and wealth and relative contentment.

Gentlemen, I didn't go to Russia to confirm that there are prison camps. We know that. I didn't go to Russia to confirm that there is oppression of religion. We know that. I didn't go to Russia to find out if there is what we call individual liberty. We know there isn't.

I did go to Russia to see what I could see, on the streets, in the country, in the cities, in the faces of the people, in the stores, the markets, and play-places and work-places. And in due course I wrote that what I had seen had surprised me and had hurled my ignorance into my face. I do not take back my confession nor my shame at my own ignorance. I suggest a capacity for surprise and shame is something that Canadians are a little short on. It seems to me we are far advanced to the point where we believe only what we want to believe; and to where we believe that only *what we like* can be successful.

Insofar as Russia and the Russians are concerned, because we deplore their ways we minimize them and belittle their achievements. On this opium we sit by in a kind of coma of ignorance, defying their success and indeed almost denying their existence.

Gentlemen, some of you hate all Russians and all their works. If you do, you should all the more want to learn about them and know what they are doing. Some of you believe with a fire-hot certainty that Russia is going to declare war on us when it suits her. You should then be vigilant in your study of her war-making potential. Some of you cling to the belief that somehow we can and must coexist. You then, above all, should be zealous in your efforts to know and to understand, to clear away the barriers of dark and of mutual mistrust, to base your hopeful policies upon facts rather than fancies and fears.

In 1956, the world was rocked when Egypt—with the tacit backing of the Soviet Union—grabbed the Suez Canal. Britain, under Prime Minister Anthony Eden, joined France in an abrupt military action to keep the canal open while Israel attacked Egypt as well.

Sir Hugh Nicholas Linstead, British M.P., with the British perspective:

Ask yourself these questions. Are we forever to see the civilized world losing ground before lawlessness and Communism? Who is to apply international sanctions if the United Nations Organization is impotent? After Tibet, what? After Indo-China, what? Great Britain negotiated a peace on Persia. Great Britain negotiated a compromise on the Suez base. Is Great Britain to negotiate a compromise on every demand made no matter by what country? If she does, to whose advantage is it? There is only one country which gains as Western powers are negotiated out of Asia and out of Africa piecemeal and that is Russia. . . .

As Britain sees it, because of the veto, U.N.O. is impotent in many vital fields. Yet if no one takes action then we play into the hands of international anarchy and of the one country that stands to profit by it. This is the background to what Great Britain is doing in Suez today.

We shall be criticized for unduly strong action, but that criticism does not concern me greatly. Once the decision has been taken that action is necessary, then half-hearted action is worse than useless. It must be, and be seen to be, ample to achieve its aim.

Why is Suez so vital to us? In brief, because our economy is shifting its base from coal to oil. Remember we are 50 million people cramped on a small island, dependent for any reasonable standard of life on exports. We can no longer export the heavy machinery of Victorian days. Our customers make it themselves. We must export the latest discoveries in engineering, physics, electronics, aeronautics, and in nuclear fission. At present our second greatest source of power for the factories that make these things is oil. We are dependent on it increasingly for heating, for road transportation and more recently for our railroads. Without it Great Britain would slowly run down. The bulk of our supplies of oil comes to us through the Suez Canal. We dare not allow those supplies to be held under the arbitrary control of one man who has already shut the canal to the ships of one country.

It may be argued that Egypt has acted legally. That is a matter for the lawyers. The point that I am certain about is that their act was by any standards a gross breach of international faith. Supposing that Panama in the purported exercise of its rights of sovereignty were to seize the Panama Canal. Then the situation would be brought home to the Americans. Co-operation in international affairs depends on good faith far more than it depends on lawyers' interpretations of documents.

Nevertheless had circumstances not gone further than seizure of the canal the question might still have been negotiable. It is true that all through Great Britain has reserved the right to use force but I am satisfied that it was at first intended to use force only in two circumstances, to protect British lives and property and secondly should it have decided to do so by the United Nations Organization.

The Israeli attack, however, put a completely new complexion on the situation. When she marched into Egypt it became essential to control the flames, it became legal for us to re-open our old Suez base and it became necessary for us to protect our shipping and keep the canal open. Would the United Nations have done this? Would it have put in forces to keep Israel and Egypt apart? Could it have kept open the canal? The answer to these questions is certainly, no. That is why we and the French have gone in. We have gone in because we have been injured by a gross breach of international good faith. We have gone in in default of there being any other instrument to do so. Certainly we are serving our own vital national interests but we hope and believe that by keeping Israel and Egypt apart we are preventing a prairie fire that would affect the interests of every other country in the world.

In the international furore that followed Suez, Eden resigned. Brigadier Claude Dewhurst, a former British intelligence officer familiar with the Middle East, spoke in January, 1957. He said that if the Brits hadn't acted as rapidly as they did, within three days Jordan, Syria and Egypt would have attacked Israel on three fronts, with the help of Soviet technicians, tanks and aircraft:

It was reckoned that within about a week Israel would have succumbed to these attacks and it would have taken quite a week before the United Nations met, before the Security Council met, vetoed and referred the question to the General Assembly, with counterclaims from Arabs and Jews to work out meanwhile. By that time Israel would not have existed!

This Intelligence information was available, and had for some time been available, but speed and secrecy were what was essential to thwart this Soviet-inspired plan.

Now the Israelis were the ones most immediately threatened, and they were the ones who at once beat the pistol by saying: "Before this happens we will hold Jordan, we will hold Syria but we will launch an attack on Egypt, for we know the stamina of her army and we believe it can be defeated within a fortnight." Actually they defeated it within five days.

This speed and secrecy, which was so necessary, did not allow of the U.S. to be consulted. They were informed 48 hours before, . . . but they were not consulted on it because it would have been quite useless to consult the U.S. on election eve. . . .

Nor really was there any point—when you look at it dispassionately—in consulting the Commonwealth. Commonwealth reaction might have shown itself in one of many decisions:—"Yes, we support you." Or it might have been a calling for documents. . . . "Produce your evidence." "Why is this a calamity?" "Why must you work swiftly?" Right oh! Then we would have had Commissions set up—people flying here and there—divulging our Intelligence—putting plans on the table. "See if you agree to this, or that." Then they would go back to their Legislative Assemblies, and so forth, and so forth! But, there was not *TIME* for this! There was no point if they disagreed because they would *HAVE* to be overruled in any case.

And when you look at it in that light, you realize the sort of differences of opinion there might have been between India and Australia, or Canada and South Africa. They would undoubtedly have been very great. There would not have been unanimity and Eden reckoned it would be better to take the risk oneself since only U.K. troops were to be involved rather than to appeal to the Commonwealth beforehand.

Now the attack was astonishingly successful. The Israelis, and later on British and French troops, shot down or destroyed on the ground 80% of the aircraft which Egypt had received from Russia and routed over 35% of her army in the Sinai Desert or near Port Said. It was amazingly successful.

And then, of course, as you know, came the Soviet bluff; the great bluff that said they would send volunteers to the Middle East in hundreds of thousands and that they would rocket-bomb England. And if she bombarded Great Britain, how do you deal with rockets? You bomb the bases. And who would do it? The American aircraft from their bases in Great Britain, and Russia would thus be at war with the Americans within 24 hours. To my mind that was a bluff and, all to our sadness, we were too fearful to call it, though it is, as I said, perfectly understandable.

Thereafter, of course, Eden had to reap the fruit of all this. He had to reap the fruit of U.S. fury and the personal jealousies of Mr. Dulles. The telegrams of blackmail—that England would be cut off from the American dollar—poured into London. There came in telegrams from Canada (as yet, luckily for Ottawa, not divulged!). And there came in telegrams from India on the same lines, that they would be prepared to leave the Commonwealth as well. And it was Great Britain who had thus to give an ultimatum to the French commander, who wanted to go ahead with the final three days of getting the Canal. Eden had to give the ultimatum to his ally to stop action with their joint work unfinished.

But do not look at the bad part, as the papers always wish us to look. Let us look at the better side:—we foiled a Soviet plot which was of far greater dimensions than most of the world realized. We drew attention to Israel's position after hundreds of unfructuous meetings of the U.N. and a solution to the Suez Canal will surely be come by which may last for years to come. However it may be worded, it will be a solution.

This led us to the resignation of Eden. Eden fell as an oblation and a sacrifice to the then Nasser-Dulles axis.

A contrast to all that sound and fury: the Soviet Ambassador to Canada in 1959, A. Aroutunian, Nov. 5, 1959:

I have in mind a new project, now under discussion in the Soviet scientific spheres, to erect a giant dam in the Bering Strait and, with its help to reorganize the whole Arctic region—change the climate, make the immense territories of eternal frost in the Soviet Union, Canada and Alaska flourishing areas with moderate climate.

Some of you very pragmatic people still think that maybe I spin yarns of a fairy tale. But in fact that is a project on which its author, a very prominent Soviet engineer, Peter Borissov, has worked for more than thirty years. He has elaborated in great detail the scientific, engineering and economic aspects of the construction of a gigantic dam in reinforced concrete of 74 kilometres in length to floor the Bering Strait. The project is designed having in mind the present level of construction engineering.

The construction of a gigantic dam in the Bering Strait is quite practical from an economic point of view. By the way, Peter Borissov's project envisages the possibility of making the St. Lawrence bay a navigable waterway throughout the whole year which means your city, Toronto, would become a year-round seaport.

The project is worthwhile thinking over. It requires international co-operation on a very solid basis between many countries—the Soviet Union, the United States, Canada, Norway, Sweden, etc. I realize that it is not realistic today, but we can work to make it realistic tomorrow by changing the whole international situation and establishing on Earth real friendship among the nations. I want to introduce the idea of radical changing of climate in the Arctic to the Canadians for their reflection.

In the autumn of 1960, the presidential campaigns of John F. Kennedy and Richard Nixon held only part of the western world's centre stage. The big scene-stealer was Nikita Khrushchev—hammering the table with his shoe and generally behaving with what seemed to be childish rage at not being able to run the United Nations the way a bully could

17 *A child in the Warsaw Ghetto*

18 (Top right) *German troops cross the Rhine at Mainz, 7 March, 1936*

19 (Bottom) *Bavaria, 1935: a greeting for Adolf Hitler*

20 (Top) *Anti-conscription demonstrators in Montreal: Canada, yes; Britain, no*

21 (Bottom) *A munitions factory in Quebec: "They work with a smile, not with grumbling"*

22 (Top) *London, 1940: "It does take your mind off the war. . ."*

23 (Bottom) *"And do, dear God, take care of yourself because if anything happens to you we are sunk"*

24 (Top) *Bombs over Germany,
and a boost to Allied morale*

25 (Bottom) *General purpose,
medium capacity and high
capacity bombs at an RCAF
Bomber Group Station*

26 (Top) *D-Day in Normandy:*
"If you want to live, get off the
beaches"

27 (Bottom) *Berlin, 1945*

28 (Top) *At the United Nations,
Nikita Khrushchev steals a
scene*

29 (Bottom) *The Princess Pats
in Korea: exceptions to an
unfortunate attitude*

30 (Top left) *Greg Clark: in the bombers' bright lights*

31 (Top right) *Mike Pearson presides over a U.N. political and security committee debate*

32 (Bottom left) *Dr. Best: the rewards are real, and great*

33 (Bottom right) *A. Y. Jackson in the Arctic, 1927*

34 (Top) *The Queen in Quebec City, 1964: "No-one has a right to insult her. . ."*

35 (Bottom) *The Queen Mother at the Empire Club head table in 1965*

run a sandbox. At least, the almost unanimous media theory was that Khrushchev's displays were childish temper tantrums. Blair Fraser, Ottawa editor of *Maclean's,* was at the U.N. He begged to differ. Oct. 20, 1960:

Uncontrolled, childish, kindergarten temper tantrums? This interpretation is a little implausible on its face. Mr. Khrushchev spent many years working very closely under a mad tyrant whom, as we now know, he hated with every fibre of his being. He was able to conceal this hatred not only well enough to survive but survive at the very top of the Soviet hierarchy and to win an engagement—a duel to the death, literally—with the most powerful and well-armed scoundrel then surviving in the whole world: Beria. And finally he emerged to his present position, as the established, if not unchallenged, director of the Communist half of the world.

It seems unlikely that a man with such a record would be unable to control his temper after what was after all a fairly petty provocation.

Even if we hadn't his record to go on, I would like to recall an incident that took place ten days ago in which he was interviewed in a television programme in New York. Toward the end of that two-hour interview for which he had no notes and the questions of which were, as far as he was concerned, spontaneous—he hadn't seen or heard them before—Mr. Khrushchev received a note from one of his aides. One is tempted in retrospect to say his face froze, became rigid with anger. I must confess I didn't think so when I saw it the first time—only later I realized this had been true.

Then came a stage break of ninety seconds. The contents of that note were a warning that the interruptions in the programme were being used for violent anti-Soviet propaganda—a type of commercial for Radio Free Europe. In the studio we did not see this—I saw one after and thought, I must confess, it was pretty crude—reminiscent of World War One propaganda. Khrushchev was furious, absolutely furious. He turned to David Susskind and said, "I have just got a note that you are using this break for anti-Soviet propaganda. How dare you, how dare you invite the head of a state and treat him in this fashion?" He gave Susskind a really severe dressing down. This was while the break was still on.

Susskind said later, "I thought the programme was over. I

thought he was going to rip up the microphone by the roots and leave me to face the camera alone to explain what had happened."

But, no. With five seconds to go, Khrushchev said, "Oh well, what do I care? I will say what I like . . . we will win anyway." And he turned to face the camera as it came alive with an expression of perfect composure and very nearly with perfect control of face and expression, he began to say to the American audience, "Thanks very much. It is getting late. It seems to me we have covered most of the ground . . . if you don't mind I will take my leave."

Here was a moment when the provocation was real, when we know—we don't have to have it reported to us—he was in an absolute fury. But I would defy anybody without the benefit of hindsight to have detected this really furious anger that was bubbling at the back of his throat when he began to make what turned out to be a long farewell to the television audience.

Well, if Mr. Khrushchev wasn't putting on childish temper tantrums because he can't control his temper, why was he behaving as he behaved? Let us remember, first, what were the political conditions back home from which he emerged to make his visit to New York? It seems as nearly certain as anybody can be on that subject that there is at this moment a deep and almost violent difference of opinion, a political argument raging within the Communist world. On one side are the fundamentalists, the people who go back to Scripture, to the Old Testament Scripture of Karl Marx and who maintain that of course peaceful coexistence or any form of collaboration with the Capitalist world is impossible—in fact a contradiction in terms of; not only will there be war, there must be war, not only must there be war, but the end of that war will be the triumph of Communism, the end of the Communist millennium. This is orthodox Communist doctrine.

Mr. K., in the last two or three years, has been engaged in developing an attractive heresy, a heresy that must be attractive to any normal human being who wants peace, as all normal human beings do. His heresy has been that it isn't necessary to have a nuclear war against the West. Capitalism will collapse of its own wants in the end, no doubt. Meanwhile, it is not only possible, it is easy to have a kind of peaceful coexistence with them.

So if we remember that politics are politics even in dictatorial regimes, we must realize Mr. K. came to the United States under a considerable emotional compulsion to demonstrate to the folks back home that he was not, as his enemies say, soft on Capitalism. When the Soviet Union lost two votes by open collusion of Western countries, including Canada, with the U.S. he had to demonstrate enmity. He had to show himself as one man alone, surrounded by enemies, and a Daniel in the den, not of lions but of rats.

If you look at his public performance in that light, it seems to me they become, if not polished, if not well advised, at least credible, at least plausible.

In 1962 Soviet freighters carrying nuclear missiles to Cuba were turned back on the demand of U.S. president John F. Kennedy, and the threat of naval action. The U.S. and the Soviet Union had seemed close to war until Khrushchev ordered the fleet home. Mark Gayn of the Toronto *Star,* one of the most able U.S.S.R.-watchers in the Western world, on Khrushchev and the "Second Revolution" in Russia, Gayn's term for the change from Stalin's repression to Khrushchev's letting in the air:

If I gave you the date May 1st, 1960, and asked you what happened on that date, you will probably remember the U-2 incident. But, there was something else that happened on that day, which serves as a wonderful illustration of the developments in the Soviet Union. On that day, *Pravda,* which is an organ of the Communist Party, published a tremendously long poem. The poem dealt with the tremendous achievements that the Soviet Union had made in the last 43 years, and many triumphs with the progress of man, and so on. Then, it came to a passage, a long segment of this poem, which dealt, in verse, with the age of terror—the age of Stalin—and it dealt with the impact that this terror has had on private lives, on relations between man and man, on sufferings of millions in the Soviet Union. This was on May 1st. On May 4th, I found myself in Kiev and made an effort to contact officials of the Writers' Union. I was taken to this comfortable mansion, to a comfortable room with comfortable furniture, and there were two very comfortable-looking men waiting for me and we engaged in a long discussion of Soviet literature and best-sellers, and so on; but, eventually, I asked the President of the Ukrainian Union of Writers—what was the outstanding work of literature produced in the previous three or four years. He said, beyond any doubt, the outstanding work was this poem published four days earlier and he said, "Let me tell you a personal story about this. I arrived in my office on May 2nd. I picked up *Pravda* and read this poem—especially the section on Stalin—and I telephoned my wife and I started reading this section to her aloud and she broke into tears, and as I was reading it I also began to cry." Then, the second man—the Secretary of the Union—said: "This is strange because this is exactly what happened to me. I, too, read the poem to my wife on the phone and both of us wept." Now, they wept; they felt this tremendous reaction to it, not because it was a great work of art but because it re-awakened a tremendous hurt which you find in the soul of every Russian today, a feeling that there was an age of terror, a dark age, from which the people are now emerging and which they cannot forget. No matter with whom you talk in the Soviet Union, you can start with any subject and, within ten minutes, you always come to the subject of what happened during the age of Stalin. . . .

There are many critical things that you can say of Khrushchev. But, for one thing, Khrushchev will be given high marks by history for understanding that new methods of government were needed. He understood that he could not deal with the Russian people as Stalin dealt with them. He faced great dangers in this. One of these was psychological. He could not tell the people that Stalin was a villain without taking great risks with his own government. He was taking political chances in that he had to reshape the whole machinery of government, the machinery of terror and suppression without, at the same time, destroying the governing machinery, and he proceeded to do this in 1956 with his famous speech of the denunciation against Stalin. There were a number of foreign communists in Moscow for this Congress, including Tim Buck, and one day they were all summoned to the Central Committee of the Party and they were told that nothing was going to happen at the Congress that day and will they, as a great favour to the Communist Party of the Soviet Union, go to the factories in Moscow and speak on any subject they choose and the subject, perhaps by coincidence, happened to be "Communism." They all went out and the doors were locked and then Khrushchev proceeded to give his memorable speech attacking a man who was, up to that point, almost God in the Soviet Union. I was told, by a participant in this Congress, that Khrushchev wept from time to time, as he spoke, and many in this great auditorium also cried because they were seeing the destruction of a man who became a demagogue.

He has been continuing this process and for a definite purpose. The purpose was to demonstrate to the Soviet people that the whole regime, the whole climate and machinery of government has changed and that a new climate has entered in Russia.

CHAPTER NINE

"Canada is not Canada for all Canadians"

Until the early 1960s, anyone identifying major Canadian concerns solely from the Empire Club speeches would have had to put relations between French and English Canada well down on the list —far behind freight rates, mountain differentials, poverty in India, British politics, bond drives and the like. A token Quebecker would show up about once a year but if he spoke of differences at all, it was rarely in real depth; sometimes in allusions so veiled that only the most alert listener would get them at all. Even those were always well larded with fulsome expressions of loyalty to Canada and to Britain.

One representative sample—C.J. Langelier of Quebec in 1907:

My family is one of the oldest French-Canadian families in the country, and I can say without fear of serious contradiction, that the sentiment of the whole mass of the population is one of loyalty to Britain, and that what was said before Confederation, ''that the last shot for the defence of England in Canada would be fired by a French-Canadian,'' is still true. We French-Canadians have, of course, a great many imperfections, but there is something else that we have; we have gratitude, and we cannot forget that here in Canada under the British crown, surrounded by a British population, we have more liberty than any other Catholics in the world. You can go into the remotest part of the French-Canadian settlements anywhere, and generally you will find the portrait of one of the Popes, and alongside it, a portrait of that good Queen Victoria, and a portrait of King Edward. . . .

There is no other country in the world which is more free. We are protected by the British Court of Justice (Judicial Committee), and I may say more than that; we would go before a Court presided over by an English-speaking judge with more confidence than before a Court presided over by a French-Canadian. I say this as a French-Canadian, and as I am the son of a farmer, and all my family were farmers, I know just as well as a man can know, the real sentiment of the people.

Such speeches seemed to express Canadian patriotism above and beyond the call of duty; very close, in Mr. Langelier's case, to being obsequious. Perhaps this could best be understood in historical terms—that by its very nature an embattled outpost of French language and thought in a largely alien continent, Quebec tended to be overly defensive, as if besieged; willing to do almost anything to deflect a threat to the long-defended linguistic and religious rights of its people.

This inward-turning was seen in other ways. In Canada's expansionist years early in the century, for instance, few French-Canadians joined the westward migration. French-Canadians, in fact, did not really participate in the optimistic euphoria of the Laurier years. If there had been a time when some of their leaders had hoped to establish a Quebec branch plant in the Canadian West, this hope had faded with the realization that Manitoba (where French-speaking Roman Catholics had been an important element in 1870 when Manitoba became a province) was an outpost of Ontario rather than of Quebec, as demonstrated by the bitter furore over the *Manitoba Schools Question*. This had convinced Laurier that the minority needed a constitutional guarantee of their rights, but when it came to the case of the newly-formed (in 1904) provinces of Alberta and Saskatchewan, the Prime Minister yielded to English-Canadian pressure and introduced an amendment to the education legislation—preserving the existing separate school system but leaving the administration of the schools under the control of the provincial governments. "Canada is not Canada for all Canadians," declared Henri Bourassa.

To document the escalation over the years of the bitterness embodied in those words, "Canada is not Canada for all Canadians," is not a function of this book. But Canada, in effect, fought two wars in one during 1914-1918; one in Europe, the other in Quebec. The early enthusiasm of Quebeckers for the war having been ruined by the anti-French blundering of Militia Minister Sam Hughes (at one time he appointed as chief recruiting officer in Quebec an English-Canadian Baptist clergyman), they lagged in enlistment despite the constant, almost week-by-week, exhortations of Laurier that they should show themselves as brave as other Canadians. While some élite Quebec units fought brilliantly in Europe, at home battalions could not find recruits, and those they had were setting a high rate of desertion. One colonel was jailed for six months for telling his men in 1916 that everybody could have a pass to leave camp, and no regimental funds would be spent hunting for those who chose not to return. Henri Bourassa, grandson of Louis Joseph Papineau and for nearly twenty years the leader of Quebec nationalism, continued to provide the spiritual guidance for those who refused to enlist and eventually took part in conscription riots. His hatred for the imperialistic side of the British character set a tone for generations to come.

Yet the first comment on all this heard by the Empire Club was couched in such general terms that no listener from another planet would have known the depth of bitterness it was based upon. It came in 1919, from Leon-Mercier Gouin, a Montreal lawyer, eldest son of Quebec Premier Sir Lomer Gouin and grandson of the late Premier Honoré Mercier:

> I referred a minute ago, gentlemen, to your motto—"Canada and a United Empire"—and when you chose it you had, of course, the right to expect Canada in the very near future to enjoy internal harmony as well as external unity. But in my opinion—and I wish to be frank—and in your opinion too, I am sure we are still very far indeed from national unity, and from interracial harmony.
>
> Read our Canadian newspapers—your papers from Toronto, ours from Montreal and Quebec—and you will see how divided we are,

how bitter still are our racial controversies, our class and clan antagonisms. Owing to very unhappy misunderstanding, many Canadians have come to look upon the others either with scorn or with hatred; and of course we have in Quebec our own fools—and thank God, they are a rare species. [Laughter] I hope I offend nobody, but at the same time I believe that in this very province of Ontario there are well-meaning citizens who are led astray by their ardent but somewhat intolerant patriotism. I believe a truly Canadian patriotism is a possible thing for both of us. [Hear, hear] and I believe that the best thing would be that we each take good care of our fields, and that you endeavour to broaden the ideals of some of your fellow citizens.

Every man in Ontario and in Quebec ought to understand that our country is large enough to harbour our different creeds and our different races.

Jean-Charles Harvey, a novelist and short-story writer who had been editor-in-chief of *Le Soleil* in Quebec City before becoming the founding editor of *La Jour* in Montreal, had a go at the Canadian unity question early in 1939, bringing certain elements up-to-date and introducing others:

In the last two or three years talk has been heard of a separatist movement in Quebec, aimed at the establishment of a French state along the St. Lawrence River. The group is now to all intents and purposes impotent, but we must not lull ourselves into thinking that the idea behind it is entirely dead. Another economic crisis, for example, would probably revive it.

Since most of the leading enterprises in our province are in the hands of English, English-Canadian or American corporations, it is only natural that the people, in times of depression and suffering, should throw the blame for their troubles on employers and producers who are known as capitalists. That is where demagogues and exploiters of racial feeling come into the picture.

They had little difficulty for a while in persuading Quebec crowds that the enemy was the Englishman, that it was he who had kept French Canada in a state of misery and that the best way to get rid of him would be by breaking away from the rest of the country and setting up a distinct social and economic organization of our own.

202

These ideas were propagated during the late crisis. They may come again during the next one and grow still more intense and more troublesome. There, as I see it, is one of the greatest dangers threatening the unity of our homeland.

I must say that nobody has the right to condemn the French-speaking Canadians for struggling nearly two centuries against formidable elements to keep alive their language, their traditions, their faith and their identity. They have shown a great deal of nobility and courage in doing it. If we can some day unite in our lands the descendants of the two greatest European civilizations of modern times without destroying the essential qualities of either French or British blood, we shall have accomplished probably one of the finest feats in human history. But if these two elements fail to come together, if they will not work together to form a powerful, respected nation, the result will be that by clinging obstinately to our respective positions we shall have aggravated the ferments of hatred, of discord and of suffering we have now. We shall also have held back progress in our own part of America and retarded the attainment of human happiness. . . .

But there are other reasons than merely provincial or ethnic reasons. The Fathers of Confederation set out to forge a nation out of the scattered settlements and waste areas in Canada. They did the best they could. . . . Unfortunately, the public men who succeeded them either would not or could not stem the tide and divert the current of Canadian development into a more unified channel. The powers assigned in the British North America Act to the Federal authority have been weakened, not strengthened, and the prerogatives reserved for the Provinces, instead of being diminished have been increased to the point where the whole framework erected by the Fathers of Confederation is threatened with disruption. Not only Quebec and Ontario but even provinces in the West which were not parties to the original pact, are encroaching more and more, in the name of autonomy, upon the central power.

The Provinces, originally the daughters of Confederation, are now in the process of devouring their mother. Every year more and more of her prestige is being stripped from her. In the central government itself, sometimes through excessive political caution, sometimes through rank indifference or even cowardice, has been let go by default many an essential prerogative. . . .

One source of tension is that many of us Canadians know so little about the rest of the country. I have friends who have been to Paris five times, yet they have never seen Toronto. An extremely intelligent well-educated young man, trained in the school of Nationalism, said to me last fall, "What can Winnipeg, Calgary and Vancouver mean to us? As far as we are concerned they do not exist because we don't know them. We can feel no loyalty except to our own Laurentians." Many Canadians, English as well as French-speaking, feel pretty much the same way, though they may not be as frank to say so as bluntly as our young patriot.

Between the wars, uneasy peace also was the rule between Quebec and the rest of Canada. With 1940 the old bugaboo was with us again. When Premier Joseph Adelard Godbout spoke to the Empire Club, Dec. 4, 1940, the title was "Quebec and Unity;" but the actual topic, unspoken, skated around, was the attitude of Quebeckers towards fighting another British war—so many of them averring that they would fight to defend Canada, but not to defend Britain. It was again a plea for understanding:

> The French-Canadians, like the English-Canadians, are a constituent part of Canada. This Canada of ours they will arm themselves to defend against the eventual aggressor, come he from where he may. Gentlemen, our servicemen have enlisted with as good heart as have your own. They are doing their duty with the same spirit of discipline as are your sons. The great voice of Canada vibrates in them from fibre to fibre. They are proud of their birthright and, accepting all the responsibilities incumbent upon them, submissive to law and devoted to a great cause, they are proclaiming the efficient accomplishment of the spirit and the letter of the Canadian constitution, not only in this or that particular part of our immense national territory, but from sea to sea, as it is blazoned on the arms of Canada. They believe themselves to be giving sufficient proof of the justice of this principle to make of it the foundation for Canadian unity.

At the end of Premier Godbout's speech he mentioned two Quebeckers who had won the Victoria Cross, reading the valiant words of the citation for Lieut. Jean Brilliant of the Royal 22nd, who died in the action for which he was awarded the V.C.

Godbout, concluding, emotionally:

> Separatists, gentlemen, we are not; nor could we be. We have made too many sacrifices for Canada. There is not a foot of the soil of the country which has not felt the tread of our people; not a town, not a village but has given birth to a nation builder, to a hero illustrious or unsung. We do not renounce a single parcel of our patrimony, for it is identified with us as we with it.

It is difficult, always has been, to strike a balance in wartime between the loyalties of Canadians of British background (loyalty to Canada and Britain, not necessarily in that order) and those of French background (loyalty to Quebec and to Canada, not necessarily in that order). The eventual compulsory military service system did not help. It rather exacerbated the dispute, because call-ups (as distinguished from volunteers) had the right to refuse to serve outside of Canada. For a call-up to accept the idea of serving abroad was called "going active." Those who refused were by no means all Quebeckers, but a large percentage were. Through press and public criticism, the pressures grew.

L'Abbé Arthur Maheux, a professor at Laval:

> I can appreciate with impartiality my own fellow countrymen and blame them when I think they deserve it. Yet, in this particular case, I have been asking myself if they deserve to be blamed. I see the French-Canadians giving their money, without grumbling; they pay the taxes, they oversubscribe the Victory Loans, they give to the various drives, such as the Red Cross and the Russian Fund. I see them giving their time and work to war purposes; they work on their farms, knowing that a large part of their farm products will go to feed the populations of Great Britain and the armies; they work in the mines, knowing that most of the output goes to war industries; and in the lumbering industry, being told that wood is necessary for war works, for military needs.
>
> I see the French-Canadians working in the various war plants, even the French-Canadian women who have always been confined

to home work, are now engaged, in great numbers, in war industry. Both the men and women of the French language work well; they are skilful workers; there is little absenteeism among them; they work with a smile, not with grumbling.   Such activities might very well deserve a word of praise on the part of their English-speaking fellow countrymen, and sometimes I am inclined to think that they receive more bricks than flowers.

But, however important may be such a participation to the war effort, what to think about giving men to the various services of the Army?

Here, also, I see French-Canadians much abused. The French-Canadians have, indeed, volunteered for the Army, the Navy, the Air Force. They were at Hong Kong. They were at Dieppe, as in the previous war, they were at Vimy, Courcelette, Passchendaele. They are found at Halifax and Debert, at Sussex, at Valcartier and St. Jerome, at Petawawa and Trenton and Brockville. I have met them in the Western provinces, as far as Victoria and Nanaimo. They have the same warlike spirit as their English-speaking brothers.

Was it possible, for them [with their backgrounds and beliefs], to volunteer in equal numbers as the others did? They have been branded as "lotus-eaters, idlers, slackers, traitors, cowards, isolationists, pacifists, defeatists," by English newspapers from Halifax to Vancouver. Is is really the best method to handle even a difficult case? I would call it the "castor oil" method. Let us suppose the French-Canadians needed a purgation; it was quite possible to choose another drug, or at least to camouflage it with some coffee or orange juice.

Louis St. Laurent spoke twice to the Empire Club, first as a young lawyer in 1920, when he examined Quebec common law with only a brief reference to wartime differences between the two founding races. In March, 1953, as Prime Minister on the eve of another election (which he won against the Tories led by George Drew) he said: "One of the things which is uppermost in all of our minds in 1953 and which is exactly the opposite of any grim prospect is the Coronation of our beloved Queen and the belief of many of us that that event will serve to strengthen the members of our Commonwealth and the links which hold us all together."

In ten years, perhaps he could not have spoken so confidently about the bonding influence of the Queen. The Not-So-Quiet revolution, as historian Mason Wade terms the period leading up to the early 1960s, had produced the Front de Liberation Québecois with its terrorist activities that upset not only Quebec but the entire nation. Lester B. Pearson, newly in office as Prime Minister of a minority Liberal government, managed to avoid directly mentioning this at all in an October, 1963, Empire Club speech on "A National Purpose."

But Louis Robichaud, Premier of New Brunswick, came along a few weeks later:

Recent months have given an unwarranted amount of publicity to a small group of dissidents in the Province of Quebec who call themselves the F.L.Q. Their violent activities, which have been met with the full force of the law, are reminiscent of the few bomb-throwing Bolsheviks who were on the loose in the United States in the 1930s. They too passed away and the Confederacy of the United States of America managed to survive.

Shallow thinking in some quarters has led people to believe that perhaps the F.L.Q. is representative of the general attitude of our fellow Canadians in the Province of Quebec. That is as ridiculous as it would be to suggest that most Toronto business and professional men are secretly affiliated with the Cosa Nostra.

Extremism leads to violence. Violence and intimidation by force have no place in our Canada, whether they emanate from the F.L.Q., the S.I.U., or any other group that endeavours to undermine the authority of the people and the nation. What should be done about it?

Each of us is entitled to many rights and privileges as a Canadian citizen. Although we are quick to claim those rights at the least provocation, too many of us are reluctant to shoulder the equal weight of our responsibilities as Canadian citizens. Too many have come to regard citizenship as a spectator sport. Too few will accept that rights and privileges must always be accompanied by responsibilities in order to give them true value. . . .

This is, without doubt, a time when the voice of reason must be heard—not in angry argument—but in the calm and rational dialect of responsibility. That voice must become predominant in *every*

207

province of the nation—in order that extremists of *all* persuasions will come to know, once again, that true Canadianism can swallow them up in its strength and leave barely a trace of their passing.

Late in 1963, Peter C. Newman, then Ottawa editor of *Maclean's:*

I think it's dangerous to oversimplify the Quebec situation. One of the generally accepted facts about Quebec today, for instance, is that René Lévesque [then a Liberal cabinet minister] is an ardent separatist. I question this assumption. Of course Lévesque is a nationalist, but he's also (and I dislike the term) a leftist.

The important point here is that all of the separatist groups are right wing groups, and I for one don't believe that Lévesque could ever ally himself with such elements.

There had never been as much said, and said frankly, about Quebec as now was being heard almost weekly at the Empire Club. In February, 1964, Peter Nesbitt Thomson, 37, chairman and president of the Power Corporation of Canada Limited:

I want to speak to you today about something which is unique to Quebec and which, in its own way, is much more insidious than other and more obvious differences. This is the predisposition of some French-Canadians to blame English-speaking Canadians and, in particular, English-Canadian business, for the emergence of the separatist movement in Quebec. I want to suggest that, by their attitudes, some English-Canadians tacitly admit this is true, with the result that we now see more compatriots than we care to mention running about like scared rabbits, patting the French-Canadian on the back and telling him of the "bad deal" he has had.

It is not a situation easy to appraise dispassionately, but . . . I suggest to you that the separatists are wrong: that the fault lies as much in themselves as in anything the English have done or have not done with respect to French-Canadians. I feel that they are developing a philosophy based upon a fallacy. . . . Since when is accomplishment based on the language one speaks?

Yet we see today the spectacle of English businessmen surreptiously taking lessons in French to hide their ignorance of the language, to appease the French-Canadian hunger for equality of language. If more French-Canadians are bilingual than are English-Canadians it is to their credit, as it is to any nationality that encourages the growth of knowledge.

But to speak French to satisfy the nationalistic feelings of some French-Canadians is merely to cover up the hard, cold facts of life. Even if all the English-Canadians in Canada learned to speak French, what of the 180,000,000 English-speaking Americans who are our closest neighbours and with whom we have to do business?

It is the very opportunity and, if you will, insistence, to do as he chooses that, ironically, has harmed French-Canadian aspirations. Guarantees of the right to their own language in all French-Canadian institutions of learning, government and law have, in fact, contributed to the very economic dependency they are now bemoaning, for it is through their language that they separated themselves from the mainstream of progress and development in North America. I am not arguing that it should have been otherwise. I merely point out that exclusive development in French has been a greater inhibiting factor than any other. . .

The different cultures of Europe separated its peoples for more than two thousand years, yet trade has brought them together for the first time in history with the formation of the Common Market—to their mutual advantage. The cultures remain—but who would have suspected not so long ago that the German, the Frenchman, the Italian, would proudly say, "I am a European," as is the case today?

Perhaps that is why the attitude of the French-Canadian today is incomprehensible to many European businessmen. They see a revival here of the nationalism that kept them at one another's throats for so many years. While they can understand nationalistic feelings in under-developed countries, it is impossible to make them understand how this could happen in a free country and in a free society with our high standard of living. To the Americans this separatist feeling is even more incomprehensible. Yet it is gratifying to see that many French-Canadians deplore the separatist movement because they realize what an independent Quebec would mean, not only to the province itself, but to the rest of the world.

Yet, have enough voices been raised by our French-Canadian politicians and business leaders? Regrettably, the answer is an emphatic "No."

Some voices are now being raised, however, and in places where they will do the most good. More and more French-Canadians are coming to believe that their future lies, not in separatism, but in a revised Canadianism within a revised constitution that will give the French-Canadian the realization that he has the right to stand equally beside the millions of other Canadians of many origins who accept Canada as their own country.

This, I think we can say thankfully, is the attitude of the Lesage government. Only the other day the most verbally vigorous member of that government, Mr. René Lévesque, rejected separatism as a solution for Quebec. Not long ago Mr. Lévesque was edging toward separatism—at least he didn't reject it, if only as a last resort. Now he definitely excludes it. Mind you, neither he nor Mr. Lesage abandons any of Quebec's claims, but they seek to assert them through a co-operative federalism, and not by way of separatism.

Guy Favreau, federal Justice Minister, added this on March 5, 1964:

May I suggest, briefly, an effective way for English-speaking Canadians to develop a sympathy, if not an empathy, for their French-speaking partners—a way to place heart and mind on the wavelength of Quebec feelings? Let them play a little game called "English Canada"—pretending that English Canadians were, and remain, a minority partner in Confederation. Pretend that in 1867, their forefathers entered a pact which, in fact, guaranteed that English would be recognized and used in all federal fields, on an equal footing with the French.

Then consider the reaction when, over many decades, their letters to the federal government were answered in French . . . when, in phoning Ottawa, calls were taken by operators unable to answer in English . . . when, finally fed up, they visited their nation's capital and found that everyone—civil servants, messengers, elevator boys, waitresses—spoke French only and considered them impudent to expect service or information in other than French. In these circumstances, would our English-speaking Canadians have felt at home in Canada? Wouldn't they have reacted collectively to the indifference of the French majority and demanded that the use of two official languages, as spelled out in the Federal compact, be respected and applied?

This is the simple request of French-Canadians today.

In the autumn of 1964 Queen Elizabeth II visited Canada, after a summer in which Topic A across the country was: Is it safe for the Queen to go to Quebec? When she attended a state dinner at the Chateau Frontenac on a Saturday night early in October, bus loads of police armed with truncheons were parked quietly on nearby streets waiting for resumption of the protests that had marked the earlier course of the Royal visit that day. Riotous scenes in front of the hotel included clubbing, running, shouting of slogans, and enough arrests to bring the day's total to more than two dozen.

A few days later, Prime Minister Pearson at the Empire Club:

I am prompted on this occasion to make a few observances about the recent visit with which, because of my office, I was closely associated—a visit which gave me, as I am sure it gave millions of Canadians, the greatest of pleasure and a feeling of privilege for having the Queen in Canada. A visit which was initiated some two years ago, when it was thought fitting and indeed it was fitting to invite the Queen and her consort to come to Canada to take part in the celebration of events which I believe were worthy of the Royal Presence, the two Conferences of 1864, a hundred years ago, in Charlottetown and in Quebec City, which led to our Confederation.

The invitations were extended at a time when conditions were a little easier in one part of the country to be visited than they have been in recent months. And because of unhappy developments in recent months I, as the head of the government, was under some worry and anxiety and indeed, pressure—whether to put this off and advise that it should be cancelled or not. The pressure came from a few extremists in *one part of Canada*. And I believe, the more so now that the visit is over, that the purpose of their crude pressures—and I was subjected to them—the very purpose of this pressure was to get the government to cancel the visit. And that would have been a great triumph for them, if it had been cancelled, and would have given them a prestige and authority in their own area which they didn't deserve and shouldn't have.

These threats were made the more significant and, I believe, the more dangerous by the publicity that they received, some of which, I think, was excessive and exaggerated and was just what they wanted. And we read, all of us, phrases such as—"subjecting Her Majesty to awful risks," "slighting the danger," "Is Quebec to be another Dallas?" All that kind of thing which was bound to stir up public opinion, which was what they wanted—the extremists. And I reaffirm that to cancel the visit in the face of threats of that kind would have been their triumph and our humiliation.

It is a fact—an unhappy fact—that the alarm that was created by this agitation and these threats did require unprecedented security measures. This was the kind of situation that those responsible for security couldn't win. If the security was excessive they lost; and if the security was not adequate they lost.

It's interesting to me—I say this in no unduly critical way—but it's interesting to me to read that among those who are now complaining most vigorously against the excess of security measures, are those who in some cases brought about by their own words and their own actions a feeling of insecurity which made, if you like, the excessive security measures seem advisable. . . .

When I was in Charlottetown, where everything was very peaceful and serene, as you would expect on Prince Edward Island, especially on the occasion of a Royal visit, there were a great many reporters there, and of course some of them came from outside the country. And those from outside the country particularly, I think, had been perhaps misled a bit by some of the publicity they read in their own countries, and a Canadian columnist was down there—and some of you may have read his column—writing on the eve of the visit had this to say: "One American reporter, captivated by the Island's serenity, was heard to comment that if he wrote about things as they actually are on the eve of the visit his editors wouldn't believe it, much less print it. So he was trying to get himself into the mood to write a tense piece and finally he talked himself into it."

The Royal visit gave us an opportunity, an opportunity of which we will take advantage, unanimously, I believe, in the House of Commons, by resolution. It gave us an opportunity to express the loyalty, the affection and the respect of all true Canadians for the person and the office of Her Majesty. But it also underlined in a particularly unhappy way—indeed a humiliating way—that there is a small minority in one part of Canada that would divide and destroy our nation. This minority, this small minority, violent and provocative minority, must be overwhelmed by the expressed and demonstrated loyalty of Canadians, English-speaking and French-speaking, to Canada, to its institutions of which the monarchy is a cherished and honoured part, and to its unity.

The problem of unity has now been dramatically put before us and it must be solved. And in solving it, the mass of the people must not be blackmailed or held for ransom by any small and violent minority. I firmly believe and I know you will join me in this belief, that such a small minority does not express the views of the people of the Province in which it is centred.

Let me read you, and you will be surprised at me using this gentleman as an authority for the arguments I am trying to make. Let me read you what the leader of the Creditistes, Mr. Réal Caouette, said yesterday in the House of Commons. And Mr. Caouette will never be accused of slavish support for the British connection or for the institutions we inherited from that connection or thought to be anything but a strong Quebec and French-speaking nationalist.

But Mr. Caouette said this, and I am quoting only one or two sentences from what he said. "Her Majesty," said Mr. Caouette, "being a guest of the Quebec government, no one has the right to insult her, even under the guise of separatism. The freedom, or licence, demanded by some of our fellow citizens would surely be the last thing that they would grant to others if they were in power." And, he went on: "Her Majesty is for us"—this is Mr. Caouette speaking—"Her Majesty is for us a symbol of a way of life which enabled us to grow by our own means according to our own wishes. If it be true that unity is strength, it is time for us to achieve it in mutual respect. And we French-Canadians of the Province of Quebec have undeniable rights, but in addition to those rights, which we claim, we also have duties to fulfil toward ourselves and others. It is not in anarchy that we will succeed, but in mutual trust and understanding."

I think those words of Mr. Caouette are abundant justification for the Royal visit in spite of some of the unhappy episodes that took place on certain occasions.

It seemed to many that this psychological moment in Canadian history demanded a leader whose life had been, however unconsciously, perfectly shaped for the occasion. In 1968, masses of Canadians believed the moment indeed had thrown up such a man: Pierre Trudeau, a man who merited the trust of both Canadian cultures. And yet . . .

In 1969 Claude Ryan, publisher of *Le Devoir* and known as one of Quebec's strongest moderate voices (still nearly a decade from agreeing to lead the Quebec Liberal party against the by then separatism-aimed government of René Lévesque's Parti Québecois) spoke to the Empire Club on ''The Unwritten Laws of Quebec's Politics.'' It stands ten years later as a valid political primer on the subject. At the time, the Quebec government was Union Nationale, under Premier Jean-Jacques Bertrand:

When I joined *Le Devoir* in 1962 Mr. Filion, the then publisher of the paper, told me that they had only one reservation about their new editorial writer and that I probably had in turn one reservation about the leadership of *Le Devoir*. ''You probably feel,'' said Mr. Filion, ''that we are too nationalistically inclined. We feel in turn that you are not enough of a nationalist to be a fully reliable associate editor.'' And he concluded wisely, ''Let us hope that the cross-fertilization of the two approaches may help produce something better in the years ahead.''

The first thing I have learned in my job is that provincial politics are far more vital to Quebeckers than they are to Canadians residing in other provinces. The people of New Brunswick, Ontario and Alberta are deeply attached to their respective provinces. But they all agree that they have one national government located in Ottawa and that the latter must be considered as the senior, more important government.

I was reading in the Toronto papers yesterday about Mr. Robarts hinting that after all the troubles he has had recently with it, he might as well turn medicare over to the federal government. Such words would be sheer political heresy in Quebec, even if they were meant as a joke.

The last one hundred years have taught Quebeckers that the Government of Quebec is the only one that they can hope to control in any stable and unequivocal way. It is the only one which they have been able to mould in line with their temperament and natural inclinations. It is the only one which they can trust one hundred per cent to defend their fundamental cultural interests in times of acute crisis and misunderstanding.

The late Daniel Johnson used to say that Quebec is the national home of French-Canadians and that the Government of Quebec must be considered in consequence as the national government of the French-Canadian people.

There was some exaggeration, some rhetorical exaggeration, in that statement. But I wish you to believe that it appealed to a deeply-rooted dimension of the French-Canadian political consciousness and that Mr. Johnson never encountered any serious trouble in Quebec for having made it.

This helps us understand that the political phenomena which we have observed in the last decade, in particular the emergence of political separatism in the Province of Quebec, have deeper roots in the political psychology of Quebeckers than has, for instance, the separatism that has emerged of late in the western provinces.

I used to say before I joined *Le Devoir* that political separatism was as remote from the French-Canadian mentality as the thought of an eventual reunion with France. I would now qualify this statement by saying that French-Canadians for practical reasons would not now opt for separation but that they would probably refuse to close the door to that option for the future.

The Prime Minister of Quebec is in a very real sense the grass-roots leader of French-Canadians in the political arena. French-Canadians will admire and support the one among them who has enough stature to be sought and accepted as Prime Minister of the whole of Canada.

But they also remember when they study history the rather bitter ending of two previous experiences of the same nature. And I would gamble that, barring grave international circumstances which would

215

momentarily supersede domestic considerations, they would, in the eventuality of an open conflict between Quebec and Ottawa, give their natural preference to the leadership offered to them by the Prime Minister of Quebec.

This explains the vital importance which Quebeckers attach to their provincial politics. For many of them provincial politics is the only politics which they understand and love. It is the only politics which makes them feel completely and irrevocably involved. Quebeckers, when they go to the polls, are mindful, like voters in all parts of the world, about taxes, economic development, social services, and the quality of education. But they also look with great attention to the ability of each party leader to stand up to the Ottawa Government in defence of the so-called prerogatives of Quebec.

Under the late Maurice Duplessis this unwritten law of our politics had been given a rather negative interpretation. Duplessis was a staunch defender of Quebec's autonomy against what he called the "encroachments of Ottawa." It was Mr. Lesage's great contribution to have given this concept a dynamic meaning, and to have turned it into an instrument for gaining important concessions from Ottawa and for implementing key reforms at home.

Need I underline also that this concept of autonomy interpreted in a dynamic way, if pursued as an end in itself, can only lead to the logical conclusion [separation] which men like Lévesque and Parizeau have espoused? The responsibility of Quebec's leaders at this juncture is particularly great. They are playing with dynamite all the time. And I am afraid that there is no escape from this game except in the positive recognition of the forces which are at work in their people, and in a deliberate effort on their part to bring the people to a higher and more exacting vision of thier future than that which is conveyed by narrow nationalism.

Another aspect of Quebec's politics is the great importance which French-Canadian voters attach to the personalities of the leaders. The most successful men of the last twenty-five years in Quebec's political life have been Maurice Duplessis, Jean Lesage, Daniel Johnson, Jean Drapeau, Lucien Saulnier and Pierre Elliott Trudeau.

You will easily grant that each of those men had a strong personality. But each was also, in his own way, a moderate; that is to say, a man with no rigidly preconceived dogmas as to how problems should be solved.

In Trudeau's case, for instance, I can say that thousands of voters who would have disapproved of many of his statements and attitudes if they had come from a different leader were swayed to his cause by his overwhelming personality.

This factor makes the next provincial election a particularly intriguing one. Of the three leaders who will be facing the voters the only one who has a strong, established personality in the eyes of the public is René Lévesque. Both Messrs. Bertrand [the premier then] and Bourassa have yet to assert themselves in this respect. They are both respected men. But they have not yet established themselves in the minds of the people as strong men who can lead in difficult moments.

In Mr. Lévesque's case his basic political option will most probably work against him, because the people also expect of their leader that in addition to being personally strong he should represent a position which is closer to a balanced view of reality than the one which is presented at the moment by Mr. Lévesque and his supporters.

How about the ethnic and the class factors in Quebec's politics? I should like to submit a couple of observations in this respect.

The National Union Party gained power in 1966 with only 41% of the total vote [beating] the Liberals, with 47% of the vote. To a journalist who was asking him a question about this, the late Daniel Johnson made this significant reply: "It is true that the English and the Jews voted overwhelmingly for the Liberals; but my party won a solid majority with the French-Canadian voters."

This factor contributed to give the Johnson Government a moral legitimacy which escaped the attention of superficial observers.

The truth is, Mr. Chairman, that English-speaking voters behave in provincial elections in Quebec almost exactly like their French-speaking counterparts do in federal elections; with the only qualification that the impact of their votes is far less preponderant in determining the results of Quebec's elections than it has been for a couple of generations in helping determine the results of federal elections.

In the next election the Liberals will lose a certain proportion of this support to Lévesque's party because a large segment of the student body and the important new intellectual class will support Le Parti Québecois, while they supported the Liberals in 1960 and in 1962. An indefinable proportion of the working people may be tempted to shift their allegiance to the Creditistes of Réal Caouette. And this would be a loss for the National Union.

This brings us to an additional factor: the role of third parties in Quebec elections. In 1966 two separatist parties were in the race, Le Rassemblement pour L'Independence Nationale and Le Ralliement Nationale.

Together these two parties got about 12% of the vote, but the RIN—that was Bourgault's party—whose strength was largely concentrated in the urban areas was very probably instrumental in causing the defeat of at least ten Liberal candidates.

Mr. Lesage had dismissed Bourgault's party as a non-entity a few weeks before the election. He was given four painful years in which to swallow back these presumptuous words which he had uttered during the electoral campaign.

On the basis of these facts it becomes extremely difficult to predict what will happen next time. It is very plausible that with a strong leader like Lévesque at the head of the "sovereignist" party, the voting age having been lowered to eighteen years, with the widely-spread discontent in connection with economic uneasiness and unemployment—it is very plausible that Le Parti Québecois should now show respectable strength.

In only one Quebec election since over thirty-five years has the impact of federal leaders been directly felt. That was in 1939 when the financial interests of Montreal made an alliance with the federal Liberals in order to get rid of Duplessis. The provincial Liberals had to pay dearly for that artificial triumph which brought Godbout to power in 1939. And they were left in the wilderness of opposition for sixteen years, between 1944 and 1960, in order that they should learn that law of Quebec's politics that they had forgotten.

They learned during those years that they cannot hope to win the confidence of the Quebec voters in the provincial field unless they can come up with a programme and a leadership that are solidly and predominantly Quebec in their orientation.

Nothing points at the moment to any direct intervention on the part of the federal Liberals in the forthcoming election. Mr. Trudeau has stated several times that he would not hesitate to step into the picture if he felt that separatism had become a central and threatening issue during the campaign. He apparently feels for the moment that the two leading parties do not pose such a problem and that Mr. Lévesque's party has very little chance of making serious inroads with the Quebec voters in the next election.

This may be taken to mean that the next election might not be, after all, as decisive as some people have suggested. It might mean that the unwritten laws which have just been evoked may continue to dominate Quebec's politics for at least another decade.

On Nov. 15, 1976, the Parti Québecois came to power in Quebec. Three days later René Lévesque was invited to speak at the Empire Club at a date of his choosing. He chose to send, instead, Jacques Parizeau, his Minister of Finance and of Revenue, who spoke on March 17, 1977:

There have been an incredible number of diagnoses of the electoral victory won by the Parti Québecois and of the meaning of that victory. It is not a simple matter. The idea and the goal of political independence are fairly recent in Quebec. During the early 1960s, at a time when Mr. Jean Lesage was making profound inroads into the powers and the resources of the central government, the independence movement, while very vocal, was in fact limited to groups. In 1966, two separatist political parties fought the election and while (not attracting a substantial vote themselves), they were instrumental in Mr. Daniel Johnson's victory. However, it is only in 1970 that the Parti Québecois took part in an election, and at one blow got 23% of the vote. I think all commentators were aware that the independence of Quebec was at the very centre of that election. At the next one, in 1973, the campaign was run essentially on the economic consequences of independence. The P.Q. got 31% of the vote. Then came the election of 1976.

Present interpretations would have it that the independence of Quebec was not the main issue. It is true, of course, that as far as the Parti Québecois was concerned, the issue of good government took precedence, and the achievement of independence was directly linked to a referendum. This, however, did not impress the government of the day. Its campaign was squarely built around the theme of "No to Separatism." And it was a washout. If some people find today some consolation in the thought that pro-separatists did not win, they must also recognize that anti-separatists quite explicitly lost.

In fact, this kind of analysis is pretty futile. The Parti Québecois is linked to the idea of independence in the minds of all. Its objective has not changed now that it's in power. Something that started more than fifteen years ago is now coming slowly to fruition.

Mr. Parizeau's tone was that the debate was over, Quebec was on the last lap of a long struggle toward independence. Premier William Davis of Ontario followed Mr. Parizeau to the Empire Club. His message was a variation of the sports colloquialism, "It ain't over until it's over":

The government of the province of Quebec, as it is now constituted, is committed to the independence of that province from Canada and to some economic association with this country thereafter. Setting aside the road blocks to independence with which the government of Quebec has itself admitted it must be prepared to deal, I think it is important that we clearly understand how far Canadians, both as individuals and as participants in the national way of life, are prepared to go in the debate and the dialogue in which we will be engaged for some time to come.

I have said this in Quebec and I said this in the Legislature of our province on Monday night and I say it again to you today.

As long as all those involved in the debate are trying to find a creative, just, and viable resolution of the problem, I believe that fair-mindedness, and a genuine spirit of understanding will prevail. As soon, however, as doors are closed, debates are ended and discussions are terminated, those who are responsible for that termination and that closing off of options would be naive to believe that the same spirit of understanding will continue thereafter.

In clear terms that means that it would be absolutely foolhardy for the government of Quebec to believe that it could have both independence and economic association with the rest of Canada.

Moreover, I would not be prepared to commit the government of this province, and the people whom we serve, to that kind of understanding with any government.

In this regard, I took particular offence, and said so when I went to the province of Quebec, at the tenor and thrust of the address offered to you by the Minister of Finance of Quebec. I asked both rhetorically and directly, who is he? and for that matter who is anyone? to say to the people of this country, to say to you, to say to me, to say to *any* Canadian that the debate is over, the discussions have ended, the time for negotiation has passed?

CHAPTER 10

The Canadians

Back in the Twenties, decades before CanLit, when English-speaking Canadians were nurtured on imported romance à la Scott and Tennyson and Presbyterian clergyman Charles William Gordon's virtuously violent adventures, by-lined Ralph Connor, were bestsellers, the contribution of certain New Canadians—Laura Goodman Salverson in particular— to Canadian letters was lauded by John Murray Gibbon of Montreal. His 1923 speech was subtitled "European Seeds in the Canadian Garden." It was a remarkable fact, he said, that one of the most outstanding books in the English language on the fall lists—Salverson's *The Viking Heart*—was written by an author (he didn't note her sex) whose mother tongue was Icelandic.

A few years later, Gibbon traced a pervasive cultural contribution, in "The Music of the People":

I find that many people here in Canada think of folksong as something remote and crude, tunes which are sung only by very elderly people on farms over in Europe, and if they are sung in Canada at all, it is only by the habitants in French Canada.

. . . Let me tell you a story about a group of German settlers near Winnipeg. Eighteen months ago I was helping to organize a New

Canadian Folkmusic Festival at Winnipeg, the object of which was to demonstrate to Anglo-Canadians in the West the wealth and charm of the folkmusic brought to Canada by the Continental Europeans. In the preliminary organization no place had been kept for the Germans, but I found that about a year before a colony of German immigrants from the Black Forest had settled about thirty miles from Winnipeg at a place appropriately called "Little Britain." The leader of this colony was a Dr. Schneider, formerly a lawyer, assisted by his wife, a doctor of medicine. When I suggested that they should present a group of German folksongs, they hesitated. "We were fighting you ten years ago," said Dr. Schneider, "we might not be welcome." When I assured him that we would not invite them if we did not want them, he consulted Frau Doctor Schneider, who said, "what do you mean by folk-song? I don't think we have any." Now, I happened to have lived at one time in the Black Forest, and had learned there some of their songs, so I hummed over one called "Jetzt geh' i ans Brunnele," and asked her if she knew that. "Sure I do," she answered. Then I hummed over another called "Muss i' denn, muss i' denn." At that she laughed and said, "that's the song we sang at Freiburg when we got on the train to come to Canada." Now this song, "Muss i' denn," is a parting song—it tells the story of a young fellow leaving the village for the town. The girl he leaves behind him is afraid that he will lose his heart to the girls in town and forget her, but he assures her that he will come back again safe and sound in heart and will not forget her. You can see why these simple Black Forest people sang this song as they got on the train for Canada.

To make a long story short, they came to our Festival, fifteen of them, driving in in their farm truck, and with their simple songs, sung with such evident sincerity, and with their quaint country dances, they completely captivated their audience. [Applause]

. . . And I wish you could have heard the Icelandic Choir with their soft mellow voices in folksongs from their little northern island—an island, by the way, which set up a Parliament a thousand years ago, and which will celebrate the millenium of that Parliament next year. I wish you could have seen the grace and charm of the Swedish dancers, who had one dance that was a students' dance dating from the time of Gustavus Adolphus, three hundred years ago. I wish that your Mendelssohn Choir could have heard the two Ukrainian Choirs from Winnipeg and Saskatoon, singing the most difficult choruses from memory, without a sheet of music in front of them. I wish you could have seen and heard the Gaelic folk play produced by Hebrideans of Vancouver.

The vigorous paintings of the Group of Seven (Tom Thomson, who died in 1917, three years before the group adopted its name; A. Y. Jackson; Lawren Harris; J. E. H. MacDonald; Arthur Lismer; Frank Carmichael; Frank Johnston; and Frederick Varley), essentially romantic but intensely nationalistic in their mainspring, encountered some well-bred resistance. Jackson, however, was a Royal Canadian Academician by 1925, when he joined in debate with Wyly Grier, a fellow Academician but no kindred spirit. Grier spoke first:

Now, it is not for me to say that no artists should form themselves into groups. I think groups should be permitted to be formed as often as artists please. Groups have their dangers, and I have seen many groups wax, wane and die. One of the main reasons for their death is that they all subscribed to some kind of central doctrine which resulted in their painting like one another, and when they recognized that, themselves, they broke up. Some of those groups might be mentioned—the Glasgow Group of 1890, known as the "Glasgow School," who were considered wild revolutionaries in their day. I knew pretty intimately, also, the Newlyn Group. These are instances of the advisability of forming groups because they stimulate art considerably when they are successful. We had a Canadian group, called the Canadian Club, which selected from among the artists of Canada those who were most affected by the traditions of Europe. I thought that was something that didn't help them. They also included in membership a number of laymen who were collectors and connoisseurs of a sort, but contact with that particular kind of individual was not helpful to artists, and I think that was one reason for their early decease. I leave it to Mr. Jackson to set forth the aims and point of view of the Group of Seven, but I take it upon myself to console their hostile critics with this thought—that the modernist manifestations of art in Europe have been very much more terrible than anything the Group of Seven have given us. [Laughter]

I have . . . modernist slides as to which, after a couple of years' experiment, I have never decided which was right side up. They are the despair of the lantern operator.

Some Americans have been greatly influenced by the European modernists. But signs of decadence are not much in evidence amongst the pictures of this continent. The country is too healthy. The Group of Seven are out-of-doors men. Most of our artists are out-of-doors men. This works for freshness, not decadence. The broad healthy brine of the Atlantic keeps us pretty deaf as to what is going on in Europe, and it is a very good thing for us.

Before I sit down I am going to give a word of admonition to our friends of the Group of Seven. They continually go further north. They have deserted the Georgian Bay, and I dare say they will emerge at the North Pole some day and give us a more simple type of landscape. They may even reproduce that solitary tree which seems to be their obsession today, but I hope that the public schools will have extended such a degree of education amongst the public in general that they will not mistake that solitary tree for the North Pole itself. [Laughter]

But to be more constructive in my admonition, I invite the Group of Seven to ponder upon this thought, that it is not the only way to be intensely Canadian in our painting to go to remote parts of the earth. There are some people of Canada who have never been far away from the rural districts of Ontario, and Heaven knows we have made Ontario domesticated and rural at the expense of considerable labour and a great deal of sweat; so then when the Group went first to Algonquin Park and then to Georgian Bay and are now verging towards Abitibi and the North Pole, they are able to tell us that Canada is only a God-forsaken country which is almost featureless. I would say that that man should be Canadian in his painting who paints the old paintless barns of Ontario, [Hear, hear] who paints the rural things of the farmyard, the things we are accustomed to, and who makes that beautiful difference which should exist between the barnyard of Canada and the barnyard of Holland or England. When we get that we will class the painter as being truly Canadian. [Applause]

Jackson's rebuttal:

After Mr. Grier's polished periods I feel as if I had been given a pair of crutches and told to overtake Nurmi. There are a great many people interested in Canadian art today—more than ever before. That interest is sometimes like that of the old lady who was hurrying rapidly out of one of our Group exhibitions, and when asked why she was in such a hurry she explained, "I hate these pictures, but I am afraid if I stay around here longer I am going to like them." [Laughter]

Today art is becoming rather a fashionable and well-organized commerce which is parading itself as culture, when art should be to us an expression of emotion. So the academic bodies, instead of looking forward, look backwards; and as Mr. Grier and I are both Academicians I can say that without hurting his feelings at all. But the academic bodies rush forward with their heads turned backwards to get direction. [Laughter] Now, Canadians are not much good at looking backwards; it hurts their necks; so we are going forward, and we are not going to sell our souls to dealers, either. There has been nothing in Canadian art at all on the material side, so, as there was no way for us to go forward with the academic element, and we could not work with the dealers, we took inspiration from Marshal Foch when he said, "My right wing is pressed back, and my left wing is pressed back; I am attacking in the centre." [Laughter]

There seems to be a certain amount of confusion in regard to the modern movement in art. We are told that we are copyists and futurists, and theories or forms of modern art in Europe are attached to us; but really the modern movement in Canada has been mostly a matter of interpreting our background. That is a fairly big proposition, as Mr. Grier has said, and we are perhaps going a little too far north. Well, after we have combed the country once we are going to start over again. [Laughter] Mr. Grier regrets our leaving the barnyard. Well there are about eighty painters in Canada, and there are only six in the Group of Seven. [Laughter]

As a student in Montreal, I remember how little faith there was in any kind of Canadian art, one authority making the statement that, "Not only was there no Canadian art but there never would be any," and such remarks were too common to cause any comment.

Before the expensive importations, the native artist had to hold

227

his breath and feign wonder. It was boasted in Montreal that more Dutch art was sold there than in any other city on this continent. Dutch pictures became a symbol of social position and wealth. It was also whispered that they were a sound investment. They collected them like cigarette cards. You had to complete your set. [Laughter] One would say to another, "Oh I see you have not a De Bock yet," "No, have you your Blommers?" The houses bulged with cows, old women peeling potatoes, and windmills. [Laughter] If you were a millionaire, you bought the Maris Brothers and Israels. If you were poor, and had only half a million, there were Dutchmen to cater to your humbler circumstances. Art in Canada meant a cow or a windmill. They were grey, mild, inoffensive things compared with the work of the "Group of Seven" [Laughter] and when surrounded by heavy gold frames covered with plate glass and a spotlight placed over them, they looked expensive. [Laughter]

When one considers that Degas, Whistler, Monet and many other famous artists' works could have been procured at that time for next to nothing, our connoisseurs with a few exceptions were a rather blind outfit with a kind of herd instinct in collecting.

But the pioneer spirit in this country is second nature. We have had to find our own way of doing almost everything and, while we may admire the way they do things in Europe, we realize our way is the way for us [Hear, hear] and it was obvious that Canadian artists were not going to stand around forever in humble admiration while our bankers turned the spotlights on their cows. [Laughter]

Our atmosphere was clear and sharp, our colours were bright,— crude if you will. The villages were scattered and the landscape untidy and ragged as you went north—swampy, rocky, wolf-ridden, burnt and scuttled country with rivers and lakes scattered all through it, and on top of this variety there were four changes of scenery such as they never know in Europe. In summer it was green, raw greens all in a tangle; in autumn it flamed with red and gold; in winter it was wrapped in a blanket of dazzling snow, and in the springtime it roared with running waters and surged with new life, and our artists were advised to go to Europe and paint *smelly canals*. [Laughter] We argued that if a cow could stay in the drawing room, then why couldn't a bull moose?

Anyway, the artist goes where the spirit moves him, and artists

canoed and camped all over Northern Ontario. If we chose Georgian
Bay and Northern Ontario, it was not that we did not realize the
beauty of other parts of Canada. It was the most accessible country.
Why did we not do pastorals? One reason is that the supply was
already greater than the demand; the other, that the farmer is clutter-
ing up his whole place with barbed wire, concrete silos, milking
machines, and other modern farm machinery, so that the artist is
crowded out. [Laughter]

I got in touch with the modern group up here—MacDonald and
Harris, Beatty, Hemming and Thomson, and decided to leave
Montreal. We started what was first called the "Hot Mush School."
Thomson was only beginning at that time, but in four years he had
become a great painter. He is the heroic figure in Canadian art,
[Applause] a strange fusion of gentleness and strength. He ranged
the north country like an Indian, alone most of the time, and found
beauty in it that haunts one.

Of business he knew nothing. His first cheque was on the Bank of
Commerce so he went to the Bloor and Yonge branch to have it
cashed. "You will have to be identified," they told him. He got sore
and went to the College and Yonge branch. "You'll have to be
identified," they told him again. And Thomson said "Go to hell,"
and tore it up. Another time up north he was out of money and wired
down to a bank where he had a small savings account to send him
some. He got a wire back, "We can't send money on an open
telegram," and Thomson, bewildered, wired back, "Send it on a
closed one." [Laughter] Thomson has gone, but he left us conscious
of the sombre beauty of the north land that few people have realized.
[Applause] . .

There are lots of people who can give an impetus to creating
things Canadian in jewelry, textiles, wall-papers and innumerable
things, but they say it won't pay. Well a few artists, with no capital
and a few friends started a movement which the British press says
breathes the spirit of Canada, and not one of them asked if it would
pay. [Hear, hear] I have been asked how do I know ours to be the
Canadian spirit in art. I may say it is spiritual because it's been
clubbed ever since it started, and it's Canadian because it can't be
killed.

Now, a last word on modern Canadian art, because tomorrow we shall all be academic. When the last cow is taken from the drawing room and the walls are alive with red maple, yellow birch, blue lakes and sparkling snow-scapes, I can hear the young modern painter up north say to his pal, "There's the trail that those old academic Johnnies, the Group of Seven, blazed." [Laughter and applause]

The expatriate writer Arthur Stringer, about the state of the other Canadian arts, and artists, in 1932:

My literary career really began in the city of Toronto, for it was here, with the simple faith of the young, I took a sheaf of manuscripts to a sad-eyed editor and asked him why I could not sell them, what was the matter with them. And that sad-eyed old editor looked them over, and then sat back in his chair. "There is an idea or two here, Stringer," he said, "but ideas, you know, are like whiskey—they should be left to ripen in the wood."[Laughter]—"So what I advise you, Stringer, is really for quite a long while to keep these ideas in your head." [Laughter]

This Dominion of ours in the earlier days of Robert Barr did not spend much money on her authors. She dud not spend much time on them either. She had enough troubles, and those authors, if they wanted to remain authors, had to look for markets outside their native country. For you know, no matter how romantic we may be about the rights of the author, the aesthetic equipment is not always an assurance of commercial prosperity or earthly well being, which recalls to me the story of the huge negro who had been tried for a particularly atrocious crime. The presiding judge asked him if before the execution of the sentence he had anything to say, where-upon he replied: "Yas sir, I thinks I has, I has just one thing to say—if youse hangs me, judge, youse hangs the best singer in all Tennessee." [Laughter] I recall how some cynical Demosthenes of the daily press once put the rhetorical question—I do not know whether it was Hector Charlesworth or not—Where are our Canadian poets? And a cynical Toronto editor said: "On the train to New York." [Laughter]

Now, it seems at first almost a fine thing to have a foreign metropolis to send your poets and authors to. . . . This young nation of ours did not need to bother much about its authors and artists.

When they got too hungry at home we shipped them away to some other country, and when we put down the hammer and the axe and forgot about ploughs and power plants and stood back from our work and wondered what it was all about, and nursed a human-enough hunger, not only for a little entertainment but also for a little enlightening as to what we were really heading for, we remembered that we had a big and benevolent neighbour right beside us who could give us all the ready-made amusement we wanted, and it looked like a lucky break to have a kind-hearted Uncle Sam ready to shovel out to us all the motion pictures and the theatrical entertainment and the *Saturday Evening Post* that we seemed to need. But it has flaws, insidious drawbacks—it has the defect of being a foreign product. It leaves us passive and subservient to something outside our own experience. It always fails to express our nationality, but it carries with it a persistent tendency to Americanize public sentiment, to cram down Canadian throats a type of character with which the Canadian does not sympathize and to impose upon Canadian youth an attitude, a rather Smart-Aleck attitude, towards both language and life. It involves the continuous danger of denationalization. It leaves us parasites and passive in a most vital cultural issue.

Canada, I am told, is proud of her authors and proud of her poets, though on more than one occasion, after bringing out a book, I stopped to wonder why pride should so express itself in wallops where it hurts most, but we now have a Canadian Authors Association and some magazines of our own, and an effort is being made to keep the Canadian author at home and not send himself across the line to luxuriate in the abysmal rootlessness of the expatriate. In the things of the mind as in the things of commerce an effort is being made to encourage and to justify a demand for the made-in-Canada label. You will become more proudly and more passionately Canadian. You are looking for something of your own, racy of the soil—something with the tang of Maple sap in it, something sinewed with the strength of the North.

In so far as this country is alert and aspiring she must be vocal and self-expressing. It is an inside job, and your authors themselves want something more than pink teas and a pat on the back and that parochialism which is proud of second best work, just because it is a local product. They want a market, because unless you belong to today you have a slim chance of belonging to tomorrow. They want a working wage. They want wool enough to cover their backs, no matter how they keep humping to cover themselves with glory, but before they can do that they must be recognized as part of your national life. They must be given a new and adequate copyright law to begin with. Their property rights must be defined and respected, and they must be regarded as the abstracts and brief chronicles of their times, and after your death better have a bad epitaph than their ill report. And since the finite word, which is also the finished word, must come from these same chroniclers, lean the closer to those who are giving their lives to express what they live and know, whether they speak in stone or form or phrase—lean closer if they are the interpreters of your soul, and in showing them you have a soul you will create not only an art and a literature of your own but an audience to breathe back into that art and that literature the breath of national life.

A decade and a half later, Arthur Stringer came back, to laud the "literary renascence" in Canada—but descry the way so many Canadians in the arts were among the first and most eloquent to take to the public platforms and claim that there was nobody here but us mice:

You know, I'm at last beginning to understand why the beaver is our national emblem. I thought, once, it was due to the industriousness of what had been designated as merely an amplified rat. But I was wrong there. For outside its industry the beaver has one peculiar and distinguishing trait. That peculiarity stems from the conviction that its home isn't habitable until it has been well dammed. And recent events persuade me the Canadian isn't happy in his home until he sees it well damned. It seems to be done mostly by our authors, authors who ought to be the mouthpiece of a magnificent young country but turn out to be merely exponents of its misery.

For only a couple of months ago, I find, Robertson Davies described Canada as a dull, dry desert and Canadians as dull and stodgy people . . . he contended (that) the only way to keep everyone from going nuts would be to paint more pictures and act in more Little Theatres and lilt more lyrics. We must wipe out that deadly conservatism of ours, and get more abandoned. And regeneration

232

may come, apparently, when we all get busy dancing in the streets.

Then not so long ago Hugh MacLennan—and this hurts because Hugh is accepted as an astute interpreter of Canadian life—told us how dull we Canadians are. We were not only living in a reign of dullness but in art and literature we were doing mighty little that interested the outside world. And due to that dullness, he claimed, thousands of young Canadians were becoming so fed up with the emotional caution of their elders that they were leaving Canada in droves.

But that's not all. Last month you had Merrill Denison here telling you how apathetic Canada was towards fine arts . . . then a few days later Will Bird proclaimed in Ottawa that Canadians were afraid to be themselves. He accused them of deferring pathetically to foreign opinion and showing a preference for magazines and books not made in Canada. We were turning, he claimed, into a nation of copy cats. And just about the same time James O'Connor intimated in the Victoria *Colonist* that the trouble with our native book-market would end when the Canadian author woke up and wrote books worth buying.

It's a sad state of affairs, about as energizing as having your doctor put away his stethoscope and telling you you'd be a dead man before the end of the week. I can't understand, as I glance around me, how you all look so happy. It leaves me wondering why you don't all emulate the lemmings of Norway and swarm down to the Bay and jump in. It leaves me puzzled that so poor a place as Canada could produce an Osler and a Banting and a Graham Bell and a Vincent Massey, could give birth to a Roberts and a Carman and a Lampman, and a half a hundred others who are today giving voice to our national aspirations and making us known both to ourselves and the outer world. And it's about time our homemade Jeremiahs lost a little of their gloom and gave up their job of selling Canada short.

It's time for a change. And the change is taking place. It has, in fact, already taken place. Yankee editors and publishers now send talent scouts into this Dominion of ink-slingers to round up authors of promise before they're tied up with Toronto publishing houses. Half a century ago those authors had to migrate or go hungry, standing as they did between the devil of impecuniosity and the deep sea of emigration. But the tide has turned. The Canadian writer no

233

longer needs to join that League of Fallen Maple Leaves whose members had to struggle along by what the circus people call "Riding Roman," with one foot planted on the Canadian beaver and his other foot on the American eagle. He can give up that sort of straddling. For today he finds himself face to face with a literary renascence, or, rather, a literary flowering, in many ways as stirring and as vital as Ireland knew half a century ago with its Celtic Revival. His country has emerged from that pioneer state in which Earl Grey said it was too busy with the plough and the axe to give much time to the pen. We have acquired a national spirit, and a knowledge of our northland vigour, and a pride in the strength of our Dominion that stretches from sea to sea. Our country has a wide beauty all its own. It has natural grandeurs that give creative impulse to the author, just as the author in turn must give those grandeurs new richness by making them recognizable. He is beginning to learn how deep the grass-roots go, how much the homeland background colours and helps to create what he craves to express.

Natural grandeurs? New richness? How deep the grass-roots go. . . . Arthur Erickson, the B.C.-born and world-renowned architect, on another part of the landscape, in 1967:

God was showing Man all the wonders of the world. But Man was not very enthusiastic. He showed him Niagara Falls, he showed him the great forests, the great canyons, the highest mountains, depths of the sea and so on. But Man only yawned until finally God became very angry and said, "Man, you can go to Hell," and so he condemned him to live the rest of his life in the contemporary apartment building.

Finally, four writers commenting on their craft. In 1954, Luella Creighton and Pierre Berton appeared at the same head table; Berton not widely known at the time. Mrs. Creighton, author of the critically acclaimed *High Bright Buggy Wheels,* published in 1951:

It is with extraordinary diffidence that I face an audience like this, with any sort of comments I may have to make on writing and fiction. . . . However, you can't write even two novels without coming to some sort of conclusions as to what it is that makes the writer operate when he is concerned with purely imaginative fiction, by which I don't mean stories about atom bombs, space ships, and so forth. As far as I know, even they might be old-fashioned by now. Nor do I mean the kind of fiction based on solid historic research. The only kind of fiction I know anything about is the kind which springs from the necessity of the author just merely to tell a story. The writer of this kind of fiction is not interested in social reform. He does not care whether the black man can live with the white man, whether the Americans can live with the Canadians or whether our educational system is bad. Social reform is nothing whatever of his concern. He is a person who, probably as much as anything, is a register of feeling, and he is also a person who is subject to what I can only think of as a minor, interior explosion of comprehension. Of course everybody is subject to this kind of thing, but the man who is going to do the writing goes a little farther than that and he is absolutely impelled to communicate to somebody the impression he has got.

Stephen Leacock who, to my mind, has done the best writing of any Canadian, used to say to people who asked, "Is it hard to write a book?" "Oh, no, it is very simple; all you do is to take a pencil and paper and you put down what occurs. The only hard part is the occurring."

Pierre Berton, whose first published book was *The Royal Family:*

I must confess to some slight feeling of schizophrenia because of the varied interests of this audience. Should I talk to the members of the Empire Club, about the Empire? Or should I address my remarks to the writers and journalists here and give them the lowdown on the best way of getting into Buckingham Palace without a program?

I wish, really, that somebody had given me the lowdown before I commenced the researches for my book. Because it's not so easy to get into Buckingham Palace. Early in the game I went to see the naval officer who, because of his twenty-five years in the silent service, is press secretary to the Queen. He very charmingly said that he would help me in any way he could. What could he do?

I said: "I'd like to see around the palace."

A look of pure horror crossed his face.

"See around the palace?" he said. "See around? My dear chap—nobody sees around Buckingham Palace!"

I went away from there, and I got a book on the palace. And I discovered that the Royal Philatelic Collection is housed at the far end of the second floor, and it occurred to me that anybody going to see the royal stamps would also cut himself in on an unofficial tour of the palace. So I phoned the Keeper of the royal stamp collection and he said that he'd be delighted to show me around. I told him I was from *Maclean's*. I didn't intend to give the impression that *Maclean's* is a stamp magazine but I must confess that, if he got that impression, I didn't correct it. At any rate, the next day I toured the palace on the way to the stamp room. And then I spent a pleasant two and a half hours looking at stamps. I don't collect stamps. But, it was very interesting.

But there was one part of the palace that I didn't see, despite the very kind remarks that some people have made about my researches: and that was the backstairs. I never got near them. And of the hundred-odd interviews that I had in preparing the book, you'll be interested to know that only one was with a palace servant. I didn't intend to interview any palace servants but a newspaper friend of mine insisted I go through the ritual. And he arranged for us to meet this man in a pub called "The Bag o' Nails," near the palace. You know every royal servant is forbidden on pain of dismissal to talk to the press. But it was at once clear to me, on entering the Bag o' Nails that the entire clientele consisted equally of Buckingham Palace servants, and of newspaper men who were interviewing them.

I must say the proceedings that followed reminded me of those interviews we read about with Igor Gouzenko. The man we were to see sidled up and sat down with us. There was some guarded conversation and then he looked over his shoulder, turned pale and he said, "Quick, we're being watched!" And then, pausing only long enough to knock back a flagon of mild and bitter, he led us out a side door, through an alleyway across some cobblestones and into a second pub. And here I again tried to ask him some questions. And he was just about to answer when he suddenly dug me in the ribs, put a warning finger to his mouth, knocked back his pint of mild and bitter and off we went again. Very exciting! But not very rewarding.

As you can see, gathering material about the Royal Family has some elements of the cloak and dagger about it. One thing I learned early in the game was that to get to see anybody in a high place, on this subject, you had to know the password. I remember I was trying to reach a man in a high financial institution who knew a great deal about the Duke of Windsor. Let's call him Gattling-Fenn; it was a name rather like that. I finally got through to his secretary's secretary and then with a great deal of difficulty I got through to his secretary.

I said, "My name is Berton, I'm from *Maclean's,* I'm researching the Royal Family and I want to interview Mr. Gattling-Fenn."

She said, "I'm sorry Mr. Maclean, but Mr. Gattling-Fenn isn't in, he doesn't know anything about the Royal Family and if he did he wouldn't tell you."

Well, there was a long discussion which got me nowhere until I finally used the password.

I said: "I'm a friend of Beverley Baxter's!"

Instantly, there was a click on the line, and a voice said: "Gattling-Fenn here!"

Now I should have used the password again. But I didn't. I started all over again, trying to give him my name and my purpose.

He said, "I'm sorry Mr. Maclean, but I'm afraid I can't help you. I don't know the Royal Family—why don't you go up to Buckingham Palace and let them show you around."

I said, "I've tried that. It didn't work."

He said, "Well, Mr. Maclean—what did you say the name of your magazine was again?—Toronto, did you say?—I'm afraid I don't recall it; well, anyway, I can't help you."

So then I sprung the password again. I said, "I'm a friend of Beverley Baxter's."

"Oh, Bax!" he said. "How is the old boy? I say, you must be from *Maclean's* magazine! You'd know Floyd Chalmers—Napier Moore, all that crowd. How are things on University Avenue?

"Why," he said, "I'll bet I can tell you what you're here for! You'll be doing something about the Royal Family: Coronation Year! Well, I can help you. I know the Duke of Windsor you know! Why on earth don't you come to see me?" So you see what I mean about the password. . . .

A flower of CanLit, Margaret Atwood, surfaced at the Club in 1973 and admitted to being in a somewhat peculiar position, which she then delineated:

My current situation is being a "thing." When I was in New York my editor said to me, "What are you in Canada now anyway? I mean, here you are a writer but what are you up there?" And he said "Are you a 'thing'?" And I said "Yes, I think I'm probably a thing." Now I must explain to you that being a thing is different from being distinguished. You can get to be distinguished without ever being a thing. As a matter of fact you can go from nonentity to distinguished without making that transitional phase. I know I thought of distinguishment as something that starts at your feet and works up and when it's got to the top you are a statue. I thought for a while that I was in danger of becoming merely distinguished; now, however, I am a thing. The difference between being a thing and being distinguished is that when you're distinguished people ask for your opinion on things but never listen to the answers because your role is simply being distinguished and it doesn't really matter what you say. Being a thing, however, is a culmination of being an icon, that is something that people worship, and being a target, that is something that they shoot at. I was informed by one of the Toronto newspapers this fall that I am the Barbra Streisand of Canadian literature. I'm not sure what the points of comparison are. To me Barbra Streisand is someone with a long nose and a very loud voice and I certainly have the wrong nose and I am gradually developing the loud voice but I had always thought of myself rather as the Mary Pickford of Canadian literature. Spreading joy. So when you're distinguished they ask but don't bother listening to the answers. And when you're a thing people make up what you are supposed to think without asking you about it and then they either praise or attack you for what they have in fact made up. This can be aggravating. It also gives you indigestion. So having found myself this kind of thing I paused and looked back over my life to see how I had become this thing. I used to be a writer. The difference between being a writer and being a thing is that writers just write books and they write away and they write away and most of the time nobody pays much attention to them because they are either ahead of their time or behind it. But if what you happen to be saying coincides with what is going on in society; then you become a thing and this is what seems to have happened to me. Now, as I've said, part of being a thing is that you are a target and people shoot at you. . . .

When *Survival* (Atwood's thematic guide to Canadian literature) was published bullets were fired from several directions, including

a very strange reaction from Quebec which went something like—if English Canada is having an identity crisis, it shouldn't, because it doesn't have an identity and even if it does it's bad for them to talk about it because that isn't humanism. Better we should be modest, virtuous and humble, labouring in our narrow sphere and leave identity crises to those who deserve it more, namely Quebec. For them separatism, for us humanism. I found this reaction sort of peculiar, especially since it came from a place which had surely been through a lot of this before and therefore ought to have recognized some of the symptoms, and I wondered, how come? And I figured, well, the usual Quebec cliché is that we are a country without a culture and they are a culture without a country and if we turn out to have a culture after all it leaves their parallelism disturbed and it leaves them odd man out. We get to have two things and they only get to have one.

From centre right (came) the cry that there is no Canadian literature anyway and another variation of this is that we are all something called "earth people," not Canadians. Earth people, I thought about that for a while. . . . I'm an earth person myself but I think if you don't pay attention to the earth that you are standing on you aren't going to get very far with the rest of it. Another version of that is that we are all earth people but somehow Canadians are an inferior kind of earth people and that we should pay attention to our biggers and betters to see how being a real earth person is done.

From the moderate left we have general agreement and from the centre, and I judge the centre by what comes in through the mail slot from people who are not literati or critics or anything like that but just ordinary readers, I gather that Canadian literature is something that they had never heard of or thought of before but when they read this book it somehow coincided with their own cultural experience, or lack of it.

[As for] cultural nationalism, there are two forms of that. One serious and one silly. The serious kind says, "Let's pay attention to what is going on in our own cultures." The silly kind says, "Let's pay attention to nothing but."

And finally, a reflection from Robertson Davies in 1972, on other oddities of authorship:

Authors are not very much in the public eye, unless they are in trouble because of some gigantic imposture about a book they haven't written, or should not have written, such as a biography of Howard Hughes. Occasionally they are deemed to be of interest if they are being divorced, especially if the cause is cruelty. There is a widespread idea that authors are absolute devils in their matrimonial lives. Sometimes the newspapers carry reports of an author's death. These often run like this: "The unknown man of shabby appearance who was knocked down yesterday by a pizza delivery van has at last been identified as Lanugo Inkhorn, an author once popular but long forgotten. Identification was possible because the sum of forty-seven cents, which was found in his pocket, tallied exactly with Inkhorn's 1969 royalties, which had been paid to him last week by a Canadian publishing firm, now under American domination." When authors die they are frequently described as "once-popular" or, more often "well-known in the 'thirties." It is unheard of for an author to be popular at the time of his death. This is part of the tragedy of my profession.

Another curious thing about authors is that they have no period of maturity. When they begin, they may be so lucky as to be referred to, for ten or fifteen years, as "promising;" after that, they are called "old-timers." Last year the *Globe and Mail* referred to me as an old-timer, and then I knew that I was a genuine Canadian author; I had passed from the bud to the yellowing leaf without any intermediate period of flowering. From now until the melancholy item about the pizza truck it will be all downhill.

In the late summer of 1953 more than 3,000 men and women from forty-eight countries met in the annual International Physiological Congress in Montreal. Other related conferences followed until on

September 15, Dr. Charles H. Best, co-discoverer of insulin (with Dr. Frederick Banting) came home to open, at the University of Toronto, the research institute that bears his name. Speaking to the Empire Club, he said:

Many people ask us the question: Why do you devote your lives to medical research? What are the rewards? They are certainly not financial. Ethical medical men do not make a penny out of their medical discoveries, and this was the course followed in Toronto. The patents on Insulin were assigned to the University of Toronto; they were given away to every country in the world. Some funds from the United States, through the companies which make Insulin, have been used by the University of Toronto to administer matters relating to insulin the world over and to support a testing laboratory which has investigated every lot of insulin made. The residue from these funds was made available for medical research in Canada. This has supplied a part of the budget for the departments which have benefited from it. If the University of Toronto had been so minded, it could have exploited insulin—legitimately from the business point of view—in all countries in the world and have secured a revenue which would have paid all the expenses of educating the 10,000 students in the University for the life of the patents. That is a conservative statement, they probably could have made more than that. This was not considered an ethical way to handle matters and I believe that the University of Toronto and Canada have profited enormously by not attempting to commercialize this medical discovery. The University would have gained some of the world but would have lost part of its soul.

Those of us who go into medical research work and other research activities must have a missionary spirit and we must certainly be dedicated to our work, because what we do must be the main reward that comes from it: opening up new pathways, some of which may lead to immediate cures of disease, some to better methods of treatment, some merely to reveal new truths which certainly will be applied later. In short, the rewards of medical research are very real and very great indeed.

The death penalty (for murder most foul, and a few other reasons) is one of the hardiest of long-running Canadian issues. Unfortunately, most is heard about it when it has become, as happens occasionally, an issue of politics rather than an issue purely concerned with human experience and the safety of society at large. Few audiences ever are treated to a debate on the subject such as the one that took place in November, 1954, between two of the land's most eminent lawyers, Arthur Maloney and Joseph Sedgwick: Mr. Maloney then only 35, a brilliant defence lawyer; and Mr. Sedgwick, at 56, a man who had been both a prosecutor and a defender, and who had served on the Royal Commission that completely revised the Canadian Criminal Code, in which capital punishment remained the supreme penalty.

Mr. Maloney, in opposing the death penalty, noted the record over the 20 years from 1930 to 1949 in Canada: 407 persons sentenced to death, of whom 220 actually were hanged. Among those released, he said, none—as far as was known—had committed a second murder, although a small percentage had been convicted for other lesser crimes:

> In a discussion on the question of the death penalty it is never out of place to remind your audience of one or two of the humorous stories that are sometimes told in connection with it.
>
> One that occurred to me to tell you today is the story of the notorious gunman who finally came into the clutches of the law and was convicted of murder and sentenced to be hanged. The night of his execution arrived, a solemn procession formed outside the cell and he was led to the foot of the thirteen steps that led to the gallows. He mounted them, one by one, until he came to the thirteenth which gave way beneath him. Fortunately, he was able to grasp the railing beside him and when about inches from the trap door he turned around to the Governor and he said, "This damned thing ain't safe."
>
> The case for the death penalty has always found adherents. As a matter of fact, in England in 1838 it was possible to hang a man who stole five shillings or more. Today you and I would be appalled if we ever heard of such a thing being done. Yet, actually it was seriously debated and debated for years before abolition of the death penalty for that crime. In order to persuade his fellow legislators to vote against the abolition of the death penalty for theft, the Lord Justice of England said in 1838, when he was asked to concur in a vote to

abolish the death penalty for theft of five shillings or more: "My Lords, if you suffer this Bill to pass we shall not know where to stand. We shall not know whether on hands, head or feet. Repeal this law and no man can trust himself for more than an hour out of doors, lest every vestige of his property be swept away by the hardened robbers."

So I say the controversy over this subject has gone on for centuries.

Now, to me there is but one basis on which the death penalty can be justified . . . that is if it proves to have a deterrent effect. I think no matter what our instincts are, no matter what our feelings in regard to it may be, if it is proved to have the effect of deterring others from committing crime we must bury our own aversions and our deep instincts and submit to the imposition of this penalty.

That leads to the question, does it deter? Too often we are inclined to answer by saying "Yes." When asked why we say Yes, we say, "Because it would deter me." That is the fallacy that lies at the root of the thinking of everyone, in my submission, who favours the retention of the death penalty. You say it would deter, because it would deter you. The fact is the average murderer is a man very unlike you, a man with whom you have nothing in common . . . a man with whom you would share no interests . . . and what would deter him would not have the slightest effect on you, and what would deter you would not have the slightest effect on him. That, I submit, is one of the real fallacies in the argument of those who would retain the death penalty and the retention of the death penalty or otherwise should not be determined by that subjective test, but it should be determined instead by a cold, impersonal study of the facts as we know them.

Now, thirty-six jurisdictions throughout the world, sprawled across Europe, the United States, South America, Asia and Africa, have experimented with the abolition of the death penalty. People of all races and creeds, people of all colours, people from cold climates and people from hot climates, people from countries mainly industrial and people from countries mainly agricultural, all have experimented with abolition, thirty-six of them, and they boast of having done so because they have done so successfully.

Surely a cross-section of so many countries is something with which we of Canada can make an effective comparison for the purpose of determining what we should do ourselves.

This is a question, as you know, which can be discussed in many aspects, under many headings. It cannot be discussed under any aspect very thoroughly in the short interval of time given to speakers at a meeting of this nature. There is one aspect, perhaps two, on which I would like very briefly to touch before I conclude.

One aspect of the death penalty that rather shocks me is the inequality of its imposition. That inequality reflects itself in a number of ways. In the vast majority of cases convicted murderers are men who are poor and in many cases . . . far too many . . . they are defended by inadequate legal help.

I have in mind the case of four convicted murderers [separate cases] who were defended by a lawyer about whose sanity we all entertained doubts. This lawyer is now dead and it makes it less embarrassing to discuss the case. In 1950 in a case tried before the late Hon. Mr. Justice Green, the wife of this lawyer brought an action to have her marriage annulled on the grounds that at the time it was solemnized her husband was insane and in the judgment given by the late Mr. Justice Green, he says in his formal judgment the marriage should be declared null and void on the grounds the man was at the time of celebration of the form of marriage incapable of contracting the said marriage by reason of his mental incapacity.

The date of the marriage was March 5, 1946. In September 1946 he defended a convicted murderer. On February 8th, 1947, he defended a convicted murderer. On March 4th, 1947, he defended a convicted murderer. At a later date, I do not have the exact date, in 1947, he defended a convicted murderer. Every one was sentenced to death, and in December 1948 he was committed to a mental institution.

Those are hard things to say but they must be said. They demonstrate the inequality of the imposition of the death penalty.

Apart all together from that, a defence of the convicted murder too often involves the first experience in the courtroom for a young lawyer, just out of law school.

That is one aspect of the inequality. Another aspect of the inequality is the difference in the vigour with which the prosecution is conducted, the difference in the fairness with which a prosecution is conducted, and with which police investigation is conducted. Contrast on the one hand, the celebrated case of Mrs. Bell, the fairness with which that prosecution was conducted by Counsel for the Crown . . . not a single detail was held from the Defence . . . there was an exhaustive preliminary hearing before the trial . . . not a single thing was done of which anyone could be critical. No matter what the outcome of that case she never could have complained about a lack of fairness on the part of the prosecution . . . Contrast that with another case which I am not at liberty to name, but with which I had personal experience, in which the very opposite occurred . . . deliberate efforts to conceal facts from the Defence, deliberate efforts to take the Defence by surprise.

So there is another aspect in which there is an inequality about the imposition of the penalty of death.

Then, too, to a lesser degree, not inequality, but the difference in men . . . the difference in trial judges. They are human . . . they have a difference in temperament . . . a difference in outlook. Some have an aversion to the death penalty, some are opposed to it, some are in favour of it. It is not disrespectful of a Judge to say that your chances, if you are defending a man charged with murder, are likely to be more successful if tried before Judge A, rather than Judge B. This is another aspect of the inequality.

Take too, the difference in locale. Urban juries are invariably more adverse to the death penalty than are rural juries.

I have in mind a case, not too long ago, of a young man in the Province of Quebec, convicted of a murder of another young man as a result of a jealous quarrel over the affections of a young lady. I suggest to you if that case had been tried before a Toronto jury and the same facts brought forward, I suggest that man would now be serving a sentence for manslaughter.

In conclusion, not having by any means exhausted the subject, as I sometimes wish I had an opportunity to do, although it would take too long a time to do, I submit a fair study of all the facts will satisfy you that the death penalty has no proved deterrent effect, that in its application it is unequal, and that in this country, civilized as we boast of being, it should be done away with and should be done away with now.

Mr. Sedgwick:

It is never easy to follow Mr. Maloney, and it is particularly difficult to do so when one is dealing with this subject which he has made so peculiarly his own. What Mr. Maloney said in his opening is quite true . . . it is difficult to approach the subject with any degree of logic. In fact, in what may well be called the classic plea for the abolition of Capital Punishment, Lord Templewood's "The Shadow of the Gallows," that humane and experienced gentlemen, who was for some years Home Secretary in England, makes it clear that most people who have any decided views on the subject have those views more by instinct than by logical process.

There are many statistics showing the incidence of capital crime in those countries that have abolished the death penalty as compared with those that have not done so. Really and truly, they prove nothing. As Mr. Quintin Hogg said in the debate on the matter in the British House . . . and it was a most helpful debate . . . he said, "Statistics are not cogent . . . patiently, honourably and scrupulously collected as they have been, they only befuddle us." He went on to say that he preferred to look into his own heart, and there he found that if he were a professional burglar, with terms of penal servitude behind him and no death penalty to fear, he would take the chance of carrying a gun and shooting any witness of his crime. He added that against the result of this heart-searching, "neither Dr. Jung nor the statistics will convince me to the contrary."

But one does get a little help, if not from statistics, at least from the experience of other civilizations similar to our own. One finds, for instance, that New Zealand did abolish the death penalty, tacitly, by not enforcing it, from 1936 to 1941, and specifically by legislation from 1941 to 1950. Then in 1950, and I believe as a result of two atrocious murders that shocked the public conscience, the death penalty was restored in that Commonwealth whose people are greatly similar to our own.

Apart from the statistical argument, which is almost always used by the advocates of abolition, there is the other argument that Mr. Maloney stressed . . . that is the awful finality of it. That is true. One cannot call back from "the unanswering legion of the dead." But it is also true that the risk of judicial miscarriage on that level of crime is so slight as to be negligible, and no proponent of abolition can cite a case within the last fifty years at least of a person hanged and later proved, or reasonably suspected to be, innocent. There are so many safeguards existing now that did not exist at the start of this century. I think I am safe in saying no person ever convicted of murder fails to appeal. In every case he does appeal, his case is reviewed with the utmost care by a bench, in this Province at least, of five judges. Then, if there is still doubt, by right in certain cases, and by leave in others, the case may be carried to the Supreme Court of Canada, where there will be an equally careful and exhaustive inquiry, by a bench consisting of nine judges, and there the matter is again canvassed with the greatest of care, and I feel confident, in my mind at least, that if there is any reasonable doubt whatsoever that doubt is resolved in favour of the accused person, even at the Appellate level.

And finally, and Mr. Maloney referred to this also, there is complete review of the matter by the Department of Justice, and there is a right exercised (in some cases) to reprieve the convicted person, even at the last moment, after all appeals have been heard and dismissed.

I can only say in my own experience at the Bar for almost a third of a century, during which time I have appeared both for the Crown and the accused, and in a number of murder cases, I cannot think of a case where the capital penalty was inflicted and there remained even a scintilla of doubt as to the guilt of the culprit.

Then another argument that Mr. Maloney did not touch on, but that I have heard many refer to, is that hanging is a brutal thing. I have never witnessed a hanging and have not the slightest intention of so doing, therefore I can have no very convincing opinion. You will hear that argument advanced and I can only tell you it is said by those most competent to judge that it is quick and painless extinction.

In England some years ago the Home Office made a careful study of the matter, and issued a somewhat macabre but interesting report which concludes, "there is no record during the present century of any failure or mishap in connection with an execution, and as now carried out execution by hanging can be regarded as speedy and certain."

I have, of course, read of hangings, I have read of electrocutions, I have read of guillotinings and also of the methods practised in some of the States of the Union, and I can only say one seems about as humane as the other, and in any event the method of execution is hardly pertinent to a discussion of whether you have executions or not. It should be no part of the argument to discuss how they should be carried out.

Of course it should be argued that the extreme privacy that surrounds executions today adds to their horror, rather than taking away from it, and we might consider the advisability of going back to public executions. I am not to be taken as saying I favour that course, but there is quite an argument to be made for it, and those who still read that great literary pundit of the eighteenth century, Dr. Samuel Johnson may recall that he defended public hangings with some vigour, as being in the public interest. He said, "They object that the old method drew together a number of spectators. Sir, executions are intended to draw spectators. If they do not draw spectators, they don't answer their purpose. The old method was most satisfactory to all parties; the public was gratified by a procession; the criminal was supported by it. Why is all this to be swept away?"

May I say a word about the economics of the whole matter. In this we are all interested, as taxpayers. If murderers are not to be executed, what then is to be done with them? If a murderer is to be incarcerated for the whole of his life, is that lingering death a more humane thing than the speedy execution of the gallows? Or, if after a period of imprisonment he is to be released, what assurance has society of his reformation? Can we be sure in a critical moment he will not again turn to the gun or the knife?

Again, to take the extreme case, and that is the case of the lifer who is confined in a penal institution, and who knows he will never be released by process of law, why should he not kill a warden or guard, or make his escape if he can, knowing nothing will be done except that he will be put back in prison if caught?

While certainly I do not want to propose to weigh human life against money, why should society pay, year after year, to keep such a person in confinement when we know there is not the slightest possibility that he will ever make any return to society, any contribution to society in return for his keep.

As Mr. Justice Keiller Mackay said, when discussing the same subject not long ago, and I must completely agree with him, "Is it not time that the state should begin by asking, not necessarily what is good for the murderer but, on the other hand, what is necessary for the good order of society and the preservation of the lives and safety of its citizens?" Or, as an eminent judge said many years ago, he had always believed if you hanged a man when he was young he would not bother you when he was old.

Finally, coming back to my starting injunction, I ask you to search your own hearts.

Consider the case of Seddon, the poisoner . . . another case in all the books on crime . . . the man who deliberately planned the murder, the painful death of a woman who trusted him and who had made over her few pitiful savings to him in return for an annuity, and he poisoned her so by shortening her life he would not have any long time to have to pay the annuity he had traded for her savings. Do you think that such a mean monster as that should be kept alive at the public expense for fifteen or twenty years, and then should be released, again to plot murder, if he so saw fit, and with no punishment to fear except being returned to prison?

Mr. Maloney says that the death penalty, that the gallows has no deterrent effect. I can only echo what Mr. Quintin Hogg said, "I think it would deter me," and when Mr. Maloney says murderers are not, generally speaking, of the class to which you gentlemen here are privileged to belong, certainly he is overlooking the case of Seddon who belonged to what is called the middle or upper class.

One could multiply examples. I have neither time nor inclination. Indeed, referring to a case that Mr. Maloney defended with ability, the case of Suchan and Jackson, who were tried for what I thought the unprovoked murder of a gallant and unarmed officer, Detective Sergeant Edward Tong, they were hanged, and I think rightly hanged. I think society owes a duty to protect itself. I think society owes a duty to its police, and I think the police are entitled to feel that taking, as they do, their lives in their hands, if one is killed by people bent on crime, that condign punishment will be visited on the murderer.

And lastly, I am not sure that I favour the compulsory death penalty . . . juries have a right or privilege, whichever you may describe it as, of recommending mercy, and in a large percentage of the cases where there is such a recommendation, the Department gives weight to it, but certainly not in all.

In some States of the Union to the south of us, and in some other jurisdictions, the jury have a final duty to decide on the penalty. They can bring in a verdict of murder in the first degree which is followed by the compulsory imposition of the death penalty or maybe some lesser degree of murder, in which case only a term of imprisonment is imposed or, in some cases, the jury may specifically recommend mercy and the Judge is bound to accede to the recommendation. I am not sure I wouldn't favour such a course. I think it may be the twelve men of the jury should have the right to say whether the convicted person is to be hanged or imprisoned.

With that limitation, I strongly favour retaining the death penalty for those cases of murder most foul.

Sixteen years later, a footnote from T. George Street, chairman, National Parole Board:

I do not believe that every vulture is a maladjusted nightingale.

Take all the political happenings in Canada in the first three-quarters of the century and pick the most startling. The choice of many would be those hours one warm night in June 1957, when the nation realized that John Diefenbaker's Progressive Conservatives had ended the twenty-two year reign of the Liberal party. One of Dief's chief lieutenants was Donald M. Fleming:

It was on the fateful 21st day of June 1957, that a group of perhaps mildly excited individuals, including one lady, found themselves at the door of Government House in Ottawa. As they entered the portals, sheets were handed to them containing the roster of officers in the new government who were to be sworn into office, and the first one read: John G. Diefenbaker, Prime Minister, Secretary of the Council . . . Donald M. Fleming, Minister of Finance and Receiver-General of Canada. It didn't make any impression on me at the time, but it was in the course of the day, perhaps when opportunity had come for some quieter thoughts, that the thought struck me as a flash: Receiver-General of Canada—that is the bloke in whose favour I have been writing cheques all these years, and I have hated him every time I did it, and now I am it! My blood chilled in my veins at the thought.

On May 17, 1967, Richard Nixon made his first visit to Canada. He had not been there before, he said, because when he was vice-president under Eisenhower he was only sent to trouble spots. In his speech he supported the war in Vietnam (which five years later he ended, and won his second presidential term partly on his promise to do so); and supported the exclusion of Communist China from the United Nations (which he later helped to reverse). He was introduced by E. B. Jolliffe, former leader of the Ontario C.C.F., the introduction touching all bases so fulsomely that Mr. Nixon began his speech with a reference to his losing the presidential campaign in 1960:

Mr. President, Colonel Drew, distinguished guests, after that very gracious and generous introduction and your warm reception, I can only conclude that I ran for president of the wrong organization.

Some politicians tend to be careful when speaking of labour unions. Premier Joseph R. Smallwood of Newfoundland, November, 1959:

I think sincerely, if you were to take a secret ballot vote in New-foundland today, except for a few cranks, a few malcontents, a few crackpots (and we have a fair share of these in Newfoundland), I doubt that more than a hundred in all of Newfoundland would vote against union with Canada.

Union, however, has brought us one or two things that are not good for us. One of these is the I.W.A., the International Wood-workers of America.

Gentlemen, I have myself organized half a dozen trade unions. I have organized a number of co-operative societies. I have been with politics for ten years. At about 47 or 48, I became a politician. Up to 45 or 46 years of age I was an executive trade union organizer, a co-operative organizer among primary producers. My sympathies have always been, I hope always will be on the side of the ordinary people, the common people, as Abraham Lincoln called them, the people God must have loved so much, He made so many of them.

But the I.W.A. is the barracuda of the trade unions of Canada . . . a savage shark of a union . . . able, extremely able, extremely clever, with enormous ability and experience. They can do a better job of brainwashing than anybody, and they are absolutely unscrupulous.

They went into Newfoundland. No one, in or out of the Government, said a solitary word to them for nearly three years. They organized and carried on all the ordinary activities of the trade union and they did it with superabundant ability and success. They called a strike and they were right, up to the moment they called the strike. They had done nothing wrong, nothing unlawful, at any rate until they called the strike, and for some short time after they called the strike. Then they made the mistake of their lives, the mistake that means that no one here today will live long enough to see the I.W.A. get a foothold in Newfoundland again.

The mistake they made was to challenge law and order. Now, that is not a very dramatic thing to do in Ontario. It is done, so I am told, almost every time there is a strike . . . maybe not every time, but very frequently. Strikes are conducted up and down this continent to the accompaniment of violence, frequently of bloodshed, so much so that that has come to be accepted as part of life itself. But not in Newfoundland.

On that last January morning, at four o'clock, at ten below zero, in a snow storm, three hundred Newfoundland loggers were led ten miles through the snow to two logging camps, occupied by other Newfoundland loggers, and these three hundred men, at four o'clock in the morning, attacked these two camps as though they were three hundred British troops attacking by stealth an encampment of German troops, as though they were foreigners to each other and with brutal violence, brutal force, attacked and beat them up and put them out into the snow and drove them before them. One man tramped ten miles in his bare feet, and they wouldn't allow them time even to put on their boots . . .

Bloody, wicked violence! Something broke inside me. I said, "I don't want to be Premier of Newfoundland, I don't want to be in the Government of Newfoundland, I don't want to be in the Legislature of Newfoundland, I don't want to be in Newfoundland if this kind of bloody violence against Newfoundland can be carried out with impunity, if they can get away with it.''

So we put our hand to the task of smashing and we smashed it. We smashed it. If we had not smashed it the I.W.A. would have succeeded. The strike would have been a great success and they would have established in Newfoundland, they would have created, they would have invited, they would have initiated, because it had never existed before, a new pattern in labour matters, the pattern being that the way to handle labour relations was by the blitzkrieg, the Hitler method . . . don't pussyfoot, don't fool about, whatever you have got, throw it all in and argue about it after. Hit with everything you've got. That pattern would have become the pattern of labour relations in Newfoundland. The I.W.A. would have become the tutors of the labour movement. They would have enjoyed enormous prestige in Newfoundland. The whole of the hundred and twenty trade unions in Newfoundland would have looked up with respect and awe to the I.W.A. and it would have become overnight the leader of the whole labour movement of Newfoundland and they from then on, instead of directing dozens from the mainland of Canada under assumed names, surreptitiously brain-washing men in midnight meetings in the camps, they could have come in quite boldly and Newfoundland would have fallen just as some other parts of Canada already have done, to this union gangsterism.

Newfoundland! I thank God for all her faults, and she has many. With all her faults, all her weaknesses, Newfoundland to this moment is cleansed of that violence and will stay so. They may refer to the I.L.O., they may refer to the United Nations, but while we are a British colony, now a Canadian Province, while the Union Jack flies over us, we will give them answer, and they will get it every time.

E. Peter Lougheed, leader of the Progressive Conservative party in Alberta, speaking in the mid-1960s, years before he began his long and powerful run as Alberta premier and oil baron:

I recently proposed to the annual convention of the political party I represent that one of our guideposts be that we should work towards an Alberta Government which considered itself Canadian before Albertan and hence promoted the cause of national unity and economic sovereignty as well as the determination of national purpose. This might not be the most popular political position for me to take in our western province, but it is, nevertheless, the position I intend to always maintain.

In 1966 Dalton Camp was national president of the Progressive Conservative Association of Canada—and he thought the party would best be served by reviewing the leadership of John Diefenbaker. This course was not popular with some Tories, including Mr. Diefenbaker. On October 20, 1966, about one year before a leadership convention ended the Diefenbaker era, Mr. Camp:

We, in Canada, must be considered by the rest of the world, if they consider us at all, as a nation of a certain fixed irresolution. Our parties are models of piety, full of ritual, liturgy and platitude, timid about change, standing forever in the shadows of history, reluctant to embrace the true spirit of the party system, free speech, open debate, the clash of ideas, and hesitant before the rising spirit of democracy.

Let me summarize that point in one statement of fact. Since 1956 the two major parties in the United States have had *six* leaders and *three* elections. Since 1956 the two major parties in Britain have had *seven* leaders and *four* elections. In Canada, in ten years, we have had three leaders and five elections, and of the five elections, four have not produced, from the Canadian electorate, a government majority.

Surely it is reasonable to say that any party that sought now to reassess its condition, its policy, its leadership and its organization after five elections in ten years, ought not to be considered headstrong, impulsive or disloyal. . . .

It is puzzling to me what all the shouting is about. There is a widespread public view that the party system is failing this country, that some politicians often seem more interested in the damnation of their opponents than in the salvation of the country.

254

All parties live like paupers between elections and squander funds during elections in the desperate attempt, not only for victory, but to force on the Canadian people the task of what they should be doing themselves, and that is their own housekeeping and their own housecleaning. . . .

Not since 1958 has any national leader had a genuine mandate to give direction and purpose to national policy, and not since Mackenzie King has there been any continuity of policy or purpose in this nation.

Thus, when one says as plainly as one can, that both major parties need to take stock of themselves, one surely is not speaking for any cabal or clique, but rather one is echoing the prayers of most, if not all, the people of this country. . . .

All I have said in speaking, not for myself, but for many members of my own party and certainly countless others, is that the Conservative Party, whose importance to this nation surely no one would deny, has a responsibility to decide for itself its future course. I want to ask the question: what is wrong with democracy? What is wrong with allowing a modern party the democratic right to express itself, its convictions and its conscience in a democratic manner?

Such questions, for example, as whether or not it is in the interests of a more realistic unity and in the interests of certain events in the near future, that the Party have a Convention in 1967. Who is it that fears a democratic expression of view and if they do, why do they fear it? . . .

I want to ask why the party, at this critical point, may not be told in candour what its future holds? Why should it not be told? If a party's leader intends to ask its continued confidence from this day through the next election, while his friends say, as they are saying, that this is not so, what is the party to believe? If the leader intends to continue, then surely he will submit this decision to the judgment of his party and allow them democratically and freely to express their wishes. If he intends to retire, as his closest supporters are saying, why do they have this intelligence when the Party does not?

The convention was held in 1967. Robert Stanfield of Nova Scotia replaced John Diefenbaker as leader and lost in the 1968 general election to Pierre Trudeau. John Diefenbaker licked his wounds, kept his seat and found that a lot of Canadians still loved him, no matter what job he held in Ottawa. Early in 1972 he was at the Empire Club:

You mentioned, Mr. President, that sometime when I am gone—there will be some part of Canada—that will have lost something. Well—we won't worry about that possibility in the immediate future. [Applause] A few years ago a Jewish congregation gave me an award—"The Tree of Life"—a magnificent thing—no Gentile had ever received one. After the presentation I naturally asked what it meant. He said it meant I would live as long as Moses.[Applause]

I had to ask, "What do you mean by that?" He said, "According to the thirty-first chapter of Deuteronomy, Moses lived to one hundred and twenty years." Mr. President, when that news got back to Ottawa [Applause]—well. . . .

I have a deep affection for Toronto, Mr. Mayor, but I have been disturbed by recent events. Who could have ever believed a few years ago or dreamed of the fact that Toronto would have an international airport 360 miles away in South West Quebec? [Laughter]

Who would ever have dreamed that in Toronto the Good in 1972 Rochdale College would be in existence, more suicides than graduates [Laughter] and they are receiving $270,000 from the LIP program. If this was not a gentlemanly meeting I would define "LIP" but I won't. There they are receiving money for all kinds of things under the sun, crackpots, parasites, draft-dodgers;—Hamilton, Mrs. Fairclough, isn't far behind. [Laughter] There, $40,000 has been made available to a chap who is to produce two Communist plays to be used in schools and libraries. And in Ottawa—I have to tell you what we have there. [Laughter] We have a chap, a French citizen, three years in Canada, who gets $280 a week to tell the people of Ottawa how to be poor. We don't need any help with taxes being at the present levels. . . .

I have never been frightened to say what I have to say because I might fear being described as a bigot. You know—I like a nice spirit of tolerance where we do not say harsh things about each other, where nobody speaks out—where everybody is happy. I was greatly disturbed recently by the confrontation between the Prime Minister of Canada and the Premier of British Columbia. They got into an argument, [Mr. Trudeau called Mr. Bennett a bigot] but it was a private argument. I would like to have seen rather a St. Valentine's day card. I thought now, isn't there some way in which they could have said these things about each other without being so personal. I place this before you for what it is worth. There is a cartoon—a Valentine—from the Prime Minister to the Premier of British Columbia: "To the great big bigot of the Big B.C., [Laughter] a handful of horseradish and a stinging bee"; [Laughter] and then I can see Premier Bennett replying: "Roses are rouge"—he never uses French—"Roses are rouge, violets are bleu, Bennett is great, the bigot is you." [Applause] Now, in that way we would have that friendly relationship that we always had. [Applause] . . .

I interpolate this. I was with Churchill in his home on the day his great political enemy died, Aneurin Bevan. Dr. Morin came in and said "Winston, Nye Bevan has just died." Churchill said, "That is very sad." Ten minutes later in came one of his secretaries and said, "The press would like to know in your heart of hearts, Sir Winston, what you thought of Aneurin Bevan?" And the reply was, "Are you sure he's dead?" [Laughter]

Oh, I think of some of the funny things in Parliament. I think of Mackenzie King. Mackenzie King was a bachelor and of course Mr. Bennett was a bachelor. We had a member by the name of Billy Assaly who was blind but he could recognize every member in the House by his voice. He loved all mankind. He left his entire estate to help the poor children in Kootenay; but the one group that he didn't like was the Doukhobors and this day he was discussing how terrible the Doukhobors were and he heard from across the way somebody laugh. Mackenzie King had a little laugh all of his own, "heh, heh, heh" [Laughter]—that was before politicians had to develop the Pepsodent look [Laughter] and he said, "The Prime Minister laughs." Sitting almost directly across, he said, "I ask him this question. What would he do some morning if he were to arrive out at Kingsmere and see half a dozen Doukhobor women totally devoid of all raiment?"

King said, "Is that a question or a rhetorical one?" [Laughter]

Billy Assaly very seriously said, "It is a question I would like answered."

And the Prime Minister said, "I would immediately call in The Right Honourable, the Leader of the Opposition" and the House chuckled and laughed.

Bennett got up in all his full pride and said, "Mr. Speaker, as usual, the Prime Minister exaggerates. [Laughter] Dispensing patronage outside of his party has never been a characteristic in the past." [Laughter]

Those are the living things. Parliament only lives so long as men and women stand for what they believe in. Parliament isn't business. Parliament has a soul. It represents the freedom of Canadians as a whole.

Mr. Diefenbaker made passing reference in that speech to Ellen Fairclough, who had served in his cabinets. Years earlier (1958) Mrs. Fairclough, in her first cabinet post—the first Canadian woman to hold one—had spoken to the Empire Club:

> I am sometimes amused by the reasons which are given for the non-admittance of women into certain groups, and one of the most common is that men like to talk among themselves and, on occasion, in rather rich language. I can only speak from personal experience. I have been in elective posts of one kind or another for some twelve years now, and before that I worked for many years in organizations where I was frequently the only woman. In that time I do not think my colleagues pulled their punches at all in the matter of language and I solemnly assure you that in that whole period I never learned one word. I am certain that would be the case with any woman who has attended co-educational institutions from kindergarten grade.

The 1972 general election was like a hung jury: the Liberals who had had a majority in the previous parliament, hung on to 109 seats to the Tories' 107, with both the New Democrats and Social Credit running strongly. Réal Caouette, leader of the Social Credit party, explained what the future held:

> It is a minority government and as a minor party I'll say this, we are

not going to play politics with the situation at all. I'm not going to. I'm going to support all the measures in the interest of the people of Canada. If they come in with abortion, definitely I will be against, as I was. I told Mr. Trudeau himself that had a Bill on Abortion been passed fifty-three years ago, probably the Prime Minister would not be sitting where he is. . . .

Now the B.B. problem—bilingualism and biculturalism—has been discussed over and over again. I think Ottawa spent, what?—nearly $50 million, on that B.B. Commission to find out what—that we speak French in Quebec and they speak English outside the Province of Quebec. A thing we knew well in advance. . . . We have some language problems—yes. But this is not the main problem. I know, and you all know, we cannot make a French out of an English or an English out of a French but we can make good Canadians out of both when we understand each other.

So when I was out west I heard, "If it's going bad it's because of the west giving too much to the east." And down east, "If it's going bad here, in the Maritimes, it's because of the east giving too much to the west." They are all complaining one against the other like that. Sometimes you will hear, "Well if it's going that bad it's on account of those pea soup from the Province of Quebec. We're giving everything to those people." And in Quebec you hear René Lévesque saying, "Well, if it's going that bad in Quebec it's because of the Anglo-Saxons. Get rid of them." And we all know that if Lévesque would become, he'll never be, but suppose he would become the Premier of the Province of Quebec to replace Bourassa, what would he be doing? Exactly the same as Bourassa—in the U. S. borrowing credit for the development of our national resources. You think he would tell the companies out there, "You speak French or else I won't borrow money from you." No! Lévesque would be on his knees—speaking English.

René Lévesque on his knees speaking English . . . an appropriate place, however wry, to mention an element that is said to be above politics (this is said by speakers of all parties, some of them believing it); namely, the crown, the British connection the Empire Club was formed to nurture.

According to Queen Elizabeth, the Queen Mother, nurturing this (among other things) is exactly what the Club has done. In 1974:

> It is through such loyal and enduring associations as yours—
> fraternal, benevolent and military—with your common attachment
> to the ideals of freedom—and your allegiance to the sovereign, that
> the unity of the British Commonwealth finds expression.

People from all over the world found rewarding lives in Canada
without forsaking their own traditions and, indeed, adding to those
older traditions something new of value:

> For you, who cherish the links between Great Britain and this
> country, help, by your example, all Canadians to see the crown as a
> symbol of national sovereignty, belonging to Canadian citizens of
> every national origin and ancestry. You are all part of a new and
> developing Canada which, at heart, is still the Canada with which I
> fell in love when I first came here thirty-five years ago. . . . I have
> great pride in your loyalty to the Queen—your Queen of Canada—
> and in your devotion to the many ideals which mean so much to us
> all. There is both room and need for ideals in our world today.

And then, also essential to the big picture, there is Canada according to
Dave Broadfoot. He says he is a nationalist, has come to terms with
himself and his roots, understands "the rhythms of this crazy, wonderful country," and doesn't mind at all passing it all on, as he did early in
1978:

> Bonjour, mesdames et messieurs. Good day, my dames and my sirs.
> Voici le spectacle de David Piedlarge . . . here is where Dave
> Broadfoot makes a spectacle of himself . . . and vous êtes bien-
> venu . . . and you're welcome to it.
>   It has been written by students of history that comedy originated
> in the sadistic pleasure that people received in observing the misfor-
> tunes of others. In other words, comedy began as cruelty. I have
> performed comedy for the past twenty-six years in Canada—that's
> not sadistic, that's masochistic—and I believe that today we have
> come along far enough to be able to laugh at ourselves. . . .

It does take a certain amount of nerve. I just don't hang around after the performance. I believe in the theory of the moving target. But I have impersonated a number of political leaders with them sitting right beside me at the head table. I remember once, Lester Pearson had to follow me. He got nicely into his speech and all of a sudden he stopped and said . . .

"You know, I don't know whether I'm doing Lester Pearson, or whether I'm doing an impersonation of Dave Broadfoot doing Lester Pearson."

He always enjoyed it. It never bothered him.

Recently during a performance in Ottawa, I was portraying a flood disaster as it would be done by television news. The City of Windsor had just disappeared in the flood-waters, and we cut to Ottawa for a reaction from Joe Clark.

He said, "I think this flood is a very bad thing for Canada, and a semi-bad thing for Windsor. If we're elected, the country I see is a place where men and women can go to bed at night without fear of flooding. The country I see is a place where there is no shortage of tall, well-built dikes. The country I see is . . . Australia."

Well, who should be sitting ten feet from the stage but Joe Clark! He loved it. He came up on the stage afterwards, and he shook me by the throat . . . by the hand. He really did enjoy it. . . .

I have parodied the RCMP right in their own headquarters. And that was an extraordinary experience. Little did I know, when I accepted the engagement, that it was going to turn out to coincide with the biggest scandal in the history of the force. . . .

(But the Mounties) roared their approval. When the Officer in charge of the evening got up to make his final speech, he said, "You know, gentlemen, looking at the scandals the force has been involved with, looking at our recent past, I'd like to use the words of Pogo—'We have seen the enemy and they is us.' "

I didn't hear one defensive remark from a Mountie all evening. That impressed me. They were all making fun of themselves. They know they have to clean up their act. Gathering intelligence is part of a Mountie's job, but they admit now that perhaps gathering intelligence from Members of Parliament was a mistake.

The interesting question for me is why would they enjoy a

character like my Corporal Renfrew so much? He's not exactly the most qualified or brilliant police officer. He relies for his intellectual guidance on his dog. Cuddles is the type of dog that would run into a burning building and emerge two minutes later with the fire insurance policy wrapped in a wet towel. But I realize that Corporal Renfrew humanizes the image of the Mountie. The material is written with no malice and performed the same way.

Whenever malice is introduced, comedy becomes self-defeating and at times very divisive.

How useful is comedy? I was asked to do a performance before Her Majesty the Queen in Charlottetown in 1964, at a time when the country was rife with rumours about a possible attempt on her life. It was an extraordinary experience. By coincidence, the day before this command performance, a union leader gangster by the name of Hal Banks who had escaped justice in Canada was seen by a Toronto reporter on a dock in Brooklyn. When I walked on stage I met an audience that was more tense than anything I had seen in my life. In the backs of their minds they had this picture of a possible assassination attempt. There were Mounties in the audience, Mounties in the corridors, Mounties on the roof, in the street.

I thought, "We have to break through this." So I just stood there for a little while, and I looked off into the wings at the Mounties there, and I looked at the Mounties up above me in the flies, standing on the gratings, and then I turned and in bewildered indignation to the audience, I said, "Why are all these Mounties here? Hal Banks has been found . . . he's in Brooklyn."

There was about fifteen seconds of the most incredible silence, and then the roof fell in. The people collapsed and you couldn't stop the laughter. The tension went right out of the audience and it was a wonderful feeling to experience that.

From then on I became totally brash and talked about every problem we had in Canada. It was a tremendous evening. There is always a need to let go.

I like to dwell on the therapeutic use of comedy. Whether it's a group or a nation or an individual, in any crisis the first casualty, even before truth, is our sense of humour. And once that's gone, we have lost our perspective on the crisis.

. . . Just last week, I was asked to appear on a talk show and to read out the winning jokes in a national joke contest. Fortunately I got there an hour and a half before show time, so I read through the jokes they were asking me to do, and almost without exception they were put-downs of minorities—either Ukrainians, Pakistanis, French-Canadians or Newfoundlanders. Talk about divisive. Whether I was right or wrong, I thought I had no alternative but to refuse to participate. The only group that I dare to put down are Anglo-Saxons, because I am one. I feel I have a right to do that. For instance, there is new evidence that Adam, the first man who ever lived, was an Anglo-Saxon. Who else would stand in a perfect tropical garden, beside a perfect naked woman, and eat an apple?

I can rationalize that. I can say I'm making fun of myself. But in a country where divisiveness is rampant I don't feel that it's a comedian's job to contribute to the problem. I want to contribute to the solution. And the best way I can do that is to do my job well. My job is to make people laugh and I do that best by giving voice to the various controversial issues that come along in our country, in the person of my alter ego, the leader of the New Apathetic Party, and member for Kicking Horse Pass.

You'll have to imagine my Stetson hat.

Do you know what the present federal government is doing about the critically dwindling supplies of energy in this country today? Exactly. Take gas. The OPEC countries say they've got to up their prices, and I would say to Alberta—up yours. (Don't get me wrong, I love Alberta.) The tragedy is that the people in the east do not understand Alberta. They don't understand Jack Horner. You know, Jack Horner was sitting so far back in the opposition back benches, that every time they filled the locks in the Rideau Canal, his ass got wet.

Little Jack Horner
Sat in the corner,
Wishing he had some pie.
So he said to Pierre
I'll sit over there
If you give me a seat that's dry.

And it took the Prime Minister a whole week to make up his mind. Then he said, "Well, I'm losing Margaret, a functionary no-no, but I'm gaining Horner, a reactionary yo-yo. A seasonally adjusted Liberal."

But in Alberta they accept yo-yos. They accept yahoos. You go out to Alberta, you stand in the foothills, surrounded by the greatest livestock the world has ever seen and you ask, "What is Alberta giving Canada?" And the answer is blowing in the wind. Natural gas is a non-renewable resource. But wind isn't. We'll always have wind. I have that direct from the horse's mouth. What we must do is harness the wind we've got.

You know, Barney Danson and Don Jamieson love to talk about Soviet nuclear capability, American nuclear capability, Chinese nuclear capability. They never talk about Holland. Why? Because, they know the Dutch have the windmill. They've been working on it for hundreds of years. But they don't want us to know about it. Today Amsterdam—tomorrow the world! With windmills in front of us, dikes behind us, we'll be up to here in tulips.

We have to develop alternate sources of energy. We have to. I'm not talking about CANDU. I'll tell you what CANDU can done. . . . We loaned money to Argentina so that Argentina could buy a CANDU reactor from us at a loss to us. And we had to pay bribe money on top of that! It's a brand new concept in economics. Never been tried before. Another Canadian first.

What's wrong with solar energy? I believe we could have solar energy in this country, and I'm convinced we could get some of it from the sun. The sun shines all day. After sundown, every man for himself. We'll have to get through the night without using any energy at all. Some of us are doing that now. We're not impotent, we're just slightly ahead of our time. . . .

If we don't find the answers to these questions, we can forget about national unity. At all these conferences all over the country, people are sitting around in rooms talking about national unity and asking, "What is Canada after one hundred and ten years?" I'll tell you. Canada is ten *big* provinces and two vast wastelands—three if you count Ottawa.

They say, "What is a Canadian?" I'll tell you that too. A Canadian is a D.P. with seniority. A Canadian owns a bit of Indian carving, a bit of Eskimo carving and a little bit of chiselling he's done all by himself. Some say, "Cast your bread upon the water, and it will return to you one hundred fold." A Canadian says, "What am I going to do with a hundred loaves of wet bread?"

Yet if you tell a Canadian he's apathetic, he'll answer, "Who cares?"

The world needs Canada. If Canada were not here, the Chinese could sail right across and invade Denmark. And you've got to pay attention to the Chinese. Any people with eight hundred million population who tell you their favourite sport is ping pong will lie about other things too.

We have people in this country who sit in envy of every other country. They've never visited South Molucca. They are indifferent negativists, and they are the same people who now say we must use force to keep Quebec in Confederation. Can you picture that? Bringing our army home from Cyprus? If we can borrow a plane. . . . Then we fly them all the way across the Atlantic, and the air traffic controllers are on strike and refuse to let them land. So they have to fly all the way back to Cyprus with the same sandwiches. Talk about no frills.

And we're supposed to think that Quebec won't do something in the meantime—like fit out some tanks with fuzz busters? There's nothing in this country could stop them. They'd roll right down 417, right into downtown Ottawa —not between 4.30 and 6.00 p.m., of course. They'd get there and go straight to the headquarters of the CBC and close it down. Then what would we do? Exactly.

They'd take the president of the CBC into a small dark room and torture him, force him to watch reruns of *The Nation's Business,* while a helpless government on Parliament Hill tries to negotiate his release . . . by mail.

I say thank God for Newfoundland. The Newfoundlanders care about where they live. They saw what was happening. The Soviet Union with their fleet were over-quota fishing on cod, herring and capelin. That's not a firm of lawyers. It's a group of fish. And they sent a delegation to the Minister of Fisheries in Ottawa, Romeo Leblanc. I didn't make that up . . . that's his name. In English it means "lover of white". Not a big name in Africa. But a very big name in Shediac.

They said, "Monsieur Leblanc, you've got to do something. Put yourself in the position of that capelin. If that was your name, would you want to be taken off to the Soviet Union? Or Newfoundland? That's the choice facing the fish. Go like hell, or come by chance."

He said, "I don't want to get in a fight with the Soviet Union. It's the only union I'm not in a fight with."

So they gave up, but at least they tried. Too many Canadians spend their time envying the rest of the world, and especially the Americans, a people who have problems we can't even conceive of. Americans have dandruff. We have Resdan in this country. They talk about their Jack Daniels bourbon. We have Red Rose tea. Only in Canada! Sure, it's a pity. Americans are plagued with organized crime. We have provincial liquor boards. American politicians can be bought. You can't buy a Canadian politician. You rent them. We have two languages. You say bilingual to an American and he thinks you're talking about a man who likes to wear women's clothing. Americans lost billions in Vietnam, while we had the Olympics right in Montreal. They put a Viking on Mars. We had trouble finding a satellite on earth.

But most important of all, Americans never know whether their leaders are telling them the truth. Now, *we* don't have that problem!

Which brings us to a thorny question. Without it, tens of thousands of Canadian luncheon club meetings never would have taken place. The question: What is a Canadian?

No problem at all for John S. Straiton, president of Ogilvy and Mathers, an advertising agency, late in 1970:

I figure I am about as Canadian as you can get.

I was born in a log house, five hundred miles north of here. Kapuskasing.

When I was a boy, we used to melt snow in a boiler on the kitchen stove to have our Saturday bath in the winter. In summer, we used the river. In the spring and fall, we just stayed a bit farther away from each other.

We had oil lamps, chopped kindling wood, carried water, and were eaten alive by mosquitoes. All the things the well-to-do buy cottages for nowadays.

266

In winter we were hauled three miles to school in a kind of covered wagon on sleigh runners, hauled by a team of buckskins. All those young bodies squeezed into a dark space on those cold winter mornings. Beats sex education.

Let me tell you about my old friend Harold Ekinswaller up in Kapuskasing. Harold was the ace salesman for the Fleet Ford Snowshoe Company. He was also an adroit marketing mind. There was this awful summer slump in snowshoe sales, so Harold developed the world's only moose-gut tennis racket. Used the same production facilities. A bloody good tennis racket it was too, if you didn't mind the flies.

Harold was taking a week off to sit on the back porch and looking at his garden. That year the circus came to town for the first time. They set up their tents in August Ridley's pasture. None of us had ever seen any of them wild animals in our lives. Well, wouldn't you know, the elephant pulled his peg out of the muskeg and runs away.

Well, old Harold was sitting on the back porch sipping a glass of goof when this elephant comes wandering into his garden and starts pulling up his cabbages with his trunk and shoving them into his mouth. Well, old Harold leaps into the kitchen and rings up old Alvin Burnby at the O.P.P.

"Cripes, Alvin," he says. "There's a big grey animal in my back yard."

"Oh," said Alvin. "What about it?"

"Well cripes, Alvin," says Harold. "It's bigger'n a moose. And it's pulling up cabbages with its tail."

"Pulling up your cabbages with its tail? What's it doing with them?"

"Gollies, Alvin, you wouldn't believe me if I told you."

Dr. George Edward Hall, president of the University of Western Ontario, took it more seriously in 1958:

Throughout the history of Canada are emblazoned the names of adventurous souls, daring people, people who sought new horizons, people who made great sacrifices, people who enjoyed competition and revelled in its excitement, people who believed in themselves, people who preferred opportunity to security, people who were not afraid to make mistakes.

No-one can truthfully say that Canadian young people have changed. No-one dare say that they are not as brave or as capable or as loyal as their parents were. That things have changed is true, but "what may have changed is our capacity (as parents) to evoke these qualities."

Andrejicka, Biagioni, Chertkoff, Demetracopoulos, Ebisuzaki, Fioravanti, Grocholski, Hayashida, Jensen, Kaspardlov, Litavaniks, Marziali, Narakas, Oleskevich, Peterson: these are not the names of members of the former French Foreign Legion nor even members of some pro football team. They are names of students at Western University, in London—a centre of Anglo-Saxon traditions. They are students at a private university. They are residents of Ontario. They are Canadians just like you and I. They and thousands like them are hard-working, eager, appreciative and responsible citizens. They deserve our respect and our commendation. They don't always receive it. Why?

Perhaps it is because they are willing to work harder than do some other Canadians. Perhaps it is because they see something which we have lost sight of—opportunity, and they are determined to strive and to risk and to look ahead. Perhaps it is because many of their parents or grandparents do not speak English quite as well as we do. Perhaps it is because they or their families have been labelled with that unfortunate tag—"D.P."

Canada is supposed to be a democratic country. Were the Tustanoffs, the Uchinos, the Von Zur Muhlens, the Zielonkos, parents of more of our students, forced to come to Canada? Certainly not. They came to Canada because they saw in Canada a land of hope, of opportunity, of freedom. They came to Canada for the same general reasons which brought our grandfathers or our great-grandfathers to this new land. They came to Canada for the same reasons that brought the Andrew Carnegies, the Meyer Guggenheims, the Kefauvers, the Eisenhowers, the Roosevelts, to the United States. They too were one-time immigrants. They too had vision, had determination, had courage and were willing to work, to start at humble beginnings—and they succeeded. They made Who's Who.

Are we, third, fourth or fifth generation Canadians losing our zest for adventure? Are we afraid of ourselves or only of hard work and competition?

Here are some of our major scholarship winners—Von Rickoff, VanderLaan, Vanslyke, Hansebout, Ondrejicka, Dohnberg, Kotorynski—all recent immigrants—now new Canadians. . . .

Certainly there are others—many others—from Anglo-Canadian and French-Canadian homes. But proportionately?

The parents of our new-Canadian students have given their children a sense of the opportunities which are waiting. The spirit of adventure is in their minds—the sense of urgency in their being—maybe because they do not have those too comfortable things which we expect and prize so highly.

Are we as parents denying our children, through a desire to protect them, those things which Canada, and the world, need more today than ever before? Are we, as parents, afraid to let our children face comparable challenges to those which our parents and grandparents faced? Are we denying that a person learns not from his successes but from his failures? Have we forgotten that even a glorious failure is worthwhile—if we survive it and push on? Those who cloak themselves in a cocoon of stability and guarantees or who are soothed by the rocking cradle of security may live a comfortable life but may never know the real thrills of living.

The present Lord Tweedsmuir once was a lieutenant-colonel in the Canadian Army, commanding officer of the Hastings and Prince Edward regiment. His father, Lord Tweedsmuir of Elsfield (John Buchan, the author) was Governor-General. At the Empire Club in 1961, the younger Tweedsmuir:

One of the things which I think has struck me most forcibly, since I first came here in 1936, is the steady growth of a Canadian identity. Canada was not then very interested in the rest of the world, nor was the rest of the world interested in Canada. It is probably true to say that most people from Britain and the U.S. found Canada rather more British, or rather more American, or rather less so, than they imagined. I remember in the war in Italy, we would creep through the darkness of the hills on night advances. The Italian villagers that we encountered would whisper: "Are you English?" "No." "Are

269

you American?'' ''No.'' ''Then who are you?'' ''Canadians,'' we would reply. That seemed to puzzle them.

But as we have seen in these selections from more than seventy-five years, the puzzlement, at least within Canadians themselves, has rarely been more than skin-deep. The Canadian is clearly distinguishable as soon as he opens his mouth and his mind, or loads his gun, or picks up his pen or paint-brush.

It is a strange outcome, in a way, that the patriotic aim of a small group of British-connected men in 1903—wanting to preserve Canada's link with Britain—brought into being a series of more than two thousand speakers who, in total, hewed out a definition of Canada, not only as a continuing British connection, but at the same time as a proudly independent nation.

THE EMPIRE CLUB OF CANADA

PAST PRESIDENTS

†1903-1905	Brig. Gen. The Hon. James Mason, K.ST.J.
†1905-1906	Rt. Rev. William Clark, D.D., LL.D., D.C.L.
†1906-1907	J. P. Murray, Esq., J.P., F.R.C.L.
†1907-1908	J. F. M. Stewart, Esq.
†1908-1909	D. J. Coggin, M.A., D.C.L.
†1909-1910	Elias Clouse, M.D., C.M., L.F.P.S. Glasgow, L.R.P.S. Edin.
†1910-1911	J. Castell Hopkins, Esq., F.R.S.
†1911-1912	F. B. Featherstonhaugh, Esq., K.C., M.E.
†1912-1913	Rt. Rev. James F. Sweeney, M.A., D.D., D.C.L.
†1913-1914	Hon. Mr. Justice James Craig, K.C.
†1914-1915	Lt. Col. R. J. Stuart
†1915-1916	Albert Ham, Esq., MUS.D., D.C.L., F.R.C.O.
†1916-1917	James Black Perry, Esq.
†1917-1918	Norman Sommerville, Esq., M.A., K.C.
† 1918	F. J. Coombs, Esq.
† 1919	R. A. Stapells, Esq.
† 1920	Arthur Hewitt, Esq.
† 1921	Brig. Gen. C. H. Mitchell, C.B., C.M.G., D.S.O., LL.D.
† 1922	Sir William Hearst, K.C.M.G., K.C., LL.D.
† 1923	Ellis H. Wilkinson, Esq.

† 1924 William Brooks, Esq.

† 1925 Rev. R. N. Burns, D.D.

† 1926 Col. A. E. Kirkpatrick, HON. A.D.V., V.D.

† 1927 Col. Alexander Fraser, LL.D., A.D.C.

† 1928 Robert H. Fennell, Esq., K.C.

† 1929 Hugh S. Eayrs, Esq.

† 1930 John D. M. Spence, Esq., K.C.

† 1931 H. G. Stapells, Esq., Q.C.

†1932-1933 Col. The Hon. George A. Drew, P.C., C.C., C.D., Q.C., LL.D.

†1933-1934 Major James Baxter, M.C.

†1934-1935 Hon. Mr. Justice Dana H. Porter, C.J.O., Q.C., LL.D.

†1935-1936 J. H. Brace, Esq.

†1936-1937 Major G. B. Balfour, K.C.

†1937-1938 Major R. M. Harcourt

†1938-1939 J. P. Pratt, Esq., Q.C.

†1939-1940 F. A. Gaby, Esq., B.A.SC., D.SC.

†1940-1941 The Hon. G. Howard Ferguson, P.C.(CAN.), K.C.

†1941-1942 C. R. Sanderson, Esq., M.A., LL.D.

†1942-1943 John C. M. MacBeth, Esq., K.C.

†1943-1944 W. Eason Humphreys, Esq.

†1944-1945 Charles R. Conquergood, Esq.

†1945-1946 Eric F. Thompson, Esq.

†1946-1947 Major F. L. Clouse

†1947-1948 Tracy E. Lloyd, Esq.

1948-1949 T. H. Howse, Esq., F.C.I.S.

†1949-1950 H. C. Colebrook, Esq.

1950-1951 Sydney Hermant, Esq.

†1951-1952 D. H. Gibson, Esq., C.B.E.

1952-1953 John W. Griffin, Esq.

1953-1954 Arthur E. M. Inwood, Esq.

1954-1955 James H. Joyce, Esq.

†1955-1956 C. C. Goldring, Esq., D.PAED., LL.D.

1956-1957 Donald H. Jupp, Esq., O.B.E.

†1957-1958 Lt. Col. W. H. Montague, O.B.E.

1958-1959 M/Gen. B. J. Legge, C.ST.J., E.D., C.D., Q.C.

1959-1960 Harold R. Lawson, Esq., F.S.A.

1960-1961 Hon. Mr. Justice Alexander Stark

†1961-1962   Dr. Z. S. Phimister, LL.D.

1962-1963   J. Palmer Kent, Esq., Q.C.

1963-1964   Major Arthur J. Langley, C.D.

1964   The Rt. Hon. D. Ronald Michener, P.C., C.C., C.M.M., C.D., Q.C.

1964-1965   Col. Robert H. Hilborn, M.V.O., M.B.E., C.D.

†1965-1966   Col. E. A. Royce, E.D.

1966-1967   R. Brelin Stapells, Esq., Q.C.

1967-1968   B. Graham M. Gore, Esq.

1968-1969   Edward B. Jolliffe, Esq., Q.C.

1969-1970   H. Ian Macdonald, Esq., O.C., LL.D.

1970-1971   H. V. Cranfield, Esq., M.D., F.R.C.P.(C)

1971-1972   Henry N. R. Jackman, Esq.

1972-1973   Joseph H. Potts, Esq., C.D., Q.C.

1973-1974   Robert L. Armstrong, Esq.

1974-1975   Sir Arthur R. T. Chetwynd, Bt.

1975-1976   H. Allan Leal, Esq., Q.C., LL.D.

1976-1977   William M. Karn, Esq.

1977-1978   Peter Hermant, Esq.

1978-1979   B/Gen. Reginald W. Lewis, C.D.

1979-1980   John A. MacNaughton, Esq.

†*Deceased*

INDEX

PHOTO CREDITS

1–Courtesy of R. L. Pocock. 2–Public Archives of Canada, C 24502 3–Public Archives of Canada 4–Archives of Ontario 5–Canadian Pacific Railway Company 6–Public Archives of Canada, PA 25088 7–Department of National Defence 8–Imperial War Museum, London. 9–Nanton Collection 10–Public Archives of Canada 11–Miller Services Limited, Karsh, Ottawa, photographer 12–The Globe and Mail, Toronto 13–Toronto Star Syndicate 16–Toronto Star Syndicate 17–Verlag Kurt Desch, München/Wien: *Hitler: Aufsteig und Untergang des dritten Reiches* 21–Public Archives of Canada, C 18734 22–Associated Press 23–Associated Press 24–Department of National Defence 25–Department of National Defence 26–Royal Canadian Navy, Department of Information Services 27–Hanns Reich Verlag, München: *Bilder Schreiben Geschichte* 28–Associated Press 29–Department of National Defence 30–Toronto Star Syndicate 31–United Nations Photo, Department of Public Information 32–National Film Board, Garnet Lunney, photographer 33–McMichael Canadian Collection, Kleinburg 34–Public Archives of Canada, C 56999 35–Courtesy of R. Hilborn

Every effort has been made to acknowledge correctly the sources of the illustrations reproduced in this book. The publishers welcome any information which will enable them to rectify, in subsequent editions, any errors or omissions which may have been made in crediting the pictures.